TEACHING COMMUNITY-BASED PARTICIPATORY RESEARCH

Rajesh Tandon is an internationally acclaimed leader and practitioner of participatory research and development. He founded Participatory Research in Asia (PRIA) in 1982 and continues to be its chief functionary. He is Co-Chair of the UNESCO Chair in Community-Based Research and Social Responsibility in Higher Education (http://unescochair-cbrsr.org) along with Professor Budd Hall. Dr Tandon has authored more than 100 articles, a dozen books and numerous training manuals. He was inducted to the International Adult and Continuing Education (IACE) Hall of Fame (class of 2011).

Budd Hall is professor emeritus with Centre for Global Studies, University of Victoria, Canada, and Co-Chair of the UNESCO Chair in Community-Based Research and Social Responsibility in Higher Education (http://unescochair-cbrsr.org). He was former dean of the faculty of education at the University of Victoria, Chair of the Adult Education Department of the University of Toronto, and secretary-general of the International Council for Adult Education. He is a member of the International Adult and Continuing Education (IACE) Hall of Fame and was selected for the 2005 Canadian Bureau of International Education Innovation in Education Award. In December 2022, he was appointed an Officer of the Order of Canada.

PRAISE FOR THE BOOK

'...brings together the experiences of several countries, especially from the Global South, on the "how-to" [of CBPR] that has been ignored thus far...an exceptional resource to have for those who are serious in ushering knowledge for change.'
– **Dzulkifli Abdul Razak**, Professor Emeritus, Universiti Sains Malaysia

'Fifty years of experience in teaching and practising community-based participatory research distilled in one book. A must-read for all educators, administrators and staff in higher education institutions who want to undertake community-engaged research and make their institution socially responsible.'
– **Prof. D.P. Singh**, Chancellor, Tata Institute of Social Sciences (TISS), and Former Chairman, University Grants Commission

'This book...reflects the experiences of many people in many parts of the world – scholars, activists, participants in social movements and community members – who are ethically committed to the struggle for social justice, to the enhancement of human rights and to the sustainability of life on the planet. [They] realize that when knowledge that derives from scientific research is put together with popular or local knowledge; when research is carried out in unison with those who suffer the consequences of inequality, poverty, discrimination and climate change; where academics and communities join in dialogue and participate on equal footing, the resulting co-created knowledge is transformative.'
– **Sylvia Schmelkes**, Honorary Researcher and Coordinator of the Chair on Educational Justice, Universidad Iberoamericana, Mexico City

'...a must-read for anyone seeking to revolutionise the teaching, research and service functions in higher education institutions. Tandon and Hall's decades of experience shine through in this inspiring book, skilfully weaving together theoretical learning with practical examples.'
– **Prof. Kevin Hall**, President and Vice Chancellor, University of Victoria, Canada

'An exceptionally timely book...[It] reminds us of the decades of painstaking work that have been undertaken across the world to develop more equitable and inclusive approaches to research. It will provide a source of inspiration and guidance to anyone committed to building purposeful, socially sensitive knowledge, at whatever stage of their journey.'
– **Paul Manners** and **Sophie Duncan**, Co-Directors, National Co-ordinating Centre for Public Engagement, UK

'This resource opens the door wider to the inclusion of knowledges that have been excluded in academic research. It provides tools, guidance and encouragement for members of those excluded knowledges to share their wisdom to maintain the health and well-being of the land and people.'
– **Prof. Lorna Wanosts'a7 Williams**, Canada Research Chair in Education and Linguistics, and Professor Emeritus of Indigenous Education, Curriculum and Instruction, University of Victoria, Canada

TEACHING COMMUNITY-BASED PARTICIPATORY RESEARCH

Socially Responsible and Ethically Anchored

Edited by

RAJESH TANDON

AND

BUDD HALL

University of Victoria
UNESCO Chair in Community Based Research and Social Responsibility in Higher Education
PRIA
unesco Chair

hachette INDIA

First published in 2025 by Hachette India
(Registered name: Hachette Book Publishing India Pvt. Ltd)
An Hachette UK company
www.hachetteindia.com

1

All images in the text have been provided by the individual contributors of the respective chapters, with the following exceptions. Figure 3.1 has been sourced from public domain. Figures 10.5, 10.6 and 10.7 have been recreated with kind permission of Prof. Prem Kumar Kalra.

Paperback ISBN 978-93-5731-304-9
Ebook ISBN 978-93-5731-560-9

Hachette Book Publishing India Pvt. Ltd
4th & 5th Floors, Corporate Centre,
Plot No. 94, Sector 44, Gurugram 122003, India

Typeset in Adobe Garamond Pro 11/14
by R. Ajith Kumar, New Delhi

Printed and bound in India
by Manipal Technologies Limited

MIX
Paper | Supporting responsible forestry
FSC™ C043100

CONTENTS

LIST OF TABLES AND FIGURES

Tables

Figures

ACKNOWLEDGEMENTS

The UNESCO Chair in Community-Based Research and Social Responsibility in Higher Education, the Knowledge for Change initiative and the Mentor Training Program – none of this would have been possible without so many friends, donors, well-wishers, administrative support staff, community members and university partners; they are too many to name. We acknowledge their generosity, time, knowledge and expertise.

This book specifically has been made possible with the intellectual contributions of John Gaventa, Sarah Banks, Darlene Clover, Walter Lepore, Irma Flores, Crystal Tremblay, Catherine Etmanski, Nandita Bhatt, Kaustuv Bandyopadhyay, Anshuman Karol, Wanda Krause, Wafa Singh, Tanya Clarmont, Tariqa Tandon, René Oosthuizen, Jyoti Gogia, Sharon Valarmathi, Luisa Pineda, Mónica Álvarez and Diksha Rajput. Thank you for making the time in your busy schedules to share your experiences of teaching and learning community-based participatory research. Thanks also to Dzulkifli Abdul Razak, Prof. D.P. Singh, Sylvia Schmelkes, Kevin Hall, Paul Manners, Sophie Duncan and Prof. Lorna Wanosts'a7 Williams for 'blurbing' the book.

The support to the UNESCO Co-Chairs and coordination for the Mentor Training Program at the University of Victoria and PRIA is unparalleled. At the University of Victoria – Walter Lepore, Director of Research for our Chair; Suriani Dzulkifli, who recently completed her PhD from the University of Victoria; Olivia Oliveira, Research Assistant; and Maeva Gauthier, Research

Scholar and Program Manager. At PRIA – Niharika Kaul, former UNESCO Chair Coordinator; Bindu Baby, General Manager; Sujit Sourav, IT and Knowledge Management Officer; and Surjeet Singh, Executive Assistant.

We would like to acknowledge the support from Kevin Hall, President; Prof. Michael Prince, Acting Dean, Faculty of Human and Social Development; Prof. Lois Harder, Dean, Faculty of Social Sciences; Oliver Schmidtke, Director, Centre for Global Studies; and Jill Chouinard, Director of Public Administration at the University of Victoria. Your commitment reflects the power and potential of mutually respectful community–university research partnerships.

To all the mentors in the 24 (and counting) K4C hubs – it is your enthusiasm to advance ethical and transparent community-based participatory research that is creating the next generation of reflexive and socially responsible students and community-based researchers.

And finally, to our fellow learners in the International Participatory Research Network – we started 50 years ago to reimagine the research process. You cheered us on as we worked to construct, strengthen and spread the dreams we had. Your encouragement has been vital to any success we have achieved in advancing socially responsible and ethically anchored community-based participatory research.

Rajesh Tandon and Budd Hall

1

INTRODUCTION

Global Policy Mandates and Urgency to Scale-up

RAJESH TANDON AND BUDD HALL

A chance phone call in 1976 by a graduate student from India studying for his PhD in the USA to a young academic teaching in Toronto was the start of a lifelong partnership in developing and disseminating the theories and practices of participatory research. Rajesh Tandon, an IIT–IIM graduate, was close to the finish line of his PhD program in Organisational Development at the Case Western Reserve University in Cleveland, Ohio. All he needed was one reference to add to the bibliography in his thesis. He had been told by a colleague at the department where he was studying about a paper written by Budd Hall, who after a stint conducting research in Tanzania had published an article in the journal *Convergence* (Hall, 1975). In this paper the phrase 'participatory research' was coined for the first time.

We (Rajesh and Budd) got an opportunity to meet for the first time in Caracas, Venezuela, in 1978. There we were introduced to the decolonial theories associated with the anti-colonial movements, and the ideas of Mahatma Gandhi, Rabindranath Tagore, Amílcar Cabral, Julius Nyerere, José Martí, Paulo Freire and Orlando Fals

Borda. Along with others who were at that conference, we asked: Was it possible to conduct research that involved academia along with social movement activists, civil society workers and the vast majorities of people who have been excluded from mainstream society? The daily lives of the excluded and marginalised for survival and advancement was creating knowledge that was valuable – how could this be 'epistemically privileged' to challenge poverty, racism, heteronormativity, domestic violence and other such 'wicked problems'? Our own experiences with rural farmers in Rajasthan and villagers in Tanzania's Ujamaa villages laid the first building block for theories about the curation of knowledge by community members, the practice of valuing such knowledge in the transformation of communities, and giving equal respect to the ideas of persons from academia, labelled as intellectuals and experts by society, and those organic intellectuals who also had expertise in solving problems while living their daily lives. This is the basis of our over-five-decade partnership in theorising, practising and promoting community-based participatory research (CBPR).

We have often been asked to write a methodological textbook on participatory research. We never did so. But when the discourses on participatory research and its many variants became more widespread and shared amongst scholar-activists in the Global North, we became concerned that the original vision of participatory research would be erased or overwritten by the unequal power of knowledge structures in the Global North. It was for this reason that we created the Knowledge for Change (K4C) Consortium, a partnership of training hubs around the world where a next generation of researchers, both university and community based, might learn together about CBPR.

The K4C Consortium was launched in 2018. It is a training of trainers model where CBPR mentors are trained by us, with the firm understanding that these mentors will in turn teach younger generations of students and practitioners. It does not teach 'how to' do CBPR using all-too-easy methods of participation to be taken up in instrumental fashion. There is no prescriptive textbook. The K4C program enables the mentors to work with communities for collective knowledge creation on a values-based ethics of justice and sustainability to harness the spiritual and emotional power of people's knowledge and bring about change in communities.

This book is not a textbook. It attempts to collate our experiences with organising and conducting the K4C program for nearly a decade now in the hope that those who want to teach CBPR to the next generation can do so with an understanding of how to do it in a way that maintains the ethical value orientations which emerged during the foundational years. While we will be credited as the authors of this book in bibliographic feeds, it is a product of all the mentors who have been part of the K4C program. These are their stories about how they teach, how they facilitate, and how they co-learn the concepts of CBPR.

In this book, we will use 'participatory research' when referring to the early phase of the development of ideas and practices of researching with communities (and not for them). From the early noughties, we began using 'community-based participatory research' – to forefront and give epistemic recognition to the community, the people's knowledge, without which there is no participatory research.

How did the foundational principles and ethical value orientations of participatory research which underpin our K4C program develop?

In less than five decades, the journey of participatory research has seen a remarkable trajectory. In the early/mid 1970s, academically trained researchers were beginning to confront several challenges around the central question of relevance of the knowledge they were producing through their research. On the one hand, academic research in all disciplines was attracting increasing attention and funding from public and private sources; on the other, the conflicts and tensions among and in newly liberated former colonies and their colonial rulers were becoming widespread.

In Tanzania, Budd was struggling with the disconnect between the vision and participation of the people in Ujamaa, where he was conducting research, and his training as a rigorous researcher from North America. Confronting his discomfort, Budd began to question his own normative and intellectual roots and began to articulate some emerging principles of an alternative approach to knowledge production, dissemination and utilisation. He first wrote about this alternative:

> *But it seems clear that research concerning itself with aspects of people's lives, particularly field research, needs to involve people in a different relationship than that of actors to be acted upon or subjects seen as objects. If change is to occur, adult educators need to be more deliberate about involving people in research. Participatory research, based on the assumption that man (sic) is a social animal, offers a process more consistent with adult education principles, more directly linked to action, and more scientific because it produces a more complex and thereby more accurate picture of reality* (Hall, 1975, pp 30–31).

In another part of the world (India), Rajesh was doing field research for his PhD thesis in rural areas of southern Rajasthan. With engineering and management education, he was beginning to experience frustrations with the disconnect between his scientific research tools and the local realities of poor tribal farmers. In his critique of the conventional research methodology that he was trained in, Rajesh found Budd as a 'reference' first in 1977, and then a lifelong colleague and friend since 1978.

The emergence of the International Network of Participatory Research in 1978 was a result of several like-minded and similarly frustrated academically trained researchers getting together from around the world. The International Council for Adult Education, where Budd was located, became the host for such regional and international networks. As the networking process grew, connections with grassroots practitioners, community organisers, educators and mobilisers began to bring to light the practice of participatory research in diverse contexts.

Between 1978 and 1980, the international network was developed and supported through a series of regional meetings in Caracas, Venezuela; New Delhi, India; Tennessee, United States, and two regional seminars in the Netherlands and Peru. When an international meeting took place in Ljubljana, in 1979, there was a consensus that despite theoretical and methodological variations, participatory research represented a three-fold activity – a method of social research, an educational act, and a means of taking transformative action (Diaz-Arevalo, 2022).

In those formative days of participatory research, key questions debated and alternatives practised centred around:

- Whose knowledge counts?
- Whose interests are likely to be served by the research?
- How can information and knowledge resources of a community be mobilised in the process of research?
- How can spaces for community participation and meaningful community engagement in the research (and development) process be created?
- How can involvement of communities facing the problems under study be catalytic in the research findings being used to improve and change their lives?

Post 1978, Rajesh continued with field research experiences that led him to empower marginal farmers by undertaking local research with them. In the process, he argued that the dominant paradigm of social science research was elitist and narrow, and mistakenly focused on objectivity and neutrality as benchmarks (Tandon, 1979). Budd continued as an academic and adult educator, influencing within the halls of academia.

The Asian Participatory Network incubated an organisation committed to the practice of and training in participatory research – Participatory Research in Asia (PRIA), of which Rajesh Tandon remains the Founder-President since 1982. During the 1980s and 1990s, PRIA promoted the practice of participatory research and participatory approaches of knowledge production in the design, planning and monitoring of development projects in India. Demystifying academic knowledge and revaluing popular knowledge were two common PRIA strategies towards empowerment. The central motto was an understanding that 'Knowledge is Power' and hence a method of both perpetuating the status quo and transforming realities.

This methodology gained substantial traction in social science research and among development professionals largely through the pioneering efforts of Robert Chambers. Chambers pushed development professionals in the UK and internationally to apply the perspective of such research in focusing on 'whose knowledge counts?' and 'who counts knowledge?'

> *There is a need to change to more participatory and open-ended social science research, with more of the agenda, appraisal and analysis carried out by local people, and the outcomes owned and shared by them. This implies also changes in relationships between funding bodies and researchers, and between supervisors and those conducting research for theses* (Chambers, 1994, p. 14).

By the mid-1990s, several phrases (including Participatory Action Research, or PAR, and Participatory Rural Appraisal, or PRA) had emerged, implying certain similar values and principles as participatory research. Efforts by PRIA at comparing action research with participatory research brought attention to the political economy of knowledge – 'whose interests does knowledge serve'?

> *Participatory researchers seek to transform the existing order and its oppressive consequences, while action researchers believe in consensus and incremental reform* (Brown and Tandon, 1983, p. 291).

We faced rejection from academia in America and India, and remained concerned about the need to find ways for participatory research to become part of academic teaching and training of young researchers even in these early days.

> *What is the role of the Academy in participatory research? What has the Academy done with participatory research? What is the status of the knowledge generated in a participatory research process? Participatory research originated as a challenge to positivist research paradigms as carried out largely by university based researchers. Our position has been that the centre of the process needed to be in the margins, in the communities, with women, with people of colour and so forth. Our experience has been that it is very difficult to achieve this kind of process from a university base; hence the need for alternative structures such as networks [and] centres. Participatory research deserves to be taught in universities. The academic community needs to discuss the role of knowledge as power to maintain status quo or transform realities* (Hall, 2005, p. 16).

In similar vein, Rajesh began to engage with academia in India from the mid-1990s. In his engagements with faculties of social work and sociology, he spoke of the primary formulations and implications of participatory research as a legitimate process of conducting research.

> *[Participatory Research] basically says, don't ignore popular knowledge; do not abandon knowledge generated through practice; do not negate emotions and actions as modes of knowing; develop tools, methods which could generate data in a research process where action and feelings are treated as legitimate modes of knowing, legitimate epistemological bases. Do take the new knowledge to those from whom we are collecting information. Can we share the findings with the so-called 'objects' for our research? Do they even have a right to know, the possibility to know, what we have discovered after we have gathered data from them? In participatory research, it is possible to have multiple uses of the same research enterprise – a researcher could publish an article and the community from where the data was generated, could use the new knowledge to integrate [it] in their own action for improving their situation. Could that use of knowledge which [the] community makes be given some legitimacy, some importance and not just [be] the printed word which the researcher [uses] for communicating new knowledge?* (Tandon, 2003).

Encouraged by his words, some students and teachers did begin to undertake participatory research in schools of social work in India from the late 1990s.

The turn of the millennium witnessed several trends which began to create a space for the more vigorous introduction of participatory research within academia. The rise of intellectual property regimes under the World Trade Organisation (WTO) began to support private capture of public knowledge and erosion of knowledge commons. Patenting local, indigenous, community knowledge became an arena of contestation. Increasing concerns about private gains from research in publicly funded universities began to enter academic discourse. When members of the International Participatory Research Network gathered for the second time in 1997 in Cartagena, they further pushed the need for cooperation between academic and popular knowledge traditions through global calls, supported by intellectuals such as Orlando Fals Borda and Paulo Freire.

In his closing remarks at Cartagena, Fals Borda was optimistic: 'In my view, this complementarity of academic and popular knowledge has been one tangible result of our discussions this week on ethics and fieldwork' (Fals Borda, 1998).

Community engagement in higher education began to move beyond the traditional colonial practice of 'departments of extension'. In University of Victoria (Canada), the first Office of Community-Based Research was set up in 2007 under the leadership of Budd (University of Victoria, 2007). In 2008, we participated in the international conference 'Higher Education: New challenges and emerging roles for human and social development' organised by the Global University Network for Innovation (GUNi). The report generated from the conference was one of the first articulations of the growing need for the social responsibility of higher education. Cristina Escrigas, Executive Director, GUNi, agreed it was time to 'review and reconsider the interchange of values between university and society; that is to say, we need to rethink the social relevance of universities'

(GUNi, 2008, p. xxviii). In the same year, at the Community-Campus-Exposition (CUExpo) in Canada, we (along with other colleagues) launched a new global alliance called Global Alliance of Community-Engaged Research (GACER).

It was increasingly becoming apparent to us that universities could become socially relevant only if they build strong relationships with the communities that lived outside their walls. As several international and regional networks of academic linkages with community and society were beginning to emerge, GACER invited them all to participate in a 'Big Tent' initiative to collaborate in promoting stronger and more equitable community-academia relationships.

At the second UNESCO World Higher Education Conference (held in 2009), GACER proposed some actions for strengthening community–university partnerships in achieving collective goals for reforming the role of higher education in sustainable development.

The Final Communiqué from the UNESCO World Higher Education Conference opens with a section on the Social Responsibility of Higher Education:

> *Higher education is a public good and the responsibility of all stakeholders...higher education has the social responsibility to advance our understanding of multifaceted issues...and our ability to respond to them...It should lead society in generating global knowledge to address global challenges* (UNESCO, 2010).

Inspired by such supportive declarations, GACER launched a study on community–university research partnerships with global perspectives, in 2011. The first global comparative research on this theme resulted in explorations of majority world roots of participatory research and articulations of knowledge democracy by de Sousa Santos (2007) and Visvanathan (2009) who found there could be 'no social justice without cognitive justice' (Hall et al., 2013).

Following the 2009 UNESCO World Higher Education Conference, we began brainstorming the idea of a UNESCO Chair with two partners, one based in an academic institution and the other in a practice-oriented organisation. Three developments converged to promote this positive idea. *First*, GUNi took an ambitious theme for its fifth World Report on Higher Education, inviting us to be the guest editors of 'Knowledge, Engagement and Higher Education: Contributions to Social Change'. In its Introduction, the Report grounds itself:

> *it hopes to explore ways in which engagement enhances teaching (learning and education) and research (knowledge production, mobilisation and dissemination); it approaches engagement in ways that accept the multiple sites and epistemologies of knowledge, as well as the reciprocity and mutuality in learning and education through engagement* (GUNi, 2013, p. xxxi).

Second, several scholars provided compelling arguments for investments in Community–University Research Partnerships (CURP). David Watson, former vice-chancellor, Brighton University, initiated a robust Community–University Partnership Programme (CUPP) at the university. He was an eloquent spokesperson for the links between lifelong learning, communities and university engagement (Watson, 2007; Watson and Maddison, 2005). Likewise, University of Victoria's Office of Community-Based Research conducted a study in Canada on the funding and development of CURP that summarised issues and challenges from the community and included a road map for collaborative advocacy on strengthening the field (University of Victoria, 2009).

Third, the Ministry of Education, Government of India and

the Planning Commission constituted a task force (of which Rajesh was nominated a member) to define features of a national policy on 'community engagement in higher education in India' (Planning Commission, 2011).

In hindsight, these were fortuitous circumstances. They supported the articulation of a UNESCO Chair with clear focus on 'community-based research' and 'social responsibility' in higher education.

We proposed to UNESCO in Paris a unique Chair – one that was based simultaneously in a higher education institution located in the Global North (at the University of Victoria where Budd Hall was teaching) and a practice- and community-oriented organisation based in the Global South (PRIA, which Rajesh Tandon continued to lead). In essence, it would be a Co-Chair.

The UNESCO Chair we were proposing described its mandate as:

> *to encourage North-South-South and South-South partnerships that build on and enhance the emerging global consensus, marking a new era of social responsibility in higher education. It will co-create new knowledge through partnerships among universities (academics), communities (civil society) and government (policy makers) leading to new capacities; new solutions to pressing problems related to sustainability, social and economic disparities, cultural exclusion, mistrust and conflict; and awareness among policy makers; enhanced scholarship of engagement; and modified pedagogy of community-based research* (Internal document, proposal to UNESCO in 2011).

Its focus on community–university research partnerships was explicit.

> *The domain of scholarship of engagement aims to redefine scholarly work from application of academic expertise to community-engaged scholarship that involves the faculty member in a reciprocal partnership with the community, is interdisciplinary, and integrates faculty roles of teaching, research, and service. While there is variation in current terminology (public scholarship, scholarship of engagement, community-engaged scholarship, community-based research, community–university research partnerships), engaged scholarship is defined by the collaboration between academics and individuals – knowledge professionals and the lay public (local, regional/state, national, global) – outside the academy for the mutually beneficial exchange of knowledge and resources in a context of partnership and reciprocity* (Internal document, proposal to UNESCO in 2011).

As our intellectual partnership entered its fourth decade, we were invited by UNESCO to co-chair the UNESCO Chair in Community-Based Research and Social Responsibility in Higher Education.

In the first four-year term of the Chair (2012–16), two global research studies were conducted to assess the state of play around community–university engagement and research partnerships. The first study focused on the question of mainstreaming and institutionalisation of CURP. Analysing global experiences in this field, the findings pointed towards the need for supportive national policies, institutional visions and appropriate structures to facilitate such partnerships (Hall et al., 2015). A particularly interesting finding was support for learning participatory research methodology for co-construction of knowledge with community, even though it continued to be university-centred and controlled.

Encouraged by such widespread reference to co-construction approaches, the second global study conducted by the Chair focused on contexts, pedagogies and arrangements for learning such approaches by the next generation of researchers. Its analysis of global 'best practices' in training next generation yielded insights about critical pedagogical principles (Hall et al., 2016). It became clear that students in academia were learning theories of co-construction of knowledge without much field practice. Practitioners, on the other hand, were learning to undertake research in support of local causes, learning by doing, without opportunities for systematisation and theorisation.

In the proposal to UNESCO to renew the term of the Chair in early 2016, building capacity for next generation of students and practitioners in CBPR was given central focus. It was argued that the movement of co-construction of knowledge will not be sustained if learning opportunities are not extensively made available in languages and contexts of the Global South and excluded North. We proposed:

> *[to] create an International Training Consortium (ITC) on participatory research approaches and methodologies that actively engage community members in knowledge production, mobilisation and research adoption processes* (Internal document, proposal to UNESCO in 2016).

We set ourselves ambitious goals – to train 5,000 community-based researchers and over 400 training facilitators in the next 5 years; and to create and support 15 hubs to deliver CBPR.

Based on our state-of-the-art research on international developments in CBPR funded by the International Development Research Centre (IDRC), Social Sciences and Humanities Research

Canada (SSHRC) and others, we responded to the question of how to create economical and sustainable structures in the Global South and the 'excluded' North for building research capacity in CBPR by developing the K4C strategy for training and capacity building of the next generation of researcher. The core of our model builds capacities through a 21-week Mentor Training Program (MTP). Academics from higher education institutions and practitioners from civil society organisations who complete the MTP go on to design and launch locally contextualised courses in CBPR.

Our approach to training university and community mentors in the co-creation of locally contextualised actionable knowledge based on grassroots resources and needs has received significant attention. The K4C was featured at the third UNESCO World Conference on Higher Education in Barcelona in May 2022 (International Commission on the Futures of Education, 2022). The K4C model has been adopted by the University Grants Commission in India as an approach for training academic staff in all the public universities in India. In November 2022, the K4C was featured in the opening UNITWIN plenary panel for the UNESCO Conference on Transforming Knowledge for Just and Sustainable Futures.

Yet, the K4C model is not yet commonly known, and that is why we have written this book. It makes available for the first time to a wider audience the unique principles, pedagogy and content of the MTP model. It is divided into two parts – the first part focuses on the content taught to the mentors during the MTP; the second part brings alive the efforts by mentors to engage in CBPR, establish new courses, and integrate CBPR perspectives and principles into existing institutional structures.

Following this Introduction, Chapter 2 by Walter Lepore and Wafa Singh continues the MTP story, giving details of the two intertwined programs, especially the pedagogical principles that underlie the training. Grounding the learning for the mentors is the understanding of power and ethics – the central values of the practice of CBPR. John Gaventa's succinct chapter 'Knowledge and Power' draws from his nearly 50 years of work in framing how knowledge is a source of power, and why it's important to recognise the various forms of power when conducting research and generating knowledge. Sarah Banks's chapter speaks to how ethical issues relating to rights, responsibilities, harms and benefits are embedded in all research. Systematising the knowledge of communities requires skills that go beyond the traditional research tools. Darlene Clover's chapter unpacks the teaching of arts-based methods in data collection and systemisation. No research should be conducted without a feminist perspective. Nandita Bhatt and Tariqa Tandon explain why the question of gender is important, showing through the example of making university campuses safe how gender considerations can be applied when undertaking CBPR. Catherine Etmanski, Kaustuv Bandyopadhyay and Wanda Krause round off Part 1 with their experience of CBPR-grounded teaching in a fully digital mode.

In Part 2 of the book, mentors who have completed the MTP share their experiences of how they have integrated CBPR's normative principles into teaching–learning programs in universities, what content in a particular subject area needs to be taught aligned with these normative principles, and the pedagogy adopted to teach the content. These experiences range from experiences in Colombia, Canada, South Africa and India.

How can one integrate Indigenous ways of knowing and learning into teaching CBPR? Crystal Tremblay and Tanya Clarmont write about the intentional ways in which they designed the upper-level undergraduate Geography course at the University of Victoria to weave Indigenous knowledges and methodologies in co-learning and reflective practice. Community engagement and service learning are well-known ways of making higher education institutions socially responsible. What can CBPR add to these well-established practices? René Oosthuizen's experience at Rhodes University, South Africa, and the efforts at Dayalbagh Educational Institute in the chapter by Jyoti Gogia show how these universities are trying to build the next generation of socially responsible students with a CBPR orientation. Sharon Valarmathi writes of Christ University's similar efforts in their service learning program. In Colombia, students are getting oriented to include CBPR in their community leadership learning, outlined by Luisa Pineda and Irma Flores in their chapter. Institutionalising the teaching and learning of CBPR brings with it a new set of challenges. Mónica Álvarez and Irma Flores's chapter gives glimpses of institutionalising CBPR at the organisational level at the University of Ibagué in Colombia, while Diksha Rajput and Anshuman Karol's chapter outlines how national policies promoting social responsibility and community engagement can be implemented through a structured training program for university lecturers to learn CBPR. The Conclusion to the book summarises the various achievements and challenges that mentors have faced in building the next generation of community-based participatory researchers. We also reflect on what we have learnt from conducting this values-based, ethically grounded training program, which holds hope for democratised learning and knowledge generation in a multi-lingual, multi-cultural world.

In the course of our work as UNESCO Co-Chairs we have been invited to deliver keynote talks to over 80 groups in 30 countries. We have seen an extraordinary growth in a global consensus in the recognition of engaged scholarship and the importance of community–university engagement. But the biggest surprise to us was the degree to which many of the principles of knowledge co-construction have made it into a range of recent UNESCO and UN reports.

1. The UNESCO Recommendation on Open Science

These recommendations released in 2021 define open science 'as an inclusive construct that combines various movements and practices aiming to make multilingual scientific knowledge openly available, accessible and reusable for everyone, and it builds on the following key pillars: open scientific knowledge, open science infrastructures, science communication, open engagement of societal actors and open dialogue with other knowledge systems' (UNESCO, 2021, p. 7). This Recommendation was adopted by the UNESCO General Conference in November 2021 by all the member states. The Recommendation has drawn on much of the thinking about engaged scholarship, the decolonisation of knowledge and the importance of multiple knowledge systems. In terms of its implications for higher education, it can be read as quite radical. Why do we say this? The Recommendation supports the principles and practices of the open access publishing movement in calling for all scientific knowledge to be freely available to everyone. It calls for the creation of open science infrastructures to provide free access to knowledge. These are principles which we would have expected to come from such a global normative statement. But the Recommendation goes far beyond this to call for open dialogue with other knowledge systems. By this they include Indigenous systems of science. The scientists behind these Recommendations are recognising Indigenous/community knowledge systems as falling within the global world of science. This has profound implications. And they go further to say that open science has an openness to societal actors. This recognises that knowledge is created in communities and throughout society.

2. Knowledge-Driven Actions: Transforming Higher Education for Global Sustainability

As a contribution to the third UNESCO World Higher Education Conference (WHEC) 2022, an independent expert group on higher education and the 2030 Sustainable Development Goals (SDG) Agenda undertook the production of a report on what needs to happen to transform higher education to support global sustainability. This report (UNESCO, 2022, p. 3) thoroughly discusses the role of higher education institutions in contributing to the 2030 Agenda, through a focus on three interrelated themes:

- the need to move towards inter- and transdisciplinary modes of producing and circulating knowledge;
- the imperative of becoming open institutions, fostering epistemic dialogue and integrating diverse ways of knowing;
- the demand for a stronger presence in society through proactive engagement and partnering with other societal actors.

3. Reimagining Our Futures Together: A New Social Contract for Education

The International Commission on the Future of Education released a report at the time of the WHEC 2022 conference, calling for '[the] need [for] a new social contract for education that can repair injustices while transforming the future. This new social contract must be grounded in human rights and based on principles of non-discrimination, social justice, respect for life, human dignity and cultural diversity. It must encompass an ethic of care, reciprocity, and solidarity. It must strengthen education as a public endeavour and a common good' (International Commission on the Futures of Education, 2021, p. 3).

4. Beyond Limits: New Ways to Reinvent Higher Education

Prepared by the UNESCO Secretariat as a working document, the roadmap prepared for the WHEC 2022, notes that 'To some extent, higher education has been built upon a unique model of thinking that prioritises an instrumental relationship with nature. This has partly led to the current climate and sustainability crisis. These views have disregarded other knowledge traditions that, for instance, have promoted a more caring and healthier relationship with our planet. It is urgent that higher education becomes open to every cultural and academic tradition and learns from them' (UNESCO, 2022, p. 29).

5. Indigenous Perspectives on Higher Education

One of the highlights of the WHEC 2022 conference was the presentation on Indigenous higher education by Dr Lorna Wanosts'a7 Williams, Professor Emeritus at University of Victoria, and Chair of the First People's Cultural Foundation. The key messages were:

- The starting point for the consultation was that higher education in its current format emerged from a narrow settlers' perspective and continues to largely exclude the perspectives and ways of knowing of Indigenous Peoples, to its own detriment and theirs.
- To favour the well-being of all people inclusively and the sustainability of societies overall, higher education systems must be deconstructed and co-created into new structures that respect and incorporate Indigenous knowledge and values and indigenous methods (Canadian Commission for UNESCO, 2021, p. 4).

The teaching and learning of CBPR is one way to achieve all these goals, for without a structured path forward these remain but lofty words.

PART 1

THE MENTOR TRAINING PROGRAM: PRINCIPLES AND PEDAGOGY

2

THE MENTOR TRAINING PROGRAM

Framework and Pedagogical Alignments

WALTER LEPORE AND WAFA SINGH

Introduction

Global developments in the recent years have led to a transformative and paradigmatic shift in the way education is imparted. The Covid-19–induced lockdown contributed to revolutionary changes in teaching and learning systems and strategies worldwide. Central to this change was the widespread and rapid adoption of technological tools and applications to aid the design and delivery of educative practices, which offer students an accessible and collaborative learning experience (Garrison, 2017). New models of education, which transcended conventional boundaries and the confines of traditional classroom teaching, began to assume increased importance in education systems around the world.

Hybrid learning has emerged as one of the most important new educational models. It represents an amalgamation of both offline and online modes of learning, delivered physically and remotely for creating innovative, flexible, creative, dynamic, and adaptable learning experience for the learners (Raes et al., 2020). In essence, hybrid learning refers to a combination of instructional modalities, which includes online learning and face-to-face classroom instruction, to provide an efficient and effective learning experience grounded in reflection and praxis (Doering, 2006; Halverson et al., 2012). It meets the needs of both the learners and educators by offering flexibility and independence in accessing and delivering courses. The learners, in particular, benefit from pacing their learning and accessing materials remotely, while also transcending from guided education to self-motivated learning in the process.

In this chapter, we present and discuss the tenets of the Mentor Training Program (MTP), which is inspired by the principles of hybrid learning and the 'Training of Trainers' (ToT) methodology, where trained mentors can effectively educate and train others, thereby creating a multiplier effect and expanding the reach and impact of the original training program. Designed and delivered by the UNESCO Chair in Community-Based Research and Social Responsibility in Higher Education (UNESCO Chair in CBR-SR thereafter), the MTP equips members of the Knowledge for Change (K4C) Consortium with the skills, knowledge and competencies needed to train others in the theory and practice of CBPR. We will delve into the structure of the MTP and its different modules; the link between the guiding pedagogical principles proposed by the UNESCO Chair in CBR-SR and content of the MTP; the MTP learning activities, assignments and expected learning outcomes; the contextualisation of CBPR training through the MTP; and the framework for assessing its impact. Our aim is to highlight the unique components of the MTP that not only ensure that mentors become knowledgeable in CBPR but are also effective in preparing them for their roles as trainers in diverse community and university settings.

Key Ideas and Significance

Initiated in 2018, the MTP represents a uniquely tailored and international curriculum for CBPR training. The program is carefully crafted as a hybrid learning experience, taking into consideration the learning needs of trainees from diverse backgrounds (i.e., academia and civil society organisations), and the need for concerted plans for scaling, replicating and formalising CBPR training, as evidenced in the UNESCO Chair's Next Gen project (Tandon et al., 2016).

The MTP is a 21-week non-credit certificate designed and offered by the UNESCO Chair in CBR-SR through the Division of Continuing Studies of the University of Victoria (Canada). The course is open to any trainee nominated and sponsored by the K4C hubs,* who can demonstrate previous experience in conducting CBPR and admissibility to the University of Victoria's non-credit programs, which normally involves graduation from a post-secondary institution. However, experienced researchers and/or community applicants who do not meet this requirement are also considered upon approval of the co-holder of the UNESCO Chair, based on their prior academic or work experience.

The MTP combines the theoretical and foundational aspects of CBPR, supervised field practices, and personal critical reflections with peers in cohorts of 20–25 learners. The 21 modules (generally one module per week) are carefully curated to build on each other, starting with the foundational concepts on CBPR, and gradually advancing to more complex topics and hands-on practice related to

---

*To be part of the K4C Consortium, a local training hub is required to be a formal partnership between one higher education institution and, at least, one civil society organisation. Each hub is led by a coordinator, who has responsibility for the development of the hub, including the selection of mentors and supervisors. Each hub selects and financially supports between three and five mentors to participate in the MTP. The selection of mentors is done in consultation with the UNESCO Chair in CBR-SR. Upon completion of the MTP, certified mentors are responsible for adapting the MTP curriculum and pedagogy to offer local educational CBPR programs in their hubs (see https://www.unescochair-cbrsr.org/k4c-2/).

teaching and practicing community-engaged research. Following a 'cascade' training model (see Figure 2.1), the main goal of the MTP is to help future K4C mentors learn to train, coach and mentor the next generation of community-based researchers (Lepore et al., 2021). To complete the program, mentors are required to design a CBPR course to be delivered in their hubs, using materials in local language and adhering to the K4C pedagogical principles (described later in this chapter). It is expected that a K4C hub will not only nominate and financially support their mentors to be enrolled in the MTP, but also facilitate the delivery of the local CBPR course within their own institutions. Thus, the MTP aims to develop individual pedagogical capacities in CBPR, as well as institutional support, structures and capacities to formally teach CBPR in the localities and institutions where the K4C hubs are located.

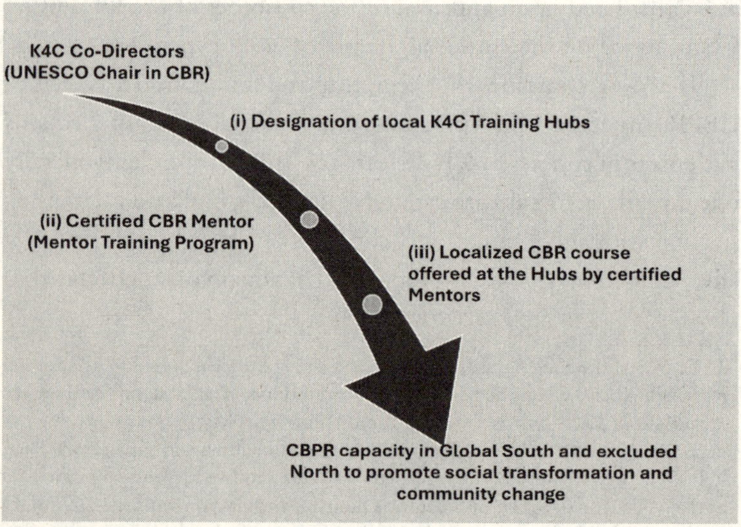

Figure 2.1 MTP cascade training model

To ensure compliance with the UNESCO Chair in CBR-SR standards, the co-holders of the Chair, Budd Hall and Rajesh Tandon, certify each local course. These courses should contain the following elements: core components of CBPR; locally customised components that meet established learning outcomes and are contextually and thematically relevant, aligning with the United Nations Sustainable Development Goals (UN SDGs); and a set of recommended components designed to cover final learning outcomes, which can be locally modified to meet students' training needs.

Structure and Design

The MTP is designed as a hybrid model for educating researchers in CBPR, which comprises the following components: (i) online learning; (ii) face-to-face learning workshop; and (iii) a field work component (see Figure 2.2). These components are supported by interspersed reflective activities, assignments, self-assessment, evaluation and reporting, throughout the 21-week learning period.

Online learning

The online modules focus on the development of **cognitive (knowledge-based) competencies** in understanding the concepts, history, development, process and methods of CBPR. This is delivered with the help of online lectures, pre-recorded videos and provision of a list of materials/literary resources as reading assignments (books, chapters, journal articles, field reports, etc.). Another important part of this learning component includes online forums, specially designed on an e-learning platform for hosting different types of activities and reflective assignments. This contributes to the engagement of mentors with the course materials and activities, and between each other, thus facilitating the creation of a community of learners in the virtual classroom, which supports critical discourse and reflection (Garrison, 2017). This is achieved through asynchronous peer discussions, sharing materials, seeking answers (from peers and course instructors), teamwork with fellow mentors from the same hub and/or geographic region, and sharing of individual experiences in community-based research work. In addition to intellectual sharings, this platform also serves as an opportunity to build rapport with peer learners and instructors.

Face-to-face learning workshop (residential component)

The two-week residential learning component is tailored to build the personal and professional competencies of the mentors in CBPR. Facilitated by the Co-Chairs and supported by local CBPR experts, this component aims to train the mentors in specific **awareness-based competencies** with particular emphasis on emotional and dialogical processes, which are critical for successfully undertaking CBPR projects in the field (Tandon et al., 2016; Palahicky et al., 2019). The residency also includes field visits and lectures by academics and practitioners with long standing history and experience in the field of CBPR on topics like value and wisdom of Indigenous knowledge keepers, real-time participatory field exercises, community mapping, participatory video, and more.

The core objective of the residency includes providing the mentors with a participatory learning environment for deepening their knowledge, both in the theory and practice of CBPR, and enhancing their facilitations skills. To further aid the consolidation of their learnings, the Co-Chairs maintain individual conversations and feedback sessions with each mentor, along with providing personalised guidance on their upcoming CBPR field projects.

The location of the residency rotates annually and is hosted by different K4C hubs, having taken place in Canada, Colombia, and

India. This offers the mentors an opportunity to connect with local knowledge workers, and to visit and learn about local initiatives aimed at co-creating knowledge with community partners and projects that contribute to knowledge democracy.

Field work component

In addition to online learning and the face-to-face residential workshop, field study is another integral part of nurturing competent CBPR mentors, considering that learning by doing is an essential part of developing and improving skills in CBPR. This third component of the MTP includes mentors conducting CBPR field projects (individually or in small teams), under the supervision of local instructors and community focal persons who provide timely guidance and feedback. As part of the field work, the mentors are expected to adhere to all the steps of a CBPR process (or parts of it, considering time and resource limitations), which includes identification of a local community partner for undertaking the project, framing research questions in partnership with the partners, jointly designing the research plan and undertaking joint data collection, analysis, and deciding on novel ways to represent and share the emergent findings and new co-created knowledge.

As such, the field work component significantly contributes to the development of **action-based competencies** needed to work with communities. The two outputs from this phase include an experience-based reflection document, and a descriptive case study on the subject matter of the research.

The broad design of the MTP and development of corresponding competencies is depicted in Table 2.1.

Table 2.1: MTP Basic Design and Components

MTP Component	Capacities
Online learning	**knowledge-based competencies** (concepts, history, development, process, and methods of CBPR)
Face-to-face residency	**awareness-based competencies** (self and social awareness; emotional and dialogical processes, reflective practice)
Field work	**action-based competencies** (planning and implementation of a CBPR project)

Pedagogical Framework, Principles and Alignment

The MTP builds on a pedagogical framework emerging from two global research studies led by the UNESCO Chair in CBR-SR (Hall et al., 2015; Tandon et al., 2016). In addition to being robust and theoretically grounded, the framework also provides flexibility for translation into effective CBPR teaching and training strategies in diverse local contexts. Figure 2.2 provides a crisp description of the five principles that form the MTP pedagogical framework and their alignment with specific training modules further described in a subsequent section of this chapter.

Figure 2.2 MTP Pedagogical Principles

1. An orientation towards research ethics and values

The first pedagogical principle emphasises the importance of orienting researchers on understanding the connotations of ethics and values in research. Its importance can be judged by the fact that it precedes any other rules, procedures and processes of CBPR training. The MTP includes a dedicated module on the ethics and values of CBPR, which follows the modules on the development of personal and professional competencies in CBPR (via the face-to-face learning workshop).

Learners delve into the concept of ethics and values and their practical application through multiple modalities, including theoretical reading materials, guest lectures by experts on research ethics, and extensive online discussions on research ethical protocols and guidelines facilitated by CBPR instructors (see Chapter 4). These efforts are aimed at nurturing the learners into ethical and value-based researchers, sensitive to and respectful towards communities (especially the marginalised ones) and community partners. An important takeaway from this learning is that, given the importance of relationality in CBPR, the impartial and detached approach to ethics that emphasises fairness – which dominates the research ethics literature, policies and codes – is inadequate on its own as an ethical framework for CBPR (MacFarlane and Roche, 2018).

2. Development of a deep understanding of power and partnerships

As a collaborative process between communities and researchers, CBPR ultimately leads to the co-construction of knowledge, aided by the weaving in of academic and practice-based knowledge cultures (Lepore et al., 2024). However, this collaboration has several subtle and dynamic underpinnings, with the most important among them being the extant power structures and differentials between research partners. This principle, therefore, emphasises equalising power asymmetries and building relationships of mutual trust before embarking on a CBPR project.

The MTP includes a full module on 'Knowledge and Power' (see Chapter 3), stressing the importance of knowledge and its role in determining positions of power and privilege, while also exploring their intersections. In doing so, it also touches upon the conflict between historically divergent community and academic knowledge cultures, and the quest for epistemic justice arising from the continued hegemony of academic knowledge epistemologies.

Acknowledging the impact of these aspects on the creation of equitable research partnerships, the MTP also includes an exclusive module on building and sustaining research partnerships. By focusing on the modalities, approaches and mechanisms for fostering reciprocal, respectful, and mutually beneficial university–community partnerships, this module guides the learners on how to navigate the contentious issues of power asymmetries to ensure desired CBPR outcomes.

3. Incorporation of multiple modes of enquiry

A collaborative approach involves multiple sources of knowledge generation as well as multiple methods to capture this knowledge. Accordingly, the third pedagogical principle advocates training researchers in multiple modes of enquiry. Here, action- and affection-based modes of data collection (such as focused group discussions, art, drama, photovoice, role-plays, and storytelling; see Chapter 5) are treated at par with other cognitive methods (such as interviews, questionnaires, and surveys).

These ideas are mirrored in the MTP as it includes a module dedicated to training learners on multiple modes of CBPR enquiry, which precedes the face-to-face residency. While this module helps the learners develop a comprehensive understanding of various cognitive, active, and affective modes of enquiry used in a CBPR process, the residency provides an opportunity for experiential learning of such approaches by practicing the different methods in real-time, in small groups, and under the expert supervision of the Co-Chairs along with other local and global experts. Special emphasis is given to practicing action- and affection-based methods (e.g., storytelling circles, community-engaged mapping), as it is observed that the learners often have little to no orientation to these approaches, while being trained in mostly traditional research methods. Additionally, real-time guidance from the experts who facilitate this learning process further enriches and improves the learner's understanding of these methodologies.

4. Participation in learning CBPR and ensuring a balance between classroom (theory) and field (practice)

The dynamism involved in a CBPR process requires the researcher to actively think, read, respond, write, and reflect. These skills cannot be developed if the teaching processes are designed in a unilateral manner. CBPR training needs to be participatory and communal with the mentors participating in the process of learning as much as the trainer/instructor, thus creating a learning community where participants assume the roles of both teacher and learner, and engage in meaningful learning activities (Garrison, 2017). This fourth principle thus calls for balancing classroom sessions and field activities in a way that the mentors participate as active stakeholders in the learning process, and take responsibility and control of their learning.

This principle is manifested in the MTP design in three ways. First, there is a dedicated module on bridging the divide between academic theory and field-based practice. Second, the organisation and structure of the MTP allows for the application of theories learnt in one module to be practised in the subsequent module(s).

For instance, the theoretical content on concepts of CBPR, such as knowledge, power, and modes of enquiry acquired in the first six modules of the MTP, is put into practice in weeks 7 and 8 during the face-to-face residency. Similarly, theoretical learnings on the CBPR steps, building and sustaining research partnerships, and knowledge representation and mobilisation are applied in real-time when the learners undertake their CBPR field project. Third, interspersed asynchronous learning activities, self-assessment tools, and assignments such as online discussions and reflection/analytical reports, ensure that the mentors actively participate in the learning process throughout the MTP.

5. The role of researchers as a CBPR facilitator

The fifth principle puts emphasis on developing a deeper understanding of the researchers' own positionality and identity. This is considered essential because development of the 'self' is crucial for growing and refining inter-personal skills of communication, facilitation and engagement, which are critical in any CPBR process (Park, 2001). The MTP embeds this principle in the entirety of its design, which gets manifested in both its theoretical and practical training components.

Interestingly, both the first and last MTP modules touch upon these aspects. The module on 'Person and Place' that marks the beginning of CBPR training, focuses on developing the learner's understanding of their positionality and how it influences their worldviews. The last module ('Becoming critical and reflexive researchers') emphasises the importance of understanding personal motivations, attitudes, and orientation, which plays a critical role in determining one's CBPR facilitation competencies and abilities. Further, underscoring the significance of reflexivity in adult education (Venneri, 2020), the MTP also embeds in its design engaged discussions among learners and with instructors (online and in-person), and reflective journaling for capturing one's own feelings, reactions and motivations in the learning process.

Grounded in theories of knowledge and adult education, these five principles relate to the various theoretical dimensions and practical aspects involved in developing training capacities in CBPR within and beyond academia. Further, they serve as broad guiding points for conceptualising and designing effective CBPR training programs, which can be adapted for producing a locally/regionally relevant CBPR training curriculum (Lepore et al., 2021). The basic design of the MTP provides visible and valid evidence on how these principles can be adapted for advancing authentic CBPR training programs.

Constituent Modules and Organisation

While the MTP builds on the tenets of hybrid learning in general, it is pertinent to examine its key constituents in detail, to be able to understand the nature of immersive learning it offers, and how the CBPR pedagogical principles described in the preceding section are embedded in the program. Table 2.2 is a snapshot of the 21 modules that constitute the MTP.

Table 2.2. MTP Modules

Module	Topic
1.	Pre-course Preparation
2.	Person and Place
3.	Introduction to CBPR
4.	Knowledge and Power
5.	Steps in CBPR
6.	Multiple Modes and Methods of CBPR
7.	Face-to-face Learning Workshop
8.	Face-to-face Learning Workshop (continued)

Module	Topic
9.	Reflections from Face-to-Face Residency and Self-Assessment I
10.	Ethics and Values
11.	Building and Sustaining Research Partnerships
12.	Representation of Knowledge
13.	Impact Assessment
14.	Reflection on the Course to Date
15.	Balancing Theory and Practice
16.	Field Work
17.	Field Work (continued)
18.	Reflections from the Field Work and Assignment I
19.	Becoming Critical and Reflexive Researcher/Mentors and Self-Assessment II
20.	Bringing K4C to Life and Assignment II
21.	MTP Evaluation and Assignment III

Module 1: Pre-course Preparation

The first week serves as an opportunity for the mentors to get familiar with the platform where the MTP is delivered (e.g., Moodle or Brightspace hosted by the University of Victoria), begin navigating it, and sort technical issues. The learners can also utilise this week to know more about the K4C Consortium and the UNESCO Chair in CBR-SR, understand the basic tenets and outline of the MTP, and access training resources. Additionally, this week witnesses personal introductions by the mentors on the online space, where they elaborate on their respective background(s), context, expectations and motivations for joining the MTP. Mentors may also choose to articulate their learning goals, based on their personal or professional backgrounds.

Learning activities/assignments

- Creation of a **learning journal** as a personal space for documenting experiences and challenges in the process. This also aids in objective self-assessments conducted later in the course.
- Discussing traditional and local approaches to community work, initial thoughts about CBPR and preliminary ideas on their forthcoming field project via the online forum.
- Initial self-assessment of competencies under the knowledge, awareness, and skills dimensions (explained below in the section 'Impact Framework of the MTP').

Learning outcomes

- Critical management of information in digital environments.
- Effective written, visual and oral communication.
- Life-long learning.
- Getting to know the fellow learners and developing inter-cultural knowledge and sensitivity.
- Familiarisation with key concepts and approaches to CBPR.
- Framing of initial ideas for CBPR field study and discussing them with instructors and peer learners.

Module 2: Person and Place

Understanding the context is a critical part of a CBPR process, and a useful place to develop this understanding is to begin with oneself. Each of us carry elements of visible and invisible identity, in relation to our place, the history of where we are working, our background, etc. Our identity shapes our worldviews, our conceptual and normative frames, which in turn influences our perception and analysis of reality (Helve, 2015). This module is dedicated to developing and consolidating the importance of explicitly reflecting on one's positionality as a part of research and teaching practices. The goal is to give mentors elements that will help them (and their own trainees) identify areas where they may hold power and privileges, discern how these may influence their research, and find ways to mitigate some tensions and ethical issues that may arise in their projects as they work with community partners. This module also serves as the first week of the structured online learning component of the MTP.

Learning activities/assignments

- Online discussions on the history of settlement on the land where one was raised and/or where one lives, and how aspects of personal identity, social class, gender, land settlement patterns and immigration relate to one's work on social justice, communities, and CBPR.
- Enlisting self-learnings on dealing with issues of diversity and inequality in the context of CBPR.

Learning outcomes

- Identifying and reflecting on aspects of one's personal location (urban-rural), gender, ethnicity, race, class, sexuality, heritage, etc.
- Becoming familiar with diverse approaches to land use and ownership.
- Understanding how issues and aspects of land and self-related identity impact and shape one's worldviews.

Module 3: Introduction to CBPR

CBPR is an overarching research approach that has originated in social movements and marginalised spaces in our societies, particularly in the Global South (Tandon, 2005). As such, it covers differing manifestations and terminologies, based on its contextual application. This module explores the history of CBPR, while introducing the basic concepts and principles of participatory, engaged research and its diverse applications.

Learning activities/assignments

- Sharing personal reflections and/or written materials on the roots of CBPR in own contexts, discussing early perceptions and reactions to the former, the reasons behind the same, own experiences of creating knowledge with the community, what led to it, and associated implications (challenges, frustrations, etc.).
- Affirming the considerations guiding one's own CBPR field research study.

Learning outcomes

- Familiarisation with the history and theoretical development of CBPR.
- Understanding the principles of CBPR and its diverse approaches.
- Integrating CBPR vocabulary into one's own field research study.

Module 4: Knowledge and Power

The study of knowledge, its creation and use, are far from being neutral. Some forms of knowledge are perceived as more credible than others, with scientists and academics often regarded as having more valid, robust and, therefore, influential knowledge than others (see Lepore et al., 2024). However, CBPR places value on the knowledge that arises from lived experiences, granting 'epistemic privilege' to those who experience discrimination or exclusion. Building on the previous module, it is crucial to pay attention to how the roles or identities assumed in the research process (e.g., the 'expert' role by academic researchers) can create power asymmetries and inequalities in relationships and partnerships with research collaborators and/or community partners (Gaventa and Cornwall, 2008). This module explores such knowledge-related power dimensions and asymmetries, examining its implication on the CBPR process and the knowledge it helps create.

Learning activities/assignments

- Online discussions on several related topics such as evolution of knowledge, its meaning and implications, interactions with aspects of power and control, and their adaptions in own contexts.
- Reflections on knowledge epistemicide and positioning of subaltern knowledge(s).

Learning outcomes

- Understanding academic and community use of knowledge, and their compatibility.
- Analysing the concepts of knowledge democracy, epistemicide, epistemic justice, decolonisation.
- Positioning CBPR as a process of building countervailing, collective or transformative power.

Module 5: Steps in CBPR

This module describes in detail the steps in CBPR processes and focuses on considerations in designing the field study in consultation with various stakeholders. It also clarifies the multiple purposes of doing research, and the special features of CBPR in each step of the research cycle.

Learning activities/assignments

- Online group discussions on co-construction of knowledge,

and the conditions which facilitate the former and aid in the achievement of social change.

- Preparation of a reflection document on the special features of CBPR at the stage of framing the research question, and the potential challenges that may arise in the process.
- Description of field study plan, and how it incorporates the different steps of CBPR.

Learning outcomes

- Becoming familiar with the processes involving co-construction of knowledge and how it plays a crucial role in each research step in a CBPR process.
- Learning the considerations in reaching agreement between community and researcher on the research question.
- Defining research question of the field study and outlining the various steps.

Modules 6: Multiple Modes and Methods of CBPR

In line with the third pedagogical principle elaborated in the preceding section, this module covers different modes of enquiry and its associated methods of data collection and analysis. Primarily, it focuses on the three most prominent modes of enquiry used in CBPR: cognition (questionnaires, surveys, interviews, case studies), action (Participatory Rural Appraisal [PRA], Participatory Action Research [PAR], Focus Group Discussions [FGDs], etc.), and affection (photo-voice, participatory video, storytelling, role-plays, theatre, poetry, etc.). As it is well explained by Palahicky et al. (2019), the affective domain is one of the most challenging teaching areas because it integrates cognition, behaviour, and emotions.

Learning activities/assignments

- Group discussion on past experiences of using different modes of enquiry (cognition/action/affection) in research.
- Discussion on the methods to be used in the field project.

Learning outcomes

- Understanding the significance of using multiple modes of enquiry in CBPR.
- Becoming familiar with the use and application of diverse set of research methods, including PRA, arts-based and action-oriented methods.
- Exploring the different considerations involved in choosing the most contextually appropriate method and applying the same in own field research study.

Modules 7 and 8: Face-to-face Learning Residency

Staggered over a period of two weeks and delivered in person, modules 7 and 8 are focused on strengthening the personal and professional competencies of mentors for achieving excellence in CBPR training. As explained earlier, this residential learning component further deepens and consolidates the development of awareness-related components through the application of experiential and context-specific learning activities and approaches. Field visits to community organisations engaged in CBPR projects, group activities and reflections on past and present experiences of one and others comprises the basis of such learning. This is complemented with active and sensitive facilitation and coaching by seasoned practitioners and experts in CBPR.

Learning activities/assignments

- Practicing CBPR facilitation, supported by video feedback.

- Group work in designing and practising various methods of research.
- Self-reflections on personal journey, values and commitments.
- Participating in field visits for learning about existing local CBPR initiatives.

Learning outcomes

- Designing, assessing and improving competencies as a CBPR facilitator, while learning norms of collaboration and joint work exercises.
- Designing and practicing methods, such as participatory resource mapping and participatory video.
- Understanding Indigenous research methodologies, and their commonalities and differences with CBPR.
- Reviewing progress of field study planning.

Module 9: Reflections from Face-to-Face Residency and Self-Assessment I

Critical reflection in adult education and CBPR helps individuals achieve deeper learning, foster collaborative and ethical practices, and drive more meaningful and impactful outcomes. This module focuses on systematising learning emerging from the two weeks of residential learning experience. This also includes the first formal self-assessment of competencies acquired up till this point in the MTP.

Learning activities/assignments

- Preparation of a reflection paper, documenting one's strengths, weaknesses, and areas of improvement for becoming a competent CBPR practitioner.
- Preparation of detailed notes on at least two new research methods learnt in the residential modules.

- Self-assessment I through online presentation of self-portfolio and identification of personal strengths and areas for further improvement, based on deliberations/feedback from the supervisor.

Learning outcomes:

- Systematising the agenda for personal and professional development of competencies in CBPR.
- Applying various new CBPR methods learnt and practised during the face-to-face learning workshop.
- Judging the development of competencies in oneself, based on the learnings acquired.

Module 10: Ethics and Values

This module explores the complex issue of ethics and values in CBPR, where the boundaries between community and academic spaces, between personal and professional spaces, and between formal and informal interactions may become more blurred, and less defined than in traditional, mainstream research (MacFarlane and Roche, 2018). This module explores various forms of ethical guidelines for working with oppressed, excluded, or indigenous communities. Recognised experts on ethics in CBPR are invited to teach this module as they hold extensive experience and knowledge about the topic.

Learning activities/assignments

- Describing and discussing the ethical issues/dilemmas one may face in CBPR projects, based on self/other's experiences.
- Outlining and discussing the ethical guidelines, protocols, practices for CBPR work at one's own organisation, community and/or region.

Learning outcomes

- Understanding research and the concept of neutrality.
- Exploring principles of Indigenous research ethics.
- Analysing approaches to ethics in different forms of CBPR.
- Understanding the limitations of traditional ethics protocol for conducting CBPR.

Module 11: Building and Sustaining Research Partnerships

Creating and maintaining trust-based relations between the researcher and the community is at the heart of CBPR. Partnerships of mutual respect and benefit can be critical to undertaking effective CBPR (Molosi-France and Dipholo, 2022). In lieu of this, this module focuses on the processes and requirements for building and sustaining reciprocal, respectful and mutually beneficial partnerships between academic researcher and community partners.

Learning activities/assignments

- Preparation of a review paper based on a critical assessment of the 'Rethinking Research Partnerships Guide and Tool Kit' (Cornish et al., 2017), exploring its strengths, weakness, and offering potential recommendations for further strengthening of community–university research partnerships.
- Sharing a short story based on one's past experiences of being involved in a research partnership, reflecting on the challenges and emergent lessons.

Learning outcomes

- Understanding the benefits and challenges of building research partnerships.

- Analysing different knowledge systems that need accommodation in nurturing strong research partnerships.
- Identifying key intermediaries, interface mechanisms, and their role in sustaining academia–community partnerships.
- Exploring the use of a formal Memorandum of Understanding (MOU) and/or Memorandum of Agreement (MOA) as potential tools in partnership management.

Module 12: Representation of Knowledge

This module delves into the multiple ways of representing knowledge and sharing research findings with diverse audiences. It puts special emphasis on how to facilitate knowledge dissemination to support action (e.g., for political/public awareness, advocacy, funding, policy change).

Learning activities/assignments

- Contribute towards the preparation of a knowledge mobilisation plan, by sharing ideas for disseminating research results based on CBPR experiences that one may have previously had or heard about. This plan should include details of the dissemination method (group meeting, mural, reports, policy briefs, etc.), stakeholders involved, intended audience, impact, etc.

Learning outcomes

- Understanding how knowledge and research findings can be represented and communicated in powerful and engaging ways to diverse audiences.
- Developing storytelling and data presentation skills.

Module 13: Impact Assessment

The impact of one's work in CBPR may manifest differently within varying timelines. While sometimes the impact is direct and obvious (such as a political or a policy change), at other times, it emerges over a longer period, including changes within oneself and others involved in CBPR, and/or changes in people who are witnesses to one's work. This module focuses on documenting the impact of CBPR, ensuring that the effects on all stakeholders, such as the community, the mentors, and the mentor's institution, are thoroughly documented and reported.

Learning activities/assignments

- Online discussions on the different ways to capture and 'measure' the impact of CBPR, and the indicators that can be used in the process.

Learning outcomes

- Analysing approaches to the assessment of impact in CBPR: institutional, political, personal, organisational.
- Demonstrating commitment and responsibility to local community, civil society, social movements and partners.

Module 14: Reflection on the Course to Date

This module serves as an opportunity for the learners to reflect on how the MTP has progressed thus far, and the expectations that have been met (or not) both individually and collectively. This reflective exercise is aimed at helping mentors to have a genuine appreciation of the skills, knowledge and abilities necessary for effective CBPR teaching, and to empower them to take control of their own learning experience.

Learning activities/assignments

- Engage in online deliberations, pose questions and ask answers on points of doubts, confusion, ambiguity and/or seek clarification with respect to future learning processes.

Learning outcomes

- Settling anxieties and nurturing hopes for further learning processes.
- Seek and receive clarifications for field work.

Module 15: Balancing Theory and Practice

As a commonplace practice, it is often observed that while academic writing is heavily focused on theory, practitioners in community organisations focus on real-time action and impact on the field. Directly informed by the fourth pedagogical principle elaborated earlier, this module helps the mentors reflect on how to bridge this dichotomy between the worlds of theory and practice in their CBPR projects.

Learning activities/assignments

- Online group discussions on the relation between knowing and doing, theory and practice, action and learning, and posting key points briefly.
- Preparation of a document, describing how theory and practice is expected to interact in one's own field study.

Learning outcomes

- Understanding the link between theory and practice.
- Understanding the issues of reliability and validity in research.
- Developing the use of praxis in field study.

Modules 16 and 17: Field Work

These modules are dedicated to advancing and completing one's own CBPR field research project in their locality, under the guidance of a dedicated supervisor and support from a community focal person.

Learning activities/assignments

- Timely progress reports to be shared with the supervisor for feedback, and actioning on the latter appropriately.

Learning outcomes

- Independent work on the field study.
- Application of CBPR learnings in a real setting.

Module 18: Reflections from Field Work and Assignment 1

Based on the various entries created in the learning journal over the weeks of the MTP and the experiences emerging from the CBPR field study, this module focuses on reflective learning, which helps mentors make sense of their experiences, enhance their understanding, and apply what they have learned in practical ways.

Learning activities/assignments

- Preparation of a 500-word reflection document, describing the different stages of the CBPR field study, focusing on what worked, what did not work, elements of surprise, coping mechanisms, etc. (Assignment 1).

Learning outcomes

- Acquiring authentic learnings based on self-reflection and one's own experience of doing CBPR in the field.

Module 19: Becoming Critical and Reflexive Researchers/Mentors and Self-Assessment II

A CBPR mentor needs to develop capacities for continuous learning in order to become a reflexive researcher and facilitator. This module focuses on exploring and aligning personal and professional motivations, analysing personal attitudes to plurality of cultures, perspectives, status and hierarchy, and examining personal orientation to issues of authority, power and powerlessness.

Learning activities/assignments

- Using a self-assessment tool to evaluate the strengths and weaknesses with respect to individual competencies and identify areas of improvement (Self-assessment II).
- Sharing stories of past experiences or attempts to conduct oneself as reflexive researchers/practitioners.

Learning outcomes

- Understanding the concept of reflexive practice.
- Learning to maintain a critical and reflexive approach.

Module 20: Bringing K4C to Life and Assignment 2

The penultimate module is dedicated to sharing ideas on how the mentors intend to take forth the learnings acquired in the MTP in their own contexts for teaching and facilitating CBPR to university students and emerging community-based practitioners.

Learning activities/assignments

- Preparation of a 5000-word case study, documenting the key research findings in local language, which would serve as teaching–learning material for CBPR courses taught and delivered by mentors (Assignment 2).
- Open online discussions on the CBPR centre/hub design, among other fellow mentors, complemented with feedback/ suggestions from the K4C advisory board.

Learning outcomes

- Presenting future CBPR training strategies.
- Learning about the process of recruiting future researchers for the CBPR training course.

Module 21: MTP Evaluation and Assignment 3

The last module presents as an opportunity to share any final ideas, feedback, suggestion, and/or comments that mentors may have about the MTP course. Ideas on strengthening the K4C network and modalities to provide continued support going forward are particularly encouraged.

Learning activities/assignments

- Complete an individual evaluation form on the contents, presentation, impact of the MTP.
- Open and reflective discussions on ways to further improve the MTP, to provide the best possible outcomes for the future researchers/mentors.
- Preparing final plans for designing and launching local CBPR courses, which are shared and discussed online (Assignment 3).

Learning outcomes

- Learning and reflecting on the overall performance of the MTP, areas for improvement and ways to ensure continued momentum.
- Firming up the plans to offer CBPR course at local levels, its design, delivery, etc.

Contextualisation of CBPR Training: MTP and Beyond

The importance of context in CBPR training cannot be over-emphasised. This aligns with the motto 'global is local and local is global', and the need to think globally but act locally for addressing contemporary social challenges (United Nations, 2011; Wadhwani and Malpani, 2023). The MTP reflects this focus by highlighting aspects of place, local issues, needs and assets, community knowledges, and research partnerships with community partners as foundational tenets of CBPR training. Thus, it helps mentors explore how the core concepts of CBPR play out in practice in their local context through CBPR projects that are socially relevant. The program is built on the premise that CBPR training and corresponding application need to be contextualised to suit local, regional and geographical needs and demands. In adhering to these considerations, MTP mentors are required to design CBPR field projects that are sensitive and inclusive of the local context, addressing immediate social concerns, and devising community-based solutions.

The link between the local CBPR courses designed by the mentors and specific UN SDGs is important for contextualising CBPR training design and its application. The MTP encourages mentors to reflect on areas of primary societal concern in their respective context/region related to the UN Agenda 2030, and to explore ways to integrate similar priorities in local CBPR training initiatives. This could range from issues related to gender, education, ecological conservation, health, water and sanitation, to name a few. Once identified, aspects related to the focal area need to be embedded within the CBPR training modules.

For instance, if gender equality (SDG #5) is identified as a potential area of concern, then it is essential for the local curriculum on CBPR to incorporate the implications of gender-related issues on different training modules on knowledge, partnerships, ethics, etc. Similarly, if quality education (SDG #4) is identified as an area of contextual concern in the region where the K4C hub is located, it is important to explore and analyse how aspects of person, place, and power are impacted by local educational contexts. Viewing CBPR from the lens of local contextual issues of mutual interest also helps to connect the abstractness of theoretical concepts with real world social relevance. Further, application of such theoretical considerations in CBPR field projects consolidates the learning and understanding of local issues, along with contributing to the generation of new knowledge, which can be actioned to bring about the desired social change at the local and regional levels.

Impact Framework of the MTP

The MTP aims to develop teaching capacities in CBPR in a way that helps K4C mentors gain relevant knowledge, skills, and experience within and beyond academia. In doing so, the MTP envisions to enhance knowledge on CBPR approaches and training pedagogies to promote social transformation and community change in a variety of contexts, as well as to influence policy and practices in the implementation of the SDGs. To achieve these higher order holistic goals, the MTP builds on a distinct impact framework that reflects the requirements, activities, competencies, and perspectives necessary for carrying out CBPR efficiently and effectively. This framework comprises five elements as depicted in Figure 2.3 and further described below.

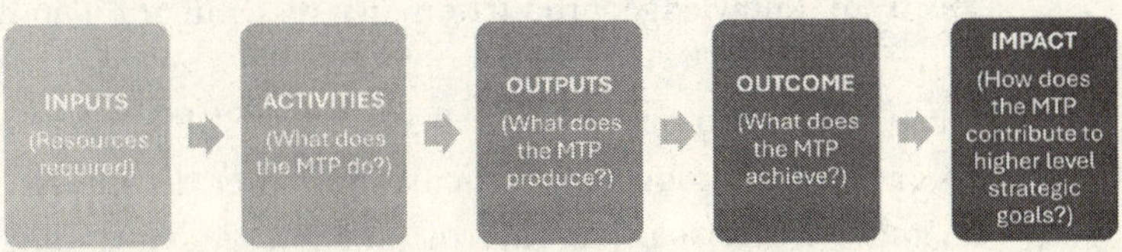

Figure 2.3 Outline of the Impact Framework of the MTP

1. Inputs

- Institutionalisation of CBPR (at CBPR hubs or centres/ embedment in departments/disciplines).
- Internationally accredited, standard curriculum for CBPR training.
- Support and mentoring from UNESCO Chair in CBR-SR.
- Access to online repositories of readings or learning materials and guidance from sectoral experts in CBPR.

2. Activities

- Overall coordination, management, and governance of MTP.
- Learner recruitment and enrolment from academia and civil society.
- Fundraising for supporting MTP activities.
- Identifying avenues for knowledge mobilisation.

3. Outputs

- Development of socially conscious CBPR practitioners, competent in the dimensions of:

  Knowledge (relating to cognitive capacities)

  a) *Digital competencies* (digital literacy, developing competencies to use information and learning technologies, use of instructional technologies).
  b) *Conceptual competency* (learning the history of CBPR, aspects of knowledge production, its dissemination and control).
  c) *Process-based competency* (how to conduct CBPR, diverse approaches for knowledge co-creation, inter-disciplinary research, CBPR steps, modes of enquiry, understanding excellence in CBPR).

Awareness (relating to affective values)

a) *Ethics, values, and social responsibility* (developing as value-based CBPR practitioners, who are ethically anchored and conscious of their social responsibilities).
b) *Developing as responsible and empathetic CBPR facilitators* (orientation to aspects of person and place, and developing as critical and reflexive researchers/CBPR facilitators).
c) *Interpersonal disposition* (exploration of personal motivations and attitudes and developing as critical and reflexive CBPR facilitators).

Skills (relating to the physical skills developed through practice)

a) *Building partnerships and ensuring engagement* (learning to build and sustain research partnerships, focusing on aspects of working in interdisciplinary settings and collaboratively in teams while ensuring authentic community engagement and participation).
b) *Listening and communicating* (development of personal and professional competencies/attitudes).
c) *Knowledge mobilisation* (exploring diverse channels of communication – internal, local, and international – and becoming well-versed in information management and documenting research impact).

4. Outcomes

- Learning to explore, collectively enquire and co-construct sustainable futures.
- Learning to foster collective action, without prejudice or preconceptions.
- Learning to live together in a communal world, and work towards shared, sustainable future.
- Learning to become self-directed learners and socially

responsible individuals, capable of fostering sustainable social change

- Learning to understand and reflect one's own values and actions, role in the community and (global) societies, and motivate oneself and others towards co-creating transformative futures.

5. Impact

- Co-creation of new knowledge for facilitating transformative social development.
- Link with UN SDGs contributes to achieving the local sustainability targets.
- Enhancement of the 'impact factor' and 'social relevance' of research.
- Production of locally relevant learning materials on CBPR (emerging from field work).
- Application of CBPR approach in different academic disciplines, especially non-social sciences (such as engineering, technology, management), which have traditionally had limited engagement with communities in research.
- Production of a young pool of CBPR researchers/mentors who can lead and champion participatory approaches to research in the future.
- Systemic transformation and reform in institutions that begin to adopt and embrace engaged scholarship approaches.

By focusing on these five elements, the impact framework provides a blueprint for institutions to curate contextual and effective CBPR training programs. In doing so, it serves as a comprehensive and a forward-thinking approach that ensures the CBPR training programs and initiatives are designed in a way that it nurtures future CBPR practitioners, capable of navigating challenges, and shaping transformative futures.

Conclusion

This chapter provides a concise yet comprehensive overview of the MTP as a cascade training model designed to enhance CBPR capacities at both individual and institutional levels. Since its initial launch in 2018 to date, the MTP has been delivered nine times, training over 150 K4C mentors across 24 hubs. According to the latest report from the UNESCO Chair in CBR-SR (2024), 4,396 individuals have completed the local CBPR courses developed by MTP graduates in their own K4C hubs.

The success of the MTP lies in its immersive design, which follows a systematic approach based on a competency-based learning framework developed by the UNESCO Chair in CBR-SR. Here, we highlight and summarise the key components that give the MTP its unique flavour and help achieve its objectives.

First, the MTP incorporates a blended learning approach, combining asynchronous and synchronous learning through digital technologies, face-to-face interactions and real-time fieldwork. This method aims to develop knowledge-based, awareness-based, and skill-based competencies. Each module within the MTP includes clearly defined learning objectives, outcomes, multiple learning resources and activities (such as readings, videos, podcasts, online discussions, and reflective assignments), which diversifies learning opportunities and caters to the needs of diverse learners.

Second, engaged and creative learning materials are a hallmark of the program. These materials include historical and contemporary readings, extensive case studies, learning videos, demonstrations of new tools for action, arts, photo and digital inquiry, and interactions with guest speakers and CBPR experts. The MTP also requires students to develop concrete deliverables such as analytical and reflection papers, research project reports and case studies of field research in local languages. These deliverables capture the learning range of the mentors and also provide the link to local SDG targets for future use as training materials.

Third, the program offers holistic competency assessment through assignment evaluation, peer feedback and a self-assessment tool, allowing for a comprehensive reflection on the learning journey. Continuous process learning is documented under the guidance of the Co-Chairs to monitor and assess the learning process. Course evaluations and feedback from peer mentors and instructors helps improve the quality of the MTP and systematises learning for future course enhancements.

Fourth, the MTP aligns with the UN-endorsed maxim of thinking globally and acting locally to address pressing societal challenges, emphasising the importance of place, local issues, and traditional community knowledge in CBPR training. By linking CBPR training to local targets under the UN SDGs, the MTP ensures that the training offered to mentors – and the deliverables mentors produce (e.g., local CBPR curricula) – is relevant to local and regional needs, thereby enhancing its social impact.

Despite the success and positive aspects of the MTP, it is also important to highlight three critical areas requiring attention and innovation in addressing the multifaceted challenges that the learners face within the context of a training program on teaching CBPR:

Opening up knowledge systems. This involves a paradigmatic shift from traditional, hierarchical methods of knowledge delivery to more inclusive, participatory, and pluralistic approaches. In a CBPR training program, this means moving away from the conventional teacher–student dynamic and creating a community of learners, where facilitators and participants work collaboratively, valuing the diverse perspectives and experiences that each stakeholder brings to the table. This approach encourages critical thinking and adaptability, essential for addressing complex community issues.

Unlearning old assumptions about knowledge hierarchies and embracing new, interactive methods of learning and teaching can lead to more meaningful and impactful community research and learning outcomes.

Contextual application of ideas. The effectiveness of a CBPR training program depends significantly on the contextual application of learning. This involves tailoring the curriculum to reflect the specific disciplines of the participants, the immediate context of their universities or community organisations, and the pressing societal challenges relevant to their communities. For example, a CBPR training program in a region facing severe water scarcity could focus on participatory research methods and projects addressing water conservation and management to better equip participants to design and implement research projects that are both socially relevant and impactful. This tailored approach ensures that the skills and knowledge gained are directly applicable and beneficial to the communities served. Further, opportunities and challenges related to creating and maintaining respectful, equitable relationships between communities and universities, and involving community members in structured pedagogical and research initiatives require careful consideration, time, and resources.

Documentation and impact assessment. These are crucial components of any CBPR training program, as they ensure that the outcomes of the training are recorded, evaluated, and communicated effectively. For participants, learning how to document their research processes and results systematically is vital for establishing credibility and validity. Impact assessment helps in understanding the effectiveness of the research interventions and provides insights for future improvements. Additionally, thorough documentation and assessment support the dissemination of findings, enabling other communities and researchers to learn from the experiences and apply similar methods in their contexts.

Reflecting on the MTP's journey, it is evident that its impact extends beyond mere training. The program has the capacity to create a ripple effect, empowering mentors and community members to address local and regional challenges through CBPR. The emphasis on place, local issues and valuing community knowledges has ensured that the training is relevant and impactful. The continuous process learning and feedback mechanisms from instructors and peers have contributed to the program's evolution, making it a dynamic and responsive model.

The past year (2024) marked a new phase in the organisation of the K4C Consortium. In response to the increased demand for training of youth in the production of locally contextualised actionable knowledge, the desire for more regionally contextualised training and lower residency costs, the decision was taken to shift the support of recruitment and training to a regional, decentralised model.

As we move forward, the MTP's commitment to fostering CBPR capacities and addressing societal challenges remains unwavering, promising a brighter future for community-based research and its contributions to sustainable development. Looking ahead, strengthening networks and partnerships, leveraging institutional support, and mobilising resources will be crucial for sustaining and expanding the impact of a CBPR training program as the MTP.

3

KNOWLEDGE AND POWER DYNAMICS IN COMMUNITY-BASED PARTICIPATORY RESEARCH

JOHN GAVENTA

Introduction

We often hear the phrase 'knowledge is power'. First attributed to Francis Bacon in 1597 (at least in Western philosophy), the theme has oft been repeated throughout history. Philosophers write about it. Political scientists and sociologists study it. Famous leaders quote it: 'Knowledge is power. Information is liberation' said the former UN Secretary General Kofi Annan (Annan, 1998). By 2017, the phrase had even become the title of a video game by the same name. But what does this phrase really mean?

For those concerned with the transformational potential of community-based participatory research (CBPR), unpacking the relationship of knowledge and power is critical. A basic premise of CBPR is that the control of knowledge is a form of domination, and that, conversely, participation in knowledge production by previously marginalised actors can be a way of challenging that domination. But to develop strategies for this means deepening our understanding of a number of key questions. Whose knowledge are we talking about? How do we mobilise knowledge to challenge unjust power relations? And what do we mean by power anyway?

To discuss these questions further, I have had the privilege over the last few years of working with the Knowledge for Change (K4C) Mentor Training Program (MTP) to offer online sessions on understanding power and knowledge. In addition, at the Institute of Development Studies (IDS), where I work, we offer a Master's course in Power, Politics and Social Change, which also teaches a lot around understanding power (McGee et al., 2020), and we have offered dozens of workshops and training programs with activists and researchers on the theme.

One framework which we have developed is the now widely applied approach known as the powercube (www.powercube.net) (Gaventa, 2006, 2021). The powercube has been widely used around the world for analysis of power, education, and awareness building, context analysis, program and strategy development, and monitoring and evaluation (Pettit, 2010). But this framework also has practical implications for how we think about knowledge strategies aimed at shifting or transforming power. In this chapter, I will briefly share this framework that can be used with academics and practitioners to reflect upon and challenge these complex knowledge-power relationships (Gaventa and Cornwall, 2006).

From the beginning, it is important to note that the idea of the framework is not simply to understand knowledge and power as abstractions, but to use it to reflect upon concrete experiences and to place oneself as a community-based participatory researcher within it. (While in this short essay, I will share one approach, further guidelines of using the powercube for teaching and learning may be found in the 'plan a workshop' section of the powercube website.)*

As Jethro Pettit, one of the creators of the site, has written:

---

*https://www.powercube.net/plan-a-workshop/

The methods are based on the experiences of practitioners and educators with broadly shared ways of understanding power and facilitating learning about it... They have some key principles in common:

- experiential knowledge: *people already know a great deal from their own experience and practice, and making this knowledge more conscious and accessible to them can itself be a form of empowerment*
- facilitating reflection: *the facilitator's role is not to transfer knowledge and skills, but to help people reflect on their own knowledge and experience, using concepts, theories and others' experiences to deepen analysis*
- questioning assumptions: *learning is deeper when contradictions are explored and dominant worldviews, values and assumptions are critically examined*
- diversity of methods: *methods for facilitating learning can take many forms and these can be combined; some applied and practical, some reflective and analytical, some creative and artistic, some embodied and emotional*
- diversity of learners: *people have different ways of knowing and learning, so using a variety of methods is more likely to meet the needs of a diverse group*
- individual and collective processes: *learning requires both individual and collective (social) processes for creating understanding*
- learning in context: *learning is more effective when related to particular contexts, questions and issues of practical relevance and urgency for learners*
- opportunities for action: *learning is consolidated when opportunities are available to apply knowledge through meaningful action*

As Pettit writes further on the powercube website, there is no '"right way" or order for using the exercises and resources. Much will depend on who is learning, what their needs are, and what time is available. For example, a short exposure for senior managers will be different from an in-depth training event. The exercises and resources can be "mixed and matched" to design your own events.'

Getting Started

With this in mind, let us turn to understanding the powercube, and the dimensions of power within it. Building on the dynamic metaphor of the Rubik's cube, the powercube approach suggests that we must examine these three aspects of power (forms, spaces, levels) not only separately, but in their interactions.

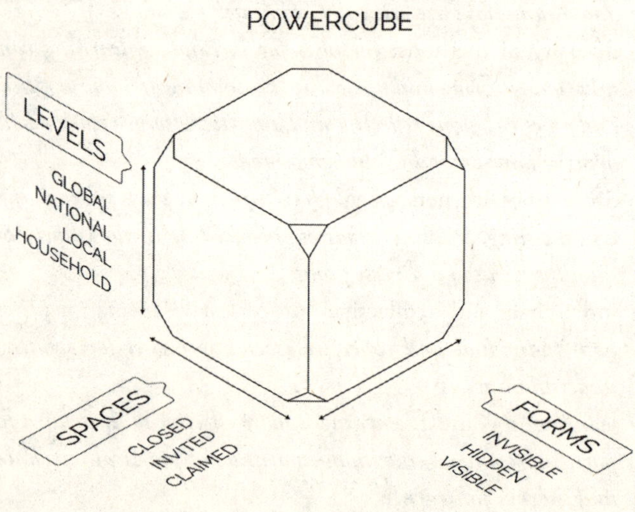

Figure 3.1: Spaces, Forms and Levels of Power*
Adapted from www.powercube.net.

---

*This is also used and discussed in Gaventa, 2006 and 2020.

The forms, spaces, and levels of power interact.

Forms relate to how power manifests itself:

- *Visible*: focuses on who participates and predominates in observable decision-making.
- *Hidden*: keeps certain issues, interests and voices out of the decision-making process or off the public agenda.
- *Invisible*: internalised beliefs and norms, or lack of awareness, which means that certain voices do not speak and certain issues and inequities go unquestioned.

Spaces of power refer to potential arenas for participation and action:

- *Closed*: decisions are made behind closed doors without broad consultation or participation.
- *Invited*: people are invited to participate in public arenas but within set boundaries.
- *Claimed*: less powerful people or groups create their own spaces where they can shape their own agenda.

Levels refer to the multiple layers of power in a global world:

- *Global*: formal and informal sites of decision-making beyond the nation-state.
- *National*: governments, parliaments, political parties, coalitions or other forms of authority, usually linked to nation-states.
- *Local*: sub-national governments, councils, and associations at the local level.
- *Household*: the micro-level, which may be outside of the public sphere, but which helps to shape what occurs within it.

In a workshop with community-based participatory researchers, be it for two hours or a full day, we would go through this model very slowly, introducing each side or dimension of the cube one by one, and drawing from participants their practical and experiential understanding of these forms of power.

If there is time, often a good warm up exercise is to ask people to imagine a moment in their lives when they felt 'powerless' and then to imagine a time when they felt 'powerful'. Then we often will push that further by asking people to name what made them feel 'powerful' or 'powerless'. Sometimes, what comes up are factors such as the lack of access to resources (money, land, contacts); sometimes the focus is on forms of behavior whether violent and bullying on the one hand, or respectful and affirming on the other. But often in this exercise the role of knowledge quickly emerges. People can usually give examples of feeling 'powerless' when their knowledge was ignored, undervalued or suppressed, or feeling more 'powerful' when it was respected, listened to and seen to count in decision-making processes.

From these warm-up exercises, we move to understanding further each dimension of power and then in turn its implications for strategies of mobilising and using knowledge for change.

The Forms of Power

Often when we think of power, we only think about what we call **'visible' power** that can be seen in public spaces, such as decision-making institutions or public fora. We would focus our attention on who participates, who wins and who loses to see who has power. In turn, when we think about strategies for change in these more visible arenas, we tend to think about using evidence and expertise that is also more visible in the public domain, and communicating that influence to influence policy makers in these public spaces. This is often referred to as 'evidence-based' policy, influenced by more traditional forms of knowledge communications, and usually assumes that knowledge is (a) available and open, and that

(b) expert knowledge is a preferred way of knowing for policy making. Inequities in knowledge access and production, or whose knowledge counts, are rarely considered in this approach.

But the powercube teaches us that not all power is visible. Various factors – lack of resources, language, threats, and coercion – may mean that power is not only about who sits at the policy table, but also about whose voices, issues and interests are not at the table at all, what we call **'hidden' power**. In such cases, actions to challenge power involve mobilising those excluding groups and empowering them to make their voices heard.

And of course there is a parallel knowledge dimension to this. One reason that certain voices or interests may not be heard is that their knowledge is not considered legitimate or 'scientific' and is relatively undervalued compared to more 'expert' forms of knowledge. Or the biases of funding, academic, media, etc., mean that relevant popular knowledge has simply not been documented or made visible in ways that it can influence policy decisions. In such cases, our knowledge strategies involve helping people to systematise and mobilise around previously suppressed or ignored knowledge to put their issues and concerns on the table. It's not just about mobilising evidence but asks the question 'whose evidence', or 'whose knowledge' is being used in the first place, and it deliberately works to overcome knowledge-based exclusions in the process.

Yet a third form of power is what we call **'invisible' power** – this is when relatively powerless groups have internalised their powerlessness to the extent that they do not question the unjust status quo, or simply do not believe that they have a right or capacity to challenge the daily inequalities they face. In its knowledge dimension, invisible power is found not simply when popular knowledge has been undervalued, as in hidden power, but when ordinary people themselves do not believe in their own experiential knowledge as the basis for action in the first place, or when the forces of exclusion are so great that important forms of popular wisdom have been erased from memory or public narratives altogether. In such cases, knowledge strategies need to involve helping people recover their own knowledge, to view it as a basis of action, to build power from within through processes of conscientisation, as Paulo Freire would say, and to change values, norms and discourses which have made certain voices and forms of knowledge invisible and unheard in public discussion.

What this analysis of forms of power invites participants to do is to think about how knowledge production itself affects power, and in turn, what knowledge strategies can be used to challenge these knowledge-power inequities. In the first instance, our knowledge strategy is simply about mobilising evidence; in the second instance, it is about mobilising to counter the biases of whose evidence is valued; and in the third it is about changing the values and discourses that systematically absent and suppress the knowledge of certain groups or of certain issues altogether. In workshops or learning sessions, we would ask people to offer examples from their own experiences of which forms of knowledge power they are addressing as participatory researchers and what strategies they are using to overcome these power inequities.

Spaces for Change

A second dimension of the powercube focuses on the spaces for participation and engagement and suggests that strategies for change may vary according to the types of space in which we are acting or engaging. By spaces we don't mean just physical spaces, but also the moments, or opportunities, where action can occur. The powercube distinguishes between 'closed,' 'invited,' and 'claimed' or 'created' spaces. Each of these in turn have consequences for the types of knowledge strategies that we might employ to bring about change.

Closed spaces refer to those decision-making arenas which have no pretence of public engagement, yet which have huge influence of people's lives. Decisions in these spaces are often taken behind closed doors, with little transparency or accountability to those affected. Examples may include board rooms of corporations or large institutions, certain policy spaces, especially those in sectors such as defence, finance or macro-economic policy, or forms of research and development surrounded by secrecy (such as corporate research on the health effects of hazardous chemicals or the impacts of fossil fuels on climate change). Faced with these spaces, knowledge strategies may involve ways of demanding transparency and accountability to bring information and decision-making into the public domain under public scrutiny. Activists and researchers have devised many approaches in this area such as citizen monitoring, investigative journalism, participatory budgeting, freedom of information policies and more. Citizen science strategies which, for instance, monitor the disposal of industrial wastes into rivers and streams offer further example of ways in which popular knowledge can expose and hold to account what might be going on behind closed doors or in secret.

Often times as formerly excluded groups demand more voice and transparency, then new public spaces may be created by authorities for consultation, dialogue and deliberation – what we call **invited spaces**. Some of these may lack any real influence or power. But some are increasingly based on the right to participation and the duty of authorities to listen or respond – leading to the potential of more empowered deliberation and engagement. While confronting closed spaces activist researchers need to think about making information available to all, the knowledge strategies for invited spaces involve being able to use information effectively and persuasively for negotiation, debate and deliberating with others. This may affect the kinds of knowledge used, the forms in which it is communicated, and the need to gain the confidence to challenge and debate others who use different knowledges. For instance, participatory action researchers may choose to enter these spaces armed with evidence from their research presented as more traditional facts and figures, or they may enter just to change the dynamics of such spaces by introducing people's own stories of their lived experience.

Finally, in every society there may be what the powercube calls **claimed** or **created spaces** in which relatively powerless groups come together to share their own knowledge and create their own narratives using their own vernaculars. These may simply be informal gathering places, whether around the community well or the tearoom; or may be within popular organisations and social movements which create alternative places for discourse; or may be in people's own homes, around the dinner table with family and friends. Knowledge within these spaces may be shared differently from the dominant discourse – for instance, through music, folklore, storytelling, or popular theatre. Such spaces often become 'safe spaces' to create, practise and deepen narratives that differ from the status quo. So here again, if our participatory research approach wants to support these popular spaces, then our strategies are about building the legitimacy of these voices, documenting and sharing the stories, learning within and across them, and/or strengthening the capacity of participants to do their own research within their own spaces for their own action and self-determination.

Each of these knowledge strategies has its own value and interact with one another. For instance, it is often through documenting knowledge in people's own claimed spaces that people gain the confidence and the evidence they can then use to enter the invited spaces more effectively, strengthened by knowledge grounded in their own experience, and empowered by speaking authentically from it.

The Levels of Power

Finally, the powercube reminds us that power happens at many levels, from within the household, to the local and national, up to the global. Decisions made at one level can often affect what happens at the other. As in the other dimensions of the cube, which level of power we want to effect also affects the choice of knowledge strategies for change.

Feminists, for instance, have taught us a great deal about the importance of the household as a space of inclusion or exclusion, and urge that we start our work by focusing on whose knowledge counts within the household. Much community-based research focuses on the importance of local knowledge (or knowledges) and to use it as a basis of popular action. But localities are affected by powerful forces behind the local, whether at the national, regional or international level. So further knowledge strategies may look at how to amplify local voices from the local to the national stage, or how to work together to build broader knowledge networks and epistemic communities at the global level. The most successful strategies often find ways of linking up across the levels, for instance, finding ways to bring local knowledge to national or global fora.

Looking at the Interrelationships

The most important insights from applying the powercube come not only by understanding the implications of each dimension of the cube for our knowledge strategies, but also at the interactions across them. For instance, invited spaces may appear to be 'open' but in fact may be surrounded by forms of hidden and invisible power which still serve to limit whose knowledge is valued and who participate within them. Champions of change inside closed spaces can be valuable allies for people demanding change from within invited or claimed spaces. However, power strategies which only focus on one element, or one dimension, often simply reproduce or strengthen power in another. For instance, mobilising expert knowledge for advocacy may seem important to win certain issues, but in the process, it may only re-enforce the sense for non-experts that their knowledge based on lived experiences is undervalued.

Given this, no one strategy for change is enough, and no one intervention or project is likely to be transformative by itself. Therefore, what is also needed are broader alliances across different actors and entry points, using multiple strategies. This means creating links between local, national, and international action and research groups, between sympathetic experts using their scientific knowledge and popular researchers building on strengthening the wisdom drawn from popular experience. Sometimes these links create their own knowledge hierarchies – the national or international groups may appear to dominate the local; the experts may dominate the non-expert; the formal may predominate over the informal ways of communicating. So, this also means creating new ways of listening and collaborating across groups that are themselves more inclusive, respectful and equal. It is when we can build this new ecosystem of knowledge actors, working across the forms, spaces, and levels of power that truly transformative change can occur.

In making this point, in our workshops we often ask participants to put themselves in the powercube by describing where they actually spend their time and energy, which forms of power their work is addressing, in which spaces, and at what levels. Very few groups or individuals can work across all of the levels and spaces of the powercube, so we also ask them to identify their allies who might be working in other spaces and levels, and how they can build collaboration with them. In workshops, this can be done in a very physical way, by playing what we have termed 'power twister', in which participants place themselves in large powercubes on the floor and describe from that position what forms of power they are trying to address.*

As mentioned earlier, while I have shared one approach to teaching and learning about power and knowledge, there are many. The key thing for those working on participatory research is to recognise that power and knowledge are deeply intertwined. Knowledge by itself is not power but the ability to use it for authentic action, grounded in the lived experiences of ordinary people, can be truly empowering.

* See powertwister_forumsyd.pdf (powercube.net)

4

TEACHING ABOUT ETHICS IN COMMUNITY-BASED PARTICIPATORY RESEARCH

SARAH BANKS

Introduction: Ethics, Normativity and Community-Based Participatory Research

Ethical issues relating to rights, responsibilities, harms, and benefits are embedded in all research. However, in community-based participatory research (CBPR), matters of ethics are arguably more prominent in that its rationale entails a commitment to transformative social change and its research process is based on principles of knowledge democracy, inclusivity, diversity and power-sharing. Indeed, CBPR could be construed as an essentially normative practice, built on a set of values, including the promotion of social justice and participation. These values entail normative ethical principles about what character traits and actions are regarded good/bad and right/wrong, such as respectfulness/disrespectfulness and equitable/inequitable treatment.

This is the subject matter of what is often called 'normative ethics' (the study of what kinds of people we should be and how we ought to act). Other types of ethics include descriptive ethics (what people actually do or believe about right/wrong and good/

bad) and meta-ethics (analysis of moral concepts such as right/wrong, good/bad, duty, rights). While all these types or aspects of ethics are inter-related and important, the teaching of ethics in research as a preparation for practice generally has a focus on normative ethics.

The aim of learning and teaching about ethics in CBPR is to develop in participatory researchers:

- Understanding of what counts as 'ethics';
- Abilities to perceive and identify ethical issues;
- Awareness of their own positionality and power; and
- Capacities to reflect on and respond to potential or actual ethical challenges and dilemmas and justify decisions and actions.

The content of a learning program, as outlined in this chapter, might include:

1. What is ethics?
2. Why is ethics an important topic in CBPR?
3. What are the ethical principles underpinning CBPR?
4. What are some of the common ethical challenges?
5. Using case examples to explore ethical challenges and dilemmas.
6. Using dilemmas cafés and participatory theatre.

What is Ethics?

The term 'ethics' may have different connotations in different cultures and languages. Therefore, it is helpful to explore what participants in a learning group associate with 'ethics' to encourage them to think broadly about its meaning. Often a 'western' conception of ethics can be dominant in the traditional research ethics literature (prioritising the choice, informed consent, and privacy of individual research participants).

Question for a thought shower (collecting people's views in a group and noting on a whiteboard/flipchart).
Ask people to shout out a quick answer to the question:
What do you associate with the term 'ethics'?

Participants frequently list associations with right and wrong behaviour, following rules, codes of ethics and maintaining confidentiality. If the group is from diverse countries, a discussion could be initiated about the words used for 'ethics' in different languages. According to Gyekye (2010), in sub-Saharan African languages there are no direct equivalents of the term 'ethics' as used in English. However, this does not mean there are no normative concepts of right and wrong conduct or good and bad character, just that these facets of human existence and behaviour are conceptualised in different ways. Similarly for some indigenous communities, respect for the natural world (of which humans are a part) is integral to their ethical worldview (Buchanan et al., 2019). A description of ethics that I use is:

> Ethics is a topic that covers questions relating to what kinds of lives we should lead, what counts as a good society, what actions are right and wrong, what qualities of character we should develop and what responsibilities humans have for each other and the ecosystem.

This is quite a broad account, encompassing several theoretical viewpoints (principle-based, character-based, relationship-based) and responsibilities for both human and planetary well-being. A brief outline of different theories, theoretical and methodological approaches to ethics is given in Banks and Brydon-Miller (2019a, pp 10–14). Depending on how much time is available and how relevant theoretical considerations are to the learning group, an introduction to various ethical theories and how they might be applied to case examples from practice might be appropriate.

Why Is Ethics an Important Topic in Community-Based Participatory Research?

Research ethics has become a specialist category of 'applied ethics' (application of ethical theories and approaches to practical life). Traditionally (in non-participatory research) this focuses on ensuring research is of benefit, that potential and actual harm to human or animal participants is minimised, that humans give informed consent to participate, and their rights to privacy and confidentiality of information are respected (for a comprehensive overview, see Iltis and MacKay, 2024). Academic or professional researchers are assumed to have a responsibility to protect research participants, and research institutions develop codes of conduct and operate research ethics committees or institutional review boards to approve research involving humans and animals.

In CBPR, however, the research is often conducted by a diverse team of 'professional' and community-based partners. Hence, attention needs to be paid to how the research team is constituted (inclusivity) and how members work together (with respect for each other, sharing power and control). Academic or professional researchers often tend to initiate the research, set the agenda at the start, and may control the finances. They have power from their institutional positions and expertise in research. Inviting learners in a teaching session to consider their own positionality and power can be a useful exercise to encourage critical reflection and reflexivity about how to make research teams more aware and respectful of each other's contributions and of their own roles (see, Egid et al., 2021, and Chapter 3 in this volume for a useful discussion of power in CBPR).

Exercise individually and in pairs: Positionality and power in CBPR

Individually

- Think of how you would describe yourself briefly in terms of your ethnicity, gender, occupation or other identities, experiences or privileges (your 'positionality').
- Think of a group or team of which you are a part. It might be a research team or it could be a team/group from work or personal life. How do you think you function in that group: what roles do you play; how much do you speak; how influential are you; how much power do you hold?

***In pairs*:**

- Each person briefly shares their self-description.
- Discuss what this means for each person for how they operate in groups/teams – give one or two examples from work or home life.
- Discuss what might be the ethical implications for each of you as members of a CBPR team (taking 'ethical' as relating to matters of harms, benefits, roles, rights, responsibilities).

The nature of academic power and ethical partnership working are often not covered by research ethics review processes, which tend to focus on regulating behaviour and reducing risk (regulatory ethics). While institutional review procedures have a role to play in encouraging and enforcing ethical practice, they have little influence over the minutiae of the everyday practice of researchers including their attitudes, demeanor, use of emotions and positional power (everyday ethics). For a discussion of everyday ethics in CBPR, see Banks et al., 2013.

Short case examples from CBPR practice can be used to stimulate discussion about positionality and power. The cases below are shortened from Banks and Brydon-Miller (2019b, pp 95–96, 66–68). They are in the format of open-ended cases, in relation to which possible courses of action can be discussed.

Case 1: Suicide and well-being research with Inuit in Arctic Canada

A research partnership involving Inuit and academic researchers in Arctic Canada was studying issues relating to suicide and well-being amongst Inuit people. The research questions and participatory methodology came from the Inuit community. A Canadian academic was working with the group. He was not Inuit and was regarded as 'white'. The Inuit Youth Committee, very much involved in the project, complained about the negative attitudes of one of the adult Inuit researchers. This man wasn't any good at doing interviews, and he also didn't like working with the women interviewers. The president of the Youth Committee asked the academic to deal with this and implied that he should 'fire' the man.

Case 2: Are you telling me this as a researcher or friend?

A UK doctoral researcher (a woman) was studying how a volunteer youth-led community radio station provided space for young people to find their voices. This research adopted a participatory design in collaboration with young people at the radio station, training them as co-researchers. She visited the station 4–5 days a week for 18 months, deciding to position herself as 'researcher as friend' – accepting young people's 'friend requests' on Facebook, sharing her mobile number, enjoying activities with them outside the station. The doctoral researcher gave an account of the situation as follows. "One day a young volunteer sat next to me, and...started telling me about his past battles with depression and drug abuse, and how the station had been his savior. 'What excellent data!' I thought. However, alarm bells rang, and I asked him: 'Are you telling me this as a researcher or a friend?' 'As a friend,' he replied, 'but you can use it in your thesis if you want.' I suddenly began to question my entire approach to this participatory research project, which had drawn me into friendships with young people, which I considered to be inevitable due to our comparable age, our liking of the same music, and our mutual interest in radio."

What Are the Ethical Principles Underpinning Community-Based Participatory Research?

Based on an express aim to maximise participation and challenge unequal power structures in society, the ethical principles that underpin CBPR have a focus on developing positive and equitable relationships between co-researchers and other participants and stakeholders. A useful set of ethical principles has been produced by people involved in CBPR associated with the Centre for Social Justice and Community Action at Durham University (UK) and the International Collaboration for Participatory Health Research, an overview of which is reproduced in Table 6.1. The principles are at a relatively general level, with the bullet points offering brief illustrations of what each principle might include. The bullet points are not meant to be an exhaustive list.

Table 6.1: Ethical Principles for CBPR*

1) **Mutual respect:** developing research relationships based on mutual respect, including a commitment to:
   - Agreeing what counts as mutual respect in particular contexts.
   - Everyone involved being prepared to listen to the voices of others.
   - Accepting that people have diverse perspectives, different forms of expertise and ways of knowing that may be equally valuable in the research process.

2) **Equity and inclusion:** encouraging and enabling people from a range of backgrounds and identities (e.g., ethnicity, faith, class, education, gender, sexual orientation, [dis]ability, age) to lead, design and take part in the research, including a commitment to:
   - Seeking actively to include people whose voices are often ignored.
   - Challenging discriminatory and oppressive attitudes and behaviors.
   - Ensuring information, venues, and formats for meetings are accessible to all.

3) **Democratic participation:** encouraging and enabling those involved in the research to contribute meaningfully to decision-making and other aspects of the research process according to skill, interest and collective need, including a commitment to:
   - Acknowledging and discussing differences in the status and power of people involved in the research and working towards sharing power more equally.
   - Communicating in a language everyone can understand, including arranging translation or interpretation if required.
   - Using participatory research methods that build on, share and develop different skills and expertise.

*Taken from CSJCA and NCCPE, 2022a, pp 10–11

4) **Active learning:** seeing research collaboration and the process of research as providing opportunities to learn from each other, including a commitment to:
   - Ensuring there is time to identify and reflect on learning during the research, and on ways people learn, both together and individually.
   - Offering all those involved a chance to learn from each other and share their learning with wider audiences.
   - Sharing responsibility for interpreting the research findings and their implications for practice.

5) **Making a difference:** promoting research that creates positive change for communities of place, interest or identity, by:
   - Engaging in debates about what counts as 'positive' change, including broader environmental sustainability as well as human needs or spiritual development, and being open to the possibility of not knowing in advance what making a 'positive difference' might mean.
   - Valuing the learning and other benefits for individuals and groups from the research process as well as the outputs and outcomes of the research.
   - Building a goal of positive change into every stage of the research.

6) **Collective action:** individuals and groups working together to achieve change through the research, including a commitment to:
   - Identifying common and complementary goals that meet partners' differing needs for the research.
   - Working for agreed visions of how to share knowledge and power more equitably and promote social change and social justice.
   - Recognising and working with conflicting rights and interests expressed by different interest groups, communities of practice or place.

7) **Personal integrity:** people conducting the research behaving reliably, honestly and in a transparent and trustworthy fashion, including a commitment to:
   - Working within the principles of CBPR.
   - Ensuring accurate and honest analysis and reporting of research.
   - Being open to challenge and change, recognising and reflecting on one's own privileges and prejudices, and being flexible and prepared to work with conflict.

Table 6.1 can be used as a stimulus for discussing what each principle means in more detail, some of the challenges to implementing them in practice, how some principles may be in conflict and the conflicts may not be easily resolved. Learners can be asked to think of examples from their own experience of, say, listening to the voices of others, encouraging diverse opinions and views, whilst also challenging oppressive attitudes. Case 1 could be used to explore tensions between promoting inclusivity versus challenging oppression. Alternatively, learners might analyse their own case examples or cases from the literature (see section 'Using Case Examples to Explore Ethical Challenges and Dilemmas') in terms of the principles.

What Are Some of the Common Ethical Challenges?

CBPR raises many ethical challenges – situations when harms, benefits, rights, and responsibilities are at stake, and it may not be easy to work out what to do. It can be productive to ask learners to think of ethical challenges they are facing or have faced in their practice. If they do not have practice experience, then cases from the literature can be analysed.

Exercise: Ethically challenging situations

Individually – Think of a situation you are finding or have found ethically challenging in your practice.

In pairs – Share your situations and discuss in relation to each situation:

- What ethical issues are/were at stake?
- What ethical principles might be relevant?
- What might you do/have done differently and why?

Based on a review of literature and the experiences of a group of community-based and academic researchers, the following common ethical challenges were identified as shown in Table 6.2.

Table 6.2 Ethical Challenges in CBPR*

- *Partnership, collaboration and power* – All CBPR involves collaboration, whether between professional researchers and community partners or a range of different community researchers. This means it is important to attend to how partnerships are established, power is distributed and control exerted. Ethical issues noted in the literature include: tackling mismatches between timelines and expectations of community organisations, funders and academics; awareness that closer research relationships also bring greater potential for exploitation; and acknowledging that co-researchers may experience moments of inclusion and exclusion in the research process.
- *Blurring the boundaries between researcher and researched, academic and activist* – Insofar as CBPR involves some degree of co-production of research and an action-orientation, this may entail community

*Summarised from Banks and Brydon-Miller, 2019a, pp 8–10, drawing on Banks et al., 2013 members taking on roles of researchers, and professional researchers taking on roles commonly associated with health, social care, or community development work. Tensions may arise for people taking on the role of both researcher and community advocate or academic and activist. Community researchers studying their own communities or peer groups may occupy the roles of both researcher and researched and have to consider whether and where to draw the lines between being researcher and friend or neighbour (see Case 2).

- *Community rights, conflict and democratic representation* – While most ethical codes and guidelines for research are concerned with the rights of individual 'human subjects' (to safety, privacy, freedom of choice to participate or withdraw), CBPR in community-based settings raises the challenge of extending rights to communities or groups. This creates issues in defining 'community', taking account of conflict within and between communities and groups, and deciding who represents a group or community interest (see Case 1). If the topic of research is controversial, for example, attitudes towards assisted suicide amongst disabled people, there are complex matters relating to democracy and community relations to be considered.
- *Ownership and dissemination of data, findings, and publications* – If multiple partners are involved in research, there may be conflicts of interest about who takes credit for findings and what channels are used for dissemination. These may manifest in decisions about co-authorship, publicity and claims for research impact, particularly as academic pressures to publish and demonstrate impact on policy and practice increase.
- *Anonymity, privacy and confidentiality* – Whilst these matters are common concerns in all social research, the close relationships developed in CBPR preclude straightforward solutions. If community or peer researchers are involved, and wide dissemination is planned within the community, identities of research participants may be hard

to conceal. Some participants may wish to be named and credited, others may not. There may be matters that some representatives of a community or group do not wish to be revealed, such as survival strategies of asylum seekers, sex workers, or indebted families.

- *Institutional ethical review processes* – A noticeable theme in some literature is the difficulty of fitting CBPR into the process and procedures for institutional ethical review. Whilst many of the assumptions underlying the ethical review process – including the predictability of research trajectories – are problematic for all social research, they pose specific challenges for CBPR. Ethical guidelines for research and forms to be completed are often premised on a clear distinction between researchers and subjects of research; require individual consent to participate; and make assumptions that an academic or professional researcher ('principal investigator') has primary control over and responsibility for the research.
- *Social action for social change* – The theoretical underpinnings of CBPR emphasise its action-orientation, and that it is an approach to research that strives for social change. However, what constitutes appropriate and sufficient 'action' is not always clear, with different partners holding varied views on what types of outcomes could be described as social action. That CBPR will involve social action is often assumed, with limited guidance available to research partners about the need to consider the nature of action, to plan for it and to reflect on where responsibility for this action lies. Research partners experience different constraints on their social change efforts, including time, resources, control and institutional mandates.

Using Case Examples to Explore Ethical Challenges and Dilemmas

The use of cases from the literature or cases written by learners is a very productive way of exploring ethics in practice in a group. 'Ethics cases' are descriptions of situations or events that foreground the ethical challenges. While short cases are often used in class for teaching, as exemplified in Cases 1 and 2 earlier, there is value in using or writing longer cases that also include the emotions and reflections of the person writing the case. Examples of cases of several pages in length can be found in Banks and Brydon-Miller (2019b). Members of the ethics working group of the International Collaboration for Participatory Health Research have published open access articles comprising longer cases and commentaries that can be used for discussion purposes (Banks and von Köppen, 2021; Narayanan et al., 2023; Tayebi et al., 2023). There are also several cases in the Appendices accompanying the guide to ethical principles (CSJCA and NCCPE, 2022b).

Table 6.3 Case-Based Exercises for Use in Learning and Teaching about Ethics*

A. Writing a case example. Learners with experience of CBPR might write a case example (about two pages) based on an ethically challenging situation they have faced, using the following guidelines:

1. *Background information.* Start with a short introduction about the context in which the case takes place – the setting, the people involved.
2. *Description of events, thoughts, feelings.* Describe what happened, including accounts of any thoughts or emotions and short reflections, if desired.

* Adapted from Banks and Brydon-Miller, 2019a, pp 22–23

3. *Anonymity.* Consider whether names of people, organisations and places should be changed and identifying features removed or changed to protect the identity of those involved.

B. Analysing a case. Learners can be given a case written by one of their colleagues or taken from the book or articles mentioned above, without the accompanying commentary, and discuss and analyse it in groups or individually. The following set of questions might be useful:

1. What is your initial reaction to this case, including any feelings you might have about it?
2. What are the ethical issues involved in this case?
3. What action would you take if you were the researcher(s)/ practitioner(s) involved?
4. How would you justify this ethically?

C. Writing a commentary. Learners can be asked to write their own commentary on a case written by a colleague or one from the literature. The following points can be used as guidance:

1. *Audience.* Consider who will be the audience for your commentary and ensure you write in language the audience will understand.
2. *Ethical issues*. Highlight what you think are the key ethical issues in the case. How can they be understood?
3. *Reflection on context*. If you are from a different country than the country of the case, or a different area of work, you might like to reflect on similar issues in your own country or area of work – to what extent are these universal/general issues in a particular context?
4. *Think about how critical or judgmental you should be*. Consider how the author(s) of the case, or other people who feature in the case, might respond to your comments.
5. *Ending.* End the commentary with a conclusion which could be your own position statement ('My opinion about this particular case is…' or 'At the heart of this problem lies…') or a proposed solution to the problem or another suitable ending to the commentary.

Using Dilemmas Cafés and Participatory Theatre

If several sessions are available for teaching about ethics, including longer sessions of two to four hours, then it is possible to engage in more intensive group exercises. Two methods that I have been involved in developing and using are dilemmas cafés and participatory theatre. Both require a level of skill and confidence on the part of the teacher/facilitator, including the ability to notice and handle sensitive issues that may arise when people are exploring their own ethical dilemmas or experiences of oppression. This is more difficult when teaching online.

Dilemmas cafés

This method asks participants to offer cases for discussion in small groups in a safe, yet critical, group of peers. The room is set up with tables, each seating around six to eight people, who engage in dialogue about different ethical dilemmas alongside the contributor of the dilemma and a facilitator. If time allows, after 30–40 minutes participants can move tables to discuss another dilemma. The whole group then discusses the issues raised and people's learning from hearing and exploring a range of diverse and sometimes conflicting perspectives. Care needs to be taken to brief the facilitators and contributors of dilemmas and to make a learning agreement with the group in advance about respectful communication and confidentiality. Dilemmas cafés can be successfully run online, using breakout rooms. Breakout room facilitators will need to be proactive in encouraging participation and it can be difficult if cameras are turned off. A guide for facilitators based on in-person cafés is freely available (CSJCA, 2015).

Participatory theatre

Short episodes from CBPR practice involving an ethical transgression or experience of oppression can be used as the basis for groups of people to act out short scenarios, and then rehearse different options for action. After agreeing on ground rules and undertaking introductory movement exercises, participants work in small groups to select an incident experienced by one of their members and rehearse acting it out, taking the roles of the people involved. Each group then performs its scenario to the larger group. Audience members ('spectactors') are invited to swap roles and try out new approaches. This exercise not only uncovers new ways of responding in difficult situations but also brings people in touch with their bodies, positions in space and real-time emotions. It illustrates how ethical being and doing engages not only our cognitive capacities (such as reasoning, deciding) but also our emotions (such as anger, compassion) and physical bodies (such as seating position, direction of gaze). A modified version of participatory theatre can be facilitated online with one small group, but the physical dimension is missing, and great care needs to be taken if sensitive issues are raised. Ideally it works best online if group members know each other and there is more than one facilitator. A guide for working in-person based on Augusto Boal's Theatre of the Oppressed is freely available (Banks et al., 2014).

Concluding Comments

This approach to learning and teaching about ethics entails drawing on the experiences of learners, rooted in principles of experiential, participatory, and action learning. It rests on the belief that engaging in collaborative ethical reflection and developing reflexivity about power and positionality enables situations to be seen from many perspectives, enhancing ethical sensitivity (noticing harms and infringements of rights, and recognising complexity and contradictions). As with the practice of CBPR, it relies on creative facilitation skills and a willingness and ability to draw out hidden knowledge, skills, and expertise in the group, and develop learners' facilitation skills by modeling the practice and engaging learners themselves in group facilitation.

Acknowledgements

Thanks to the many cohorts of students on the MTP, the numerous other participants on courses and workshops, and all the community-based researchers, postgraduate students and colleagues who have contributed to the materials and ideas presented here and to developing my thinking on ethics in CBPR.

5

TEACHING ARTS-BASED RESEARCH METHODS IN COMMUNITY-BASED PARTICIPATORY RESEARCH

DARLENE E. CLOVER

Introduction

For the past two decades I have taught arts-based research and knowledge mobilisation methods to graduate students at the University of Victoria, Canada, as a visiting instructor to other universities and for the past six years to participants in the Knowledge for Change (K4C) Consortium. The field of arts-based research and knowledge mobilisation methods is multifaceted and continually evolving. As umbrella terms they encompass a range of genres, investigative tools, interpretive strategies, and epistemological and dissemination approaches. While no single definition exists, Greenwood (2019) identifies two key unifying features of arts-based research: 'it is research; and one or more art forms or processes are involved in the doing of the research' (p. 1). A key feature of knowledge mobilisation is public outreach and accessibility. Central to both fields is art making, representation and aesthetics, our senses, emotions and intellectual processes.

Similar to feminist- and community-based participatory research (CBPR), arts-based research and knowledge mobilisation offer a richness of opportunity as well as challenges. Eisner (2008) called making a case for arts-based research as important as it is daunting. The students and K4C participants I have taught come from around the world and bring a range of disciplinary backgrounds, socio-cultural knowledges, research experiences and trainings, and aesthetic sensibilities. Equally varying is their involvements with the arts and responses to arts-based research and knowledge mobilisation methods.

Some students and participants self-identify as artists or use the arts in their organisations and simply lack the language and methodical approaches of research. I have taught academics and community members who actually do CBPR using arts-based methods but have never positioned or articulated their work within the field. There are students and participants who get excited when they realise arts-based research and knowledge mobilisation are legitimate approaches used by hundreds of scholars worldwide, which they too can employ. Others, however, had any artistic and creative proclivities educated out of them through schooling or fine arts museums and feel great trepidation at venturing into an unknown world that may make them appear foolish or incompetent. For others, my teaching taps into a creativity that still exists but has laid dormant or kept well away from their academic work. There are participants and students who have been so traditionally trained that they truly struggle, failing to see arts-based research as 'proper' research and/or how they would fit it within their disciplines. The list goes on, but this demographic information illustrates that when teaching arts-based and knowledge mobilisation methods there will be a range of experiences and reactions, from unbridled enthusiasm to caution to hope to utter contempt.

This chapter focuses on how I teach arts-based and knowledge mobilisation primarily to participants in the K4C, but I also include instructional methods from my graduate courses because future instructors will teach in their own workplaces and there are differences in time and access to materials, artists and arts-based researchers. I begin with my own background, and the questions I use to create an understanding of the group I am teaching. I then discuss academic critiques of arts-based research and knowledge mobilisation and how I respond. Following this, I outline how I teach key features and characteristics of arts-based research and knowledge mobilisation, placing an emphasis on the use of project examples which bring to life what can be opaque or confusing and illustrate the field's creativity and breadth. I then share some of my methods that enable students and participants to practise arts-based investigation. I conclude with some challenges, suggestions, and why this type of research is needed in what Greenwood (2019) calls 'our repertoire of tools for understanding people and the world' (p. 16).

This chapter will be useful to researchers already working with and through the aesthetic, but it is aimed primarily at instructors who have gone or will go through the K4C or similar kind of CBPR training and are actually planning or simply hoping to include arts-based and knowledge mobilisation methods in their own investigations and teaching portfolios.

Background and Relationship to the Arts

I begin each class with my background because situatedness provides insights (Whitson, 2017). In my case, these are insights into how I teach and what I believe education and research are for as a feminist adult educator who has worked for over four decades toward a more socially, ecologically, economically, decolonised and gender just world. My experience of working with the arts and artists around the world speaks to their potential. I have seen art projects not only inspire and transform the participants involved but help to bring down municipal councillors, contribute to the prevention of the construction of a power plant, and enable workplaces to unionise (e.g., Clover, 2005, 2003). Some arts-based projects receive bomb threats, so powerful is their ability to represent and voice what some do not wish to see or hear (Schönweger and Clover, 2020).

Equally important to share is my own relationship to art. I do not self-identify as an artist and neither do the majority of students or K4C participants. This positioning helps them to understand, however, that they too could use arts-based and knowledge mobilisation methods without the identity or 'special' capacity. Moreover, everyone has creative capacities as people doodle, read poetry, speak in metaphors and through body gestures, use signs and symbols, tell stories, take photographs or videos, and so forth. Once disabused of the idea that 'art' means drawing like Caravaggio, hope and creativity can emerge.

I also speak to the value of bringing community-based artists into the classroom. Their aesthetic sensibilities and teaching methods enable students and participants to hone art-making skills and focus on artistry while I concentrate on how to conduct research. Both research and art are about process, but also about product. Just as you would never publish a poorly designed research report for public consumption, nor would you produce a sub-standard art product. I do not speak of some fine art measurement but to care and attention to the art to receive the respect you and your research are due.

Starting with a Question

In order to comprehend the experiences, knowledge and openness of the group I teach and as a measure for change as we progress, I begin with a question. The one I use most often is: When I put together the words 'art' and 'research', what comes to mind? I have students or participants turn to their neighbour and share their thoughts and then we discuss those as the larger group.

How people respond to the question is contingent upon the demographics I outlined in the introduction. The last time I taught for the K4C I noticed two participants sitting silently and looking about the room with worried expressions. Concerned they did not understand, I asked if clarification was needed. Their response, however, was 'we have no idea because we have never seen these two words together.' It was satisfying when following my presentation, they approached exclaiming 'now we get it!' But I have watched students and participants who were uninterested or dismissive in the beginning remain so throughout the class.

Addressing Academic Critiques

Running parallel to the evolution of the field of arts-based and knowledge mobilisation are critiques which warrant addressing because they provide a platform to showcase the breadth, creativity and value of these methods. How I deal with the critiques will make the most sense once I outline them. One is that compared to the quantitative method's straightforward claim to objectivity and impartiality, arts-based research is impressionistic, anecdotal and influenced by researcher's bias (e.g. Greenwood, 2019). Therefore, it offers nothing more than a subjective interpretation of data which is so open to interpretation as to be meaningless. Linked is the challenge that since the arts are meant to be free and about creativity, there can be no method, meaning people simply create what and how they want which would not meet any 'reliable' scientific standard. Third, the arts can only capture what is 'known' and, therefore, cannot supply new data or statistical or quantitative data. Fourth, the research is so localised and small scale it can never be generalisable or address wicked problems. Other challenges are related to the quality and thus credibility of the research products and the assumption that the researcher must be an artist. Finally, some scholars are concerned that arts-based research is too political (theoretically grounded and aimed toward social justice) whilst others query if it is mere therapy for the downtrodden. In sum, arts-based research and knowledge mobilisation are practices that lack breadth, statistical prowess, new knowledge creation capacity, objectivity, quality (without artists), rigorous method and, therefore, will never replace tried and true 'tradition'.

How I address critiques and queries depends upon time. If I have little, I simply present a list and provide counter critiques myself. An example is to remind the group that no research is ever 'objective', nor can it work outside some type of lens or theoretical framework. To try to collect facts in an undirected way would see you disappear beneath a mountain of irrelevancies. Moreover, politics are everywhere; climate change science is not neutral; and engineering projects are never about building something with no purpose (bias) in mind.

My second teaching approach is to list the critiques and invite participant and student reflections and then expand the discussion with my own experiences and examples. My third method is to identify the critiques and respond to them by using examples of arts-based and knowledge mobilisation projects. For example, a participatory research project at the Women's Museum in Argentina gathered both statistical and anecdotal data on women who had been murdered by intimate partners during the Covid-19 pandemic and used a mask-making approach (good for questions of identity). The quantitative data, which included each victim's name to humanise the statistics, was displayed through a stunning and haunting wall installation. This project has dropped the jaws of many a statistician in my classes who have acknowledged how this representation may be much more effective than their graphs and charts.

Teaching Features, Characteristics and Genres

Arts-based research literature outlines a diversity of approaches, purposes, ethics and 'different stages and ways that art may utilise' (Greenwood, 2019, p. 2). How I teach these also depends on time. When short of time, I simply highlight the most well-trodden arguments and salient characteristics. I use paraphrasing and direct quotations from the literature. For example, Greenwood (2019) presents an excellent argument for what arts-based methods bring and do:

> The intention for using arts-based tools is to open up different, and hopefully more empowering, options for exploring the specific problem or issues, and for expressing participants' perspectives in what they can bypass participants' discomfort with words or unconscious compliance with dominate discourses, or perhaps to represent findings in ways that better reveal their dynamics and complicity than written reports (p. 6).

When I have more time, I place students into small groups with class readings and give them 30–40 minutes to share their reflections and identify questions. We then discuss these in the larger group, and I highlight features missed or tackle basic assumptions such as arts-based researchers must be artists. More visual methods I use are to have students write selected quotations from the literature onto Post-it notes and create a narrative collage and/or use magazines to find images that represent ideas in the literature. There is much more written on arts-based research than knowledge mobilisation, so I have students create zines or exhibitions based around a research question and/or invite arts-based researchers who work with artists to create graphic novels to research data (e.g., Schallié, 2022). Alongside this I always provide a list (or have students identity them from the readings and add to this) of all the different arts that can and have been used including music, poetics, exhibitions and exhibits, zines, masks, theatre, video, photography, installations, sculptures, quilts, and so on.

I also draw attention to a number of critical aspects of arts-based research and knowledge mobilisation that help to position the potential of the field and arts' relationship to research. First, these are not methods in opposition to more traditional approaches of enquiry. They work well together as they play different roles and bring different knowledges and experiences.

The mask project is a case in point, as it gathered statistics through a survey as well as anecdotally (participants knew the women in their communities), based itself on actual numbers, and addressed an uncomfortable topic in a poignant and compelling way. Articles can be written about projects like this, and they will be read by a few scholars but hundreds of people, including politicians who visit these types of installations. Mentioning this speaks to impact.

Second, no methodology is perfect; each comes with trade-offs. It is incumbent on each researcher to know what is gained and what is lost in methods chosen.

Third, in a complex and often unknowable social world we need answers to problems that are different to what conventional methods are able to produce (e.g., Knowles and Cole, 2008). We need not simply knowledge but knowing, a process made in pursuit of a problem that will yield varied conclusions that reflect complexity (McNiff, 2008).

Fourth and linked, most scholars have been schooled in rigorous, scientifically informed practice, from identifying ontological and epistemological assumptions, writing detailed and focused research questions, selecting appropriate (scientific/objective) methods of data collection, ensuring research has ethical approval through to robust methods of analysis. While this is important and valuable, 'rules, processes and procedures have intentionally and unintentionally stifled academic knowledge, creativity and innovation' (Ward and Shortt, 2020, p. 1).

Fifth and equally important, arts-based research is research (Greenwood, 2019). Like any study, these projects are guided by a clear and explicit purpose and a research question. In other words, they make explicit what is being investigated, why and how either by the researcher or the collective as in CBPR. Also, like all studies, the method (in this case the art form) depends on the purpose. Equally, like all qualitative researches, arts-based projects are framed theoretically and, sometimes, hypothetically grounded. Let us remember that people hypothesise and theorise all the time in their attempts to explain and understand the world. Arts-based and knowledge mobilisation projects are often grounded in the literature and therefore they attempt to fill a gap, but when used in the context of CBPR, their aim is to address a real-life issue such as homelessness or violence against women. Arts-based research projects follow steps which are transparent and there are ethical considerations which require attention. For example, when undertaking a photography project about homelessness, you cannot simply photograph people without their consent. This is where creativity is so useful to capture the essences of homelessness. In an installation created from photos from a research project with homeless children, images of lone seagulls and picnic tables reflected feelings of isolation, a police car caught in a review mirror illustrated confrontation, a motel sign spoke of precarity, and so forth.

It is also important in my teaching to speak to the issue of trustworthiness in the findings of arts-based research, which like all research is built in at the design stage and is dependent upon the clear alignment made between the purpose of the research and the methods selected. Having said this, Greenwood (2019) reminds us that although choices, strategies, aims and boundaries of the investigation are clearly outlined and explained, this 'does not imply need for a rigid and static design. Art is an evolving process, and the research design can well be an evolving one…Nor does it imply that all data or findings need to be fully explicatable verbally' (p. 6).

Different from other research methods, arts-based research projects are more embodied, visual, tolerant of ambivalences and ambiguities, and able to communicate at different levels from just the written word (or graphs) (Bagley and Cancienne, 2002; Leavy, 2017). One of the primary reasons for choosing arts-based methods 'is to allow the operation of aesthetic and subconscious understandings as well as conscious and verbalised ones' (Greenwood, 2019, p. 6).

Interpreting the Visual

For Lisahunter (2017) 'visual texts, visual methods, and representation of research using visual genres have had a long history and at times a close relationship with narrative research. Visual methods can contribute particular depth to what we can understand from a story and a teller' (p. 89). Some research arts are narrative, e.g., poetry and métissage, but many others are more visual and, therefore, a key element of my teaching is visual interpretation and analysis. Visuals, like documents can be read and, as noted, it is the purpose and research question(s) that enables the reading. I create a collage of diverse images. I begin with the research questions which in this case were: What does feminism look like? How do you visualise its central elements? Students search the internet, magazines and sometimes from their storied photos for images. The images are put together and then mined for their themes, just as interview transcripts would be. In the collage, there are visual themes of humor, celebration, struggle, resistance, agency, strength, complexity, and colouring outside the lines.

I have also taken students for a walk around campus or a community or sent them on their own or with an artist armed with a research question. They take photographs, videos or make drawings if they are themselves visual artists that respond to the question and come back to share the 'data'. Students can also create tableaus or theatre pieces from what they see and hear. A concrete example comes from teaching in the K4C in Italy. I sent the students into the park where we were meeting with their iPhones for two hours to capture visually the research questions (How does the park educate the public about environmental issues? What strategies are being used?) and put them together in presentation. Despite having the same question, their videos, still shots, and reflections were extremely diverse but all visually captivating.

Examples of Arts-Based Research Projects

Two other elements central to my teaching are to provide examples of arts-based research and knowledge mobilisation projects and outline their uses, elements, purposes, and stages to offer the opportunity to practise one or more arts-based methods. As I have strong connections to arts projects, community artists, and feminists in museums around the world, I have access to many examples, but the literature itself has many examples and there are artists working in your community or academics in your universities who can be invited to discuss their work. Often, there is someone in the class who has expertise too. Despite my access to so many diverse and interesting projects, I always draw on the knowledge and skills of guest speakers.

Some of the projects I share are large scale, such as taking over a house slated for demolition and re-creating it through visuals based on findings from a study. The purpose of this project titled *Wasteland* was to provide a space for young people from a secondary school, teacher candidates, artists, and community members to explore and visualise their anxieties and fears about climate change (e.g., Sanford and Clover, 2022). Other projects are longer term, such as a CBPR arts-based study with a group of homeless and street involved women over a two-year period (Clover, 2011). The purposes of this project were to explore through creativity the impact of being homeless on their lives, to create a strong community of women, to re-position the women as artists, and to use their artworks to challenge negative stereotypes about who they were and how they ended up on the streets. We created a number of individual artworks (paintings and masks) and collective works (a quilt, a mosaic, a collage and sculpture) and showcased these works in three different galleries across the city of Victoria.

There are also smaller projects such as zines. I pass examples around (such as one of a project with women domestic workers in India and one that uses graphics to share the findings of a study called 'Barbie Expo' we did of how women are portrayed in exhibitions), and explain their use in capturing and sharing data in accessible forms such as photos and drawings. The zine of the women domestic workers consists of verbatim quotations about their experiences of public transport, with images of the women themselves and their drawings.

After years of teaching and using arts-based practices and meeting others doing the same, we decided to publish the *Feminist adult educators' guide to aesthetic, creative and disruptive strategies in museums and community.* Fully open source, this edited volume is a collection of arts-based education and research methods, strategies, and approaches being used in communities and institutional settings. It is an excellent resource to generate ideas and shows how to do many practices (Clover et al., 2020).

Practising Arts-Based Research

The story from Italy shared earlier illustrates one way I teach arts-based research and knowledge mobilisation. As noted, I give an entire group one or two art forms and a research question. Another method, as noted above, is to hire artists to work with the group over the period of a day. These artists are selected for the different genres (e.g., photographer, theatre artist, fabric artist). It is the students and I who identify the research question to be investigated, as the role of the artists is to teach the artform and pay attention to the artistry. A third is to have the participants sign up under a genre such as theatre, video, poetry, and collage. It is important to keep the size of the group small as it is easier for them to work together and to provide a diversity of genres. To practise knowledge mobilisation, I have had students design an installation, exhibition, or zine based on a research question. The depth of the research questions I provide, or that students and participants generate, and the artform(s) selected depend upon length of time and resources (materials to create something).

Critical after each group presents their 'art' are the reflection questions. I ask about the degree of difficulty or ease, what the practice opened up for them, what they might have seen due to the genre, the role of metaphoric and symbolic thinking in capturing difficult or complex questions, and how they might use this in their own teaching and/or research practice in the university or community. I also ask what adaptations they might make to the process, what they learnt from the artists, or what other genre might work and why?

Final Thoughts: Challenges and Suggestions

Like Hein (1990), I believe that purely because the arts make research much more interesting and energising is reason enough to employ them. But they also yield important results in terms of what critical and feminist scholars of CBPR aim toward which, to borrow from Marx, is not solely to investigate and interpret the world but to change it. Having taught arts-based and knowledge mobilisation methods for many years, I can say that for the most part arts-based projects are exciting, exhilarating, and joyfully creative, such as a powerful and highly creative theatre piece designed in response to a question about human effects on the environment. But there are challenges and conflicts, and I conclude with those and some suggestions.

Always keep in mind that not everyone will understand or even want to use arts-based research and knowledge mobilisation methods. It is important not to force people, but to try to get them excited and let them practise and reflect on what they have learnt. Ethics and respect must be a baseline of arts-based research projects, like any other. For example, a group of participants selected to use video and decided to interview their fellow participants who were actually working on their own projects. These participants became very upset by the intrusiveness of cameras that were shoved into their faces and it took away from the approach and quality of what was produced.

Students tend to choose the artwork with which they are most familiar and comfortable, and this means photography and/or video. They are important arts, but requiring students to pair these technologies with poetry or theatre encourages experimentation. It will also tap into the artistic abilities of the diverse research participants they will meet. Moreover, reducing the world to being only about technology may be the way things are going, but we still have a world full of other genres like theatre, music, and poetry, and it is important to keep them alive. Having said this, while the artform you choose is totally contingent on the purpose, and they can be mixed and matched, much will depend on the length of time you have to teach them. Designing and making a quilt will take much longer than writing poetry.

Like me, you may never become a professional artist, but you can use arts-based research method and knowledge mobilisation methods to provoke new ways of seeing and capturing problems that tap into the human aesthetic side.

6

UNDERTAKING FEMINIST COMMUNITY-BASED PARTICIPATORY RESEARCH

Gender and Safety on University Campuses

NANDITA PRADHAN BHATT AND TARIQA F. TANDON

Introduction

In 2017, the #MeToo movement erupted across the world, where people, especially women and sexual and gender minorities, came forward with their stories of sexual harassment and sexual abuse, exposing the magnitude of the issue. The unsaid was out in the open. Many that came forward spoke specifically of sexual harassment in the workplace, where the power differentials were amplified and where survivors felt that there was no mechanism in place for them to report what they had been through. It highlighted the underlying patriarchal culture that has allowed this issue to fester in our societies, and survivors demanded more accountability from institutions that should have safeguarded them.

In India, the #MeToo movement reached academia when a law student's crowdsourced list of Indian professors, unverified but meant to serve as a cautionary list, went viral online, and it brought to the forefront the issue of safety in higher education institutions (HEIs) in the country.

A law against sexual harassment at workplaces has been in place since 2013 in India,* which extends to educational institutions. The law provides for civil remediation (as opposed to a criminal case) to cases of sexual harassment at workplace, which are adjudicated by an Internal Committee (IC) (created at an organisation level) or a Local Committee (created at a district level). The law thus puts the onus of creating safe workplaces for employees on the employer and/or organisation.

In 2015, the University Grants Commission (UGC) published an additional notice on the prevention, prohibition, and redressal of sexual harassment of students in HEIs.† These guidelines came out of a concern that there were increasing reported instances of sexual harassment at HEIs in India. A taskforce was created by the UGC, which conducted gender audits of certain HEIs across the country, to assess the situation on the ground; from this, the Saksham Report was created, which outlines the measures for ensuring the safety of women on campus, and how HEI campuses can be more gender sensitive. The Saksham Report highlighted the need for a context-specific set of guidelines for HEIs on sexual harassment, from which the 2015 guidelines were created.

The UGC guidelines are a comprehensive set of responsibilities that HEIs must adhere to, in order to make campuses safe for students and employees. It reinforces the 2013 Sexual Harassment of Women at Workplace law, but goes beyond the provisions of the law to contextualise how sexual harassment impacts HEIs

---

* More information on the Sexual Harassment of Women at Workplace (Prevention, Prohibition and Redressal) Act can be found here: https://www.indiacode.nic.in/handle/123456789/2104?sam_handle=123456789/1362

† More information on the guidelines issued by the UGC can be found here: https://www.ugc.gov.in/pdfnews/7203627_UGC_regulations-harassment.pdf

specifically and, unlike the law, it is applicable for students of all genders.

The guidelines also led to the creation of a Saksham portal, where HEIs are mandated to submit annual reports on the cases of sexual harassment reported and addressed in HEIs. In India, there are more than 1,000 universities and over 42,000 colleges that form the HEI ecosystem, yet data from the Saksham portal show that in 2022–23, only 238 HEIs had reported cases of sexual harassment that were addressed (Khan, 2024), and data on how many HEIs are complying with the guidelines is sparse. The issue of sexual harassment is largely silenced, and cases of sexual harassment remain underreported; the weak compliance by HEIs to the guidelines and the law led to the UGC issuing another directive in 2024 to submit compliance reports and take a more proactive stance towards sexual harassment in HEIs.

The case of India highlights the chasm that exists between the creation of laws and policies on sexual harassment, and its implementation in reality. On the one hand, robust laws and policies exist in the country, understanding the intricacies of sexual harassment and governing various types of workplaces, and which have been created from research done at the ground level. Yet, compliance to and governance of these laws and policies have been very weak. The safety of marginalised genders is often relegated to the backburner, and institutions have failed, even with comprehensive laws in place, to ensure that all individuals are safe at workplaces and HEIs.

Thus, one of the biggest issues in HEIs is the lack of institutionalisation of gender sensitivity, a failure to comply with laws and guidelines, and the lack of effective redressal mechanisms. To address this gap, a feminist community-based participatory research (CBPR) approach to safety on campuses can be an effective way to gather voices from all parts of the campus community and encourage them to be a part of the solutioning for safer campuses.

This chapter explores how feminist CBPR methodologies can be applied to HEIs to make them safer and more conducive spaces for learning, and where all community members feel responsible for upholding the safety of the community.

First, we explore the confluence between CBPR and feminist approaches to research, and the need for a feminist lens in CBPR; second, we understand the issue of sexual harassment in HEIs and the impact it has on survivors; finally, we delve into how a feminist CBPR approach can be used to make HEIs safer, illustrating the same with two case studies.

A Feminist Approach to Community-Based Participatory Research

Community-based participatory research breaks away from traditional, positivist research that is prevalent in academia, moving away from a top-down methodology of research. Challenging the subject-researcher dichotomy and questioning the inherent power dynamics in traditional research methodologies, CBPR shifts power back to communities (Lokot et al., 2023), who are not just subjects in research, but emerge as co-researchers. CBPR is thus community led and driven, with the objective not just to conduct research for knowledge production, but with the goal of social change and action, empowering the groups engaged in the research during the research process.

Feminist research also emerged as a counter to the traditional research methodologies, and principles of feminist research are present in theories of CBPR. Like CBPR, feminist theories 'have acted as an intentional counter to dominant theories about human experiences and strategies for change' (Frisby et al., 2009, p. 16). Ollivier and Tremblay (2000) state that one of the objectives of feminist research is 'the construction of new knowledge *and* the production of social change' (cited in Brayton et al., n.d., para 3) (emphasis added). Hence, similar to CBPR, feminist research challenges unequal social realities, and has an actionable component to it.

Feminist researchers also reject the researcher-subject dichotomy, valuing the knowledge of participants as expert knowledge (Cook and Fonow, 1986). Further, feminist research questions the power imbalance between researchers and subject, and challenges the social inequality present in communities (Brayton et al., n.d.).

Feminist approaches to research also posit that no research is objective, and that researchers cannot maintain objectivity during the research process. Indeed, subjectivities during the research process affects how the researcher conducts the research, and feminist methodologies emphasise a reflexive research practice, which takes into consideration the 'biographical journeys of researchers [which] greatly influence their values, their research questions, and the knowledge they construct' (Banks, 1998, p. 4). This reflexive process is also built into CBPR, in which communities are the researchers, and hence the direction of the research is driven by reflexive processes within the community.

Feminist research methodologies have been a major influence on various paradigms of action and participatory research, along with other critical theories (Darroch and Giles, 2014). Thus, there is a natural confluence in the basic principles of both CBPR and feminist research – they both challenge the inherent power structures in society and the objectivity of research.

However, CBPR has been critiqued – especially by feminists – for its failure to ensure the challenging of power structures, and reifying power relations instead (Darroch and Giles, 2014). CBPR and other participatory approaches to research are especially weak in challenging power structures within those communities which do not want to emphasise or work towards the empowerment of the most marginalised (Cooke and Kothari, 2001). Power imbalances reinforce themselves in the research process when more dominant members of the community take it over (Darroch and Giles, 2014).

Nowhere is this clearer to see than when looking at gender and the participation of women and gender minorities in CBPR. This is especially the case when a CBPR project takes a gender-blind or gender-neutral approach to research – failing to explicitly include a gender lens can reinforce gender relations and gender power dynamics, resulting in 'superficial outcomes only' (Lenette, 2022). Without taking on a critical feminist lens, CBPR is ineffective at including all members of the community.

Bringing feminist principles together with CBPR, the Martha Farrell Foundation (MFF), in partnership with the UNESCO Chair in Community-Based Research and Social Responsibility in Higher Education, has been working for over a decade on the issue of sexual harassment in HEIs. MFF and the UNESCO Chair have been part of the latter's Mentor Training Program (MTP), to create the next generation of community-based researchers, focused on sexual harassment in workplaces and HEIs.

Nandita Pradhan Bhatt, one of the authors of this chapter, has been a mentor of the MTP, and is responsible for mentoring a hub in the programme. MFF's hub has been Pt. Ravishankar Shukla University, a public university in central India, and the focus of the hub is on SDG 5 – gender equality. Mentors from the faculty of the university have been trained in CBPR with a special focus on gender and are encouraged to take their learnings forward with students to co-create safe learning spaces for all. Students from the initial cohorts, trained by faculty mentors, now train younger students in feminist CBPR frameworks. The hub has also launched a course for all of the students at the university to learn methods of CBPR, which emphasises feminist CBPR and the importance of a gender lens.

Sexual Harassment in Higher Education

A major part of the work being done by MFF, especially through this MTP hub, has been to ensure gender equity in educational spaces, especially HEIs, and that they are safe spaces for all genders.

Globally, individuals of marginalised genders* have been able to access HEIs, with their enrolment numbers consistently increasing. UNESCO's 2020 Global Education Monitoring gender report found that since the adoption of the Beijing Declaration in 1995, female enrolment in HEIs has tripled, from 38 million in 1995 to 180 million in 2018 (Global Education Monitoring Report, 2020). Though the trend in every country is different, global figures indicate a significant improvement in enrolment and graduation statistics for women from HEIs.

Yet, this increase in the presence of marginalised gender in HEIs has not translated to a change in the environment in higher education. As noted by Johnson et al. (2018), 'higher education, currently and historically, has been a male-dominated environment, with men in most positions of power and authority' (p. 14). Further, HEIs are spaces 'characterised by asymmetrical power relations and a gendered hierarchical structure' (Joseph, 2015, p. 136). This combination of entrenched hierarchies, asymmetry of power, and strong male authority in HEIs has made it so that while marginalised genders are able to access tertiary education, as students and as faculty their success in these spaces is limited by structural and cultural factors.

The UNESCO report notes that women and girls are more likely to face sexual harassment and gender-based violence in

---

*The term 'marginalised genders' refers to individuals who experience marginalisation due to their gender. This includes women, queer people, trans people, and those that do not conform to the gender binary. Most global data on gender focuses on women and girls, and often overlooks other marginalised genders; due to this, the terms 'women,' 'women and girls' and 'marginalised genders' are used interchangeably in this chapter, especially when referencing secondary texts.

educational institutions, which can limit their educational attainment and their success in these institutions (Global Education Monitoring Report, 2020). Sexual harassment in HEIs is 'not a new phenomenon' (Joseph, 2015, p. 125), but persistent definitional differentiation and cultural norms have made it challenging to establish a comprehensive, global understanding of sexual harassment in tertiary education.

The approach by most HEIs to increase the presence of marginalised genders at their institutions has been to 'add and stir' them to the existing structures, without much consideration of whether these structures work and are relevant to those whom these institutions were not built for. This is not different from how other institutions and structures have dealt with issues of gender representation and including marginalised genders in their folds. However, as is the case with other institutions and spheres where this was applied, this approach does not work.

As Harding (1995) notes, this is because gender differences 'were thought to be more or less caused by biological differences and the term "gender" was usually taken to refer to "women's problems" that were assumed somehow or other to be an affect [sic] of women's biology' (p. 296). Yet, gender is not a biological issue, but one of cultural and social relations, and are 'local cultural arrangements that assign different access to social and natural resources to women and men' (ibid., p. 296) and those that fall outside this binary. A rational and objective approach to gender cannot be taken, and HEIs have to realise that they are embedded in these very social relations.

The result is that the institutional mechanisms reinforce the societal marginalisation of marginalised genders in higher education spaces, and they often face various forms of gender-based violence during their education. Hence, any progress made in closing the gender gap in enrolments in higher education 'is jeopardized by the persistence of sexual harassment and its adverse impact on women's careers in...colleges and universities' (Johnson et al., 2018, p. 1).

Starting Feminist Community-Based Participatory Research in Higher Education Institutions

HEIs are usually sites where traditional forms of knowing and research are emphasised, and where hierarchies are entrenched deeply. They are spaces where individuals with authority (including faculty) can make or break a student's future, and this concentration of power in a few individuals makes the fear of retaliation against them higher. In addition, HEIs are also workplaces, in which power is highly stratified and usually gendered. Thus, employing a feminist CBPR project in such spaces can be contentious, especially if the community part of and being researched is the HEI itself.

In such situations, it is important that a gender champion emerges from the community, especially from a position of power, who can take forward the issue of gender, and especially campus safety. It is imperative that this gender champion understands that safety on campus goes beyond legal compliance. CBPR, as a research methodology and process, takes time and resources, and it is only seriously motivated gender champions that can advocate for such an approach to campus safety.

Often, many campuses have various services and assistance, including peer mentorship, faculty mentorship, psychosocial counselling and helplines, offered to students to help them deal with the myriad problems that they are facing. Yet, these services are underutilised, especially in relation to issues of campus safety and sexual harassment, because students' inputs and perspectives have not been considered. The rules are coming from the top, and there are often many gaps in their policies.

When it comes to socially entrenched issues such as gender roles and relations, it is important to address attitudes and behaviour changes. But, in a space with thousands of people with different attitudes, behaviours, and boundaries, how do you ensure that it is safe for all? Merely having mechanisms in place to address sexual harassment does not mean a higher education institution is safe; having no complaints does not mean that there is no sexual harassment on campus. Thus, what is *not* being done must be considered, and this will only be known if the whole community of the HEI is involved and heard, including students. Solutions for safety on campus must come from different sections of the community, which will address the issues most pertinent to them.

The Martha Farrell Foundation has worked extensively in HEIs in India and globally to create safe campuses for all. While in those countries, different authorities, regulatory bodies and legal institutions have formulated policies, laws, declarations, and statements on the issue of campus safety in HEIs, there has been a lack of a substantive and gender sensitive approach to safety on campuses.

Administrative bodies of HEIs understand that they need to make their campuses safe – but they do not understand who they have to make it safe for, what gender is, and how marginalised genders are disproportionately impacted by unsafe campuses. A feminist CBPR approach to campus safety, which involves all parts of the HEI community, but especially students, can be a solution to this.

Steps to Creating a Safe Campus

Step 0: Establishing a safe space

Before starting any CBPR with HEIs on campus safety, it is important for the facilitator* to note that such a project is usually

---

*This facilitator can be an external facilitator or a gender champion from within the campus community. It is better if the facilitator is from within the campus

charged with emotions, and it is important to lay ground rules for all community members* – at the forefront, this project must be sensitive, and rooted in respect and dignity. Thus, it is essential that a safe space is created for all community members. But what does a safe space mean?

Creating a safe space is the duty of the facilitator, to ensure that every member of the community feels welcome and an equal member of the CBPR project. To establish this, it is important that the facilitator holds a non-judgemental space for all, where people can speak their minds freely. Here, we are guided by the principles of adult education and learning (Hall et al., 2022) – everyone comes with their own experiences, and this must be validated. Hence, it is imperative that no one is put down for putting forth their point of view – instead, the facilitator must probe them and make them re-examine their worldview.

The role of the facilitator: The facilitator's role in creating a safe space is crucial – the facilitator must understand that they are not there for their own purpose, but for the community, and they must de-centre themselves from the process. Understanding and appreciating different points of views (even when one may disagree with them) is important.

Given that gender, violence, and safety are personal and painful topics, facilitators must take a survivor-centred and trauma-informed approach to facilitation, to ensure that the process does not re-traumatise any survivor. This means that the survivor is at the centre of the designing of redressal and support mechanisms,

---

community and is someone who holds a position of authority, since the likelihood that gender is then institutionalised within the HEI is higher. The facilitator can also be a group of gender champions, which includes faculty, non-teaching staff and students.

* In HEIs, the community members of a campus include all management, faculty, non-teaching staff, support staff, students and others that interact with the HEI.

and the focus is on how survivors want to be addressed and helped. Further, there must be an understanding of how trauma impacts persons, keeping their interests at the forefront. Thus, it is an approach that is not based on assumptions, but rather based on actual reflections and inputs from survivors. This can be done by de-personalising situations and comments, and presenting case studies and learnings to the community more generally, without singling out one person's experience.

Facilitators must be well-versed in the principles of CBPR, but also in gender, gender-based violence and sexual harassment. Respect, trust, dignity, participation, voice are some of the guiding principles, along with the mutual ownership of knowledge, that define and design solutions. An understanding of power relations is key, and must be assessed at each step. Principles of gender equity must be weaved into the understanding of CBPR, and not added as a post-script.

Sexual harassment is one of the most underreported forms of harassment globally, and it is swept under the carpet in many HEIs. Yet, feminist CBPR tells us that some of the biggest data points that you can get is no data – the silence of data is important to see and understand, especially when it comes to gender marginalisation and sexual harassment. The facilitator must pick up on the silences and probe further to find out the truth. Hence, the facilitator's understanding on gender is very important.

Finally, the facilitator must not use language with a lot of jargon, as that can alienate many of the community members. Simple language which the community at large can understand must be used, and complicated concepts must be broken down.

Step 1: A conversation on gender

After establishing a safe space, the facilitator should gather various sections of the campus community to have discussions on gender, violence and safety on campus.

Some questions that the community can be asked to consider is: what is safety for them, for whom is this safety, from whom do they have to be safe? If safety is for students, is it only extended to women students?

The conversation is de-personalised by using case studies – this allows community members, especially survivors of sexual and gender-based violence to detach themselves from a personal situation and be a part to the conversation, without having to disclose their own experiences.

Ideally, the presentation of the case studies would happen in smaller community groups; however, if there is a time limitation, then the whole campus community can be brought together in one room. While the presentation of the case studies happens with the whole group, the reflections on the case studies should take place in smaller groups with different communities of the campuses breaking out into their own sessions. This can include administrative staff, permanent teaching staff, contract teaching staff, support staff, younger students, and older students. The facilitator must consider their own institution, and cultural and social factors when determining the different groupings of the campus community. Unless specifically requested, it is encouraged to have mixed-gender groupings of persons of equal status for the conversations.

The goal of the conversation is to build an understanding on the pertinent issues, and to broaden the community's understanding of safety and community. The facilitator can offer further reading materials to those who are interested in learning more about the issue but must ensure that the focus of the conversation is on exploring the predominant ideas and thinking, and then challenging this thinking to break the socio-culturally influenced gender stereotypes.

During these conversations, the facilitator must consider that there is a thin line between protecting and moralising. Depending on the cultural context, HEIs can be over-protective spaces, especially for women students, which can lead to moralising them. While ensuring that campuses are safe is important, it is equally important to note that those attending these HEIs are adults who are at a stage in life where they are exploring their independence, freedom and sexuality. Instead of repressing these feelings, the facilitator must probe the community groups to think about what these mean for them, and how students can explore these in a safe manner.

Step 2: Reviewing policies

The next step is for different groups in the campus community to review the safety-related policies that are in place at the institution. This process of the validation of policy is important to understand the gaps in the policies, so that more effective solutions can be put in place.

Different groups are provided with the policy, and they are asked to read it and give their comments on it. The facilitator must be available to probe and encourage them to think about the gaps in the policy, and where improvements can be made. The goal is not just to critique the policy, but to envision solutions for the problems at hand. Hence, all members of the campus community, especially the students, are part of the solutioning process, and are equal stakeholders in developing or reviewing the policy.

If there are no policies in place, then the different campus community groups can start by reviewing national laws and policies, or specific guidelines issued in their country on the issue of sexual harassment in HEIs. This allows the campus community to understand the gaps in their own laws and policies, and how they can move to address them. The different campus community groups should then be given space to voice their concerns about safety and provide solutions to the issues. The formulation of the policy must be participatory in nature – the facilitator must hear what every group is saying about their safety and ensure that their voice is a part of the policy that is drafted.

The policy is created by the campus community, and different campus community groups give their suggestions on how the campus can be made safer for marginalised genders. The resulting policy is strong and contextually relevant, precisely because it has been tailor-made for the particular HEI and is informed by the experiences of survivors. It is written by and for the campus community, with solutions coming from different community groups.

Step 3: Implementing new (revised) policy

Once the policy is written and/or revised, it must be rolled out across the HEI. This is spearheaded by the gender champion(s) from within the campus community who facilitated the process, and have the responsibility of taking it forward.

This includes sharing the policy with all campus community stakeholders, to ask them for their inputs and their assistance in enforcing the policy. The reporting and redressal mechanisms must be strong and robust, so that people feel free to report their grievances or complaints.

The gender champions must also engage with the management and administration of the HEI, whose support is integral for the effective implementation of the policy. Without their backing, the policy will not be implemented and a gender-focused approach to safety on campus will not be institutionalised.

The participatory and community-driven process ensures that all campus community groups are responsible for safety on campus; responsibility does not lie with a single group or committee. The facilitator must emphasise this shared responsibility while facilitating conversations during the policy drafting stage of the process with all members of the campus community.

Step 4: Staying updated

The final step in making HEI campuses safe is ensuring that campus community members continually engage in conversations around safety, gender sensitivity and sexual harassment.

One way this can be done is for the campus community to engage with a trained facilitator at periodic intervals to continue to keep having structured conversations on the issues of safety and gender on campus, such as consent, boundaries (how they can draw a boundary, what they can do if a boundary has been crossed), etc. This trained facilitator can be an outsider, but the conversations are more impactful if they are a gender champion from within the campus community. These conversations are especially important for students to discuss.

At the same time, the facilitator should engage with the faculty and management of the HEI and should keep the students informed of how the management of the institution is taking the issues and concerns seriously. Often, there is mistrust between the students and the management, and the facilitator can help bridge this gap by continuing their engagement with both groups and addressing their concerns.

Another way to continue to engage the campus community on these issues is by creating mechanisms within different groups in the communities and encouraging peer learning within them. At MFF, we have found that peer learning is an effective way to have difficult conversations around issues of gender, violence, and sexual harassment with young people. Peers, who take on this issue and emerge as gender champions, are trained further on these topics. They then create peer groups, where they talk to their fellow students and give them information in a language and manner which is relevant to them. If any complaints are raised, they can route them through the appropriate channels and can provide support to the complainants.

Finally, the gender champion(s) from within the campus community must remain updated with the changing laws and policies that govern their country and HEI, to ensure that they are not only complying with these in name, but are taking the spirit of gender equity forward, to ensure that all members of the campus community feel safe.

This continued engagement is integral to fostering an environment in HEIs which supports open conversations on issues of safety and violence and creates a space where people who have complaints feel safe to report.

Case Study: Community-Based Participatory Research for Safe Campuses in India

In 2020, MFF started its Safe Campuses Programme with the Association of Indian Universities (AIU). The initial training was held at Pt. Ravishankar Shukla University, our MTP hub, and we invited faculty from HEIs across the country to attend a two-day intensive training on creating a practical understanding of sexual harassment in HEIs.

After this intensive training, a request for more such trainings was voiced by members of the different HEIs. Due to the COVID-19 pandemic, the programme was moved online. This included a six-hour online training session, open for all university faculty and staff, on creating a practical understanding of gender, safety, gender challenges and sexual harassment, with the intention of creating gender champions within the staff at HEIs who would actively work towards making their campuses safe.*

*MFF continues these trainings to date, pivoting online completely due to the ease of the mode. The trainings are held regularly, and have been condensed to a three-

After the initial training sessions were held, some universities who found the discussion pertinent and interesting requested for more intensive training at their campuses. MFF received an invitation by an engineering and technical university in a Tier 2 city in India to work on the issue of making their campus safe and gender-sensitive, using a CBPR approach. The residential, co-educational university has been operational for over 15 years, has over 1,500 undergraduate and post-graduate students, with one-third of the student population being female.

MFF was invited by the university's legally mandated IC,* members of which had attended the Safe Campus Programme training, and who were particularly proactive at the university.

The university had all the necessary processes in place and complied with the pertinent laws and statutes for campus safety. The IC had decided to mandate that everybody on campus must have awareness on gender issues, and hence MFF, as an expert in the field, was brought to facilitate trainings on the same.

Initially, the university wanted MFF to discuss their code of conduct with their students, to encourage them to follow the rules outlined in the code. However, MFF suggested that the focus should instead be on providing a space for students to voice their opinions and concerns of safety on the campus, and to open a conversation on consent and boundaries, and institutionalise a culture where students felt safe to express themselves. This was especially important given the cultural realities of Indian society, where there is a lack of discussions on consent and boundaries.

---

hour session, followed up by intensive face-to-face training, upon request.

*The Sexual Harassment of Women at Workplace (Prevention, Prohibition, and Redressal) Act, 2013 of India mandates that any workplace with 10 or more employees is required to set up an Internal Committee for the prevention, prohibition and redressal of sexual harassment. Any institution without an Internal Committee can be penalised for non-constitution and non-compliance with the legal provisions of the Act.

It becomes more important in the context of the Indian *guru-shishya parampara* (teacher–student tradition), which denotes that a teacher can only impart their teachings to the students through the development of a relationship with the disciple. Though it is meant to be a model of mentorship, it has been used as a way for teachers to exert their power over their students, often through various forms of abuse. Given this cultural context, it became imperative to establish an effective approach to campus safety.

When MFF came to the university, there were around 300 students gathered in a hall for the initial session. Though ideally the training would be done with all parts of the campus community, this was not possible in this case – hence, it was decided that since student voices often go unheard in universities, they should be the target community for this training, to get their thoughts and ideas on campus safety. We avoided lecturing the students on gender and safety – instead, we started off by giving some background, and then got them to anonymously write down if they felt the campus was safe or not.

In the large group, we then watched a video on sexual harassment, safety, and spaces. After watching the video, we broke out into smaller community groups to converse on the video and discuss their thoughts about it. Representatives from each group brought their views forward, speaking for the collective.

After the discussion, some students volunteered to draw a map of the 200-acre campus of the university. This map was then put up in the main hall, and everyone in the university was invited to write their safety-related concerns or queries on the map. People were also encouraged to provide their solutions on making unsafe areas safer.

With the data collected, we assisted the university IC to decode and understand the data, to devise effective solutions for the campus. The IC got to see the areas students found safe and unsafe, and how the students interacted with their campus. Solutions were presented by the students on the map – which included increased patrolling and lights in unsafe areas; training of faculty on gender, marginalisation, and safety; and sensitivity training of the campus guards, who held power but also deep-seated gender stereotypes, which were harmful to students.

A major issue that came forward through the conversations and mapping exercise was that the campus was not a safe space for gender and sexual minorities – the queer community was facing prejudice by faculty and bullying by students. A recommendation that came out of this mapping exercise was to create a more inclusive campus. An actionable item devised was that counsellors and mentors at the university must be given more awareness and sensitivity on understanding sexual and gender minorities, being the first point of change in becoming more inclusive.

Since then, refresher trainings have been held annually with the students and the IC on campus, to ensure that a culture of gender sensitivity and safety continues to be built and institutionalised.

Tools To Create Safe Spaces

Participatory mapping exercises can be an important and empowering tool to create safe physical spaces for campus community members. Either the campus community can create their own map, or the facilitator can bring a map and ask the campus community to contextualise it. The facilitator then needs to probe the campus community members to share their experiences of safety in various parts of the campus space.

A safety map does not need everyone's individual stories – it can be a joint story that many voices contribute to. Since talking about violence is highly personal and intimidating, it may be easier for survivors to lend their voice to a collective story – there is safety in anonymity, so the stories that come out can be attributed to the whole campus community, rather than an individual.

Feminist CBPR tools must be contextually relevant and allow campus community members to express themselves creatively. Videos can be used to start conversations, or photos can be used to get a mood of the room. Photos and videos which talk about a scenario helps de-personalise the situation, which can be used to probe the campus community – groups can then be asked if such situations have arisen in their community, or have they heard of such instances, and what can be done if something similar is happening in the campus community. This allows the campus community to discuss an action plan, which can be taken forward by representatives of different community groups.

Art-based methods (see Chapter 5) can be used to help survivors express their experiences and come to terms with them.

With any tool used, it is important that no individual is under pressure to say anything – everyone must share only what they are comfortable with sharing, and those are the data points that the community and facilitator have to work with.

Conclusion

With more marginalised genders entering HEIs, it is the imperative that these institutions ensure their campuses are safe for everyone. HEIs are spaces where hierarchy is revered, power differentials are entrenched, and gender stereotypes are embedded. For effective solutions to issues of sexual harassment and campus safety, it is integral, then, that HEIs undergo a reflexive process, and challenge their traditional ways of thinking, researching and structuring.

A feminist CBPR lens can be an effective way of addressing sexual harassment, campus safety and power differentials. Applying a feminist CBPR approach to safety at HEIs requires the presence of a gender champion at the institution, who holds considerable power in the hierarchy of the institution and can wield this power to make their campus more gender sensitive.

The participation of diverse community members in the process is imperative – without this, any policy that is made and implemented will be ineffective at addressing sexual harassment and campus safety. Of utmost importance is that those community members whose voices have remain unheard – especially students – are given space, so that they can be equal participants in ensuring the safety of their campuses.

The facilitator plays an integral role in the feminist CBPR process in HEIs for campus safety, and they must be well versed in gender, violence, sexual harassment and the principles of CBPR. The facilitator should apply a sensitive, trauma-informed and survivor-centred approach to create a safe space for all members of the community to voice their concerns and opinions.

The ultimate goal should be not just to create safe spaces, but to go beyond and create empowering spaces and a system which does not condone any violence or harassment. These issues have deep socio-cultural roots, and cannot be eliminated overnight; however, what must be done, as a first step, is to create a space where survivors feel they can share their experiences, and that they can access justice.

7

TEACHING COMMUNITY-BASED PARTICIPATORY RESEARCH DIGITALLY IN PARTNERSHIP WITH COMMUNITY

CATHERINE ETMANSKI, KAUSTUV KANTI BANDYOPADHYAY AND WANDA KRAUSE

Introduction

As major sectors of the world moved online at the onset of the global COVID-19 pandemic, educators of all kinds were challenged to reimagine their curricula for a digital audience. Educators of CBPR typically reject the 'banking' model of education where teachers simply deposit knowledge in the minds of their students (Freire, 2003). Such educators were doubly challenged to design online learning experiences that promoted values inherent to CBPR (e.g., justice, equity, participation, inclusion, empowerment and democracy) in both content and process. This chapter documents our efforts to rise to this challenge in the context of a master's level course in Global Leadership, where Canadian, mid-career professional students were meant to participate in a field school in India to learn about leadership in a range of community-based settings. When international travel was not possible, we pivoted all field school activities online.

The lessons learned are applicable to the Mentor Training Program (MTP) in at least four significant ways, including when educators are (a) facing travel restrictions preventing a planned field excursion; (b) wishing to engage in participatory digital inquiry with community groups from different parts of the world; (c) choosing to reduce their carbon footprint by limiting travel; or (d) wanting to create a more physically and financially accessible learning experience than a typical field school would entail due to the cost of travel and potential for physical barriers. Further, inclusion for visually impaired learners could be achieved by opening each session with an enhanced description of what others were seeing on the Zoom screen. Closed captioning could also be used to support deaf or hard-of-hearing students.

The course this chapter documents aligned with some, though not all normative CBPR principles in both content and process. The course content centred on values and concrete examples of participatory engagement, research, and governance; the empowerment of women, Indigenous Peoples, and youth; the struggles of communities from disadvantaged backgrounds; South-North solidarity; and other topics related to CBPR. With regard to the process and design of the course, the transformative pedagogy highlighted a variety of learning activities (individual, team-based, synchronous, asynchronous); the diversity of voices included as experts (community leaders from various settings in India, faculty from India and Canada, and students themselves); and our willingness as instructors to see education as a mutual process (Freire, 2003) whereby we too were learning as we shared 'in the…growth of our students' (Hooks, 1994, p. 13). However, we intentionally say that the course aligned with 'some, though not all' normative CBPR principles since the digital format did not promote experiential learning, nor did it allow for building relationships beyond those between the authors of this chapter.

Since Indian participants could not interact directly, in-person with Canadian students and faculty, we relied upon Participatory Research in Asia's (PRIA's) long-term relationships built on trust and sustained ethical practice. Therefore, the extent to which Canadian students experientially understand the value of relationships in CBPR cannot be determined given the short-term nature of their interactions.

Nevertheless, transformative pedagogy is essential to this course as a means of shaping global leaders who, in turn, are called to promote the principles of CBPR in their own spheres of influence.

A Note of Gratitude

An earlier version of this chapter was originally published in T. Cappiali and J. Jean-Pierre (eds) book, *Promoting Inclusion and Justice in University Teaching* (see Etmanski et al., 2024). We would also like to thank and acknowledge Amit Bhatt and Lisa Corak for their incredible efforts in supporting the digital platform and coordinating logistics for the various people involved in this course from both India and Canada. Finally, we extend our deep gratitude to all the facilitators at PRIA, guest faculty and community members who shared their expertise and experiences to extend the learning. This includes but is not limited to Rajesh Tandon, Anshuman Karol, Sumitra Srinivasan, and Yashvi Sharma from PRIA; Nandita Pradhan Bhatt, Nitya Sriram Srinivasan, Samiksha Jha from Martha Farrell Foundation (MFF); Suheil F. Tandon and Kabeer Arjun from Pro-Sport Development (PSD); Swapni Shah from UNNATI, and too many others to name here. MFF, PSD and UNNATI are the partner organisations of PRIA involved in several joint community-based interventions. Thank you for your generosity and good work in the world.

Context for the Digital Field School

As members of PRIA and Royal Roads University (RRU), we, the authors of this chapter, have a long-established relationship and have been collaborating on a range of curricular projects and internship exchanges since 2005. Our collaborations include co-designing an online course in 2005 titled, 'International Perspectives on Participatory Research and Evaluation'. This course later formed the foundation of a subsequent online course, 'Foundations of Community-Based Research', taught by both Catherine and Budd Hall at the University of Victoria. Both of these previous online courses informed how we approached the digital field school described in this chapter. The key difference being that this field school allowed students to interact directly with PRIA's community partners, as will be described below.

Since 1982, PRIA, a civil society organisation (CSO) based in India that pioneered participatory research and learning, has been supporting leadership to evolve from the most marginalised communities in Asia (Tandon, 1988; 2002; Tandon and Mohanty, 2002; Jha, et al., 2011). Through the work of Dr Martha Farrell, PRIA contributed to the development of the Master of Arts in Global Leadership (MAGL), which launched in 2015 and, from its inception, has included experiences that intentionally bring people from diverse cultures together to learn from and with one another. Prior to this field school collaboration with RRU, earlier in the pandemic, PRIA had also worked with academic partners at the University of Glasgow and the Michigan State University to provide site visits to their students. With both PRIA and RRU's prior experience designing online learning opportunities, we were able to build on past successes in designing this new opportunity.

Since this field school was situated in the context of a graduate leadership program (GBLD 535: International Cultural Field

Trip), the number of assignments remained consistent, but the specific leadership focus and design of the course changes every year depending on the host country and nature of the partnering organisations' work. Given PRIA's emphasis on participatory processes, the purpose of this year's field school was to demonstrate how leadership is developed from below, especially among the most disadvantaged and marginalised communities. By creating opportunities for students to interact with and learn from the work of PRIA and its partners, this course demonstrated how participatory inquiry leads to leadership development and how these leadership catalyse collective actions for the empowerment of the marginalised. PRIA has demonstrated that this approach to leadership begins with community members' reflections on their own experiences and challenges. From there, a collective identity is built as people see that their individual experience is shared by others and is therefore the result of systemic challenges. Through PRIA's facilitation process, community members learn to articulate their challenge in a collective voice and take leadership action by engaging with the institutions that are meant to support them and advocating for their needs. From women's experiences addressing domestic violence to community members in informal settlements advocating for better sanitation, this process of participatory inquiry leading to collective action was demonstrated repeatedly throughout the course.

As both PRIA and RRU have experience teaching online, the transition to a digital mode was not difficult in and of itself. Nevertheless, designing meaningful content that would keep students engaged and inspired throughout the course was our goal. As such, from 31 August to 17 October 2021, students participated in one digital site visit per week for five weeks. These digital site visits were with PRIA's partnering community groups in India working on topics such as:

- Strengthening women's leadership in local governance, using the progressive provision in the Indian constitution for reserved seats for women in local governments;
- Building leadership capacity of women domestic workers vin demanding dignity of their labour (Bibi, 2020; Domestic Workers' Action Network, 2020; Farrell, 2014);
- Building leadership in urban informal communities by organising them into Settlement Improvement Committees to access basic public services like water and sanitation (Nagpal and Bandyopadhyay, 2020); and
- Encouraging youth leadership to promote the safety of girls and women in public spaces and using sport for development (S4D) to support gender equality.

In selecting topics for these site visits, PRIA facilitators considered four kinds of diversity:

- Diversity of participants based on age, gender, social location, and more;
- Diversity of leadership approaches, e.g., those who have acquired formal positions of leadership, especially women's leadership in the panchayat (local government) versus leadership from informal communities and domestic workers, interacting with district administrators and state actors. Each approach required different skills, including public speaking, engaging with and responding to the community, taking care of administrative details, and more;
- Diversity of leadership context such as rural/urban settings, place-based communities, and communities of affiliation (e.g., elected female officials, domestic workers); and
- Diversity of participatory leadership strategies, e.g., community organising, advocacy, becoming an elected official, as well as arts-based and sports-based methods.

These site visits were scaffolded by a range of resources, synchronous and asynchronous activities as will be described in the sections that follow.

Teaching the Principles of Community-Based Participatory Research

As described throughout this book, the methodological umbrella of CBPR draws from a range of traditions and goes by many names. Various authors in this methodological space have identified normative principles, e.g., Israel et al.'s (2003) list of nine principles of CBPR. As Etmanski et al. (2014), summarised, 'there are two defining characteristics of this body of scholarship: it is action-oriented and it is participatory' (p. 8). In the tradition of participatory research developed by Rajesh Tandon and Budd Hall, the word *participation* has a distinct meaning insofar as the intended beneficiaries have decision-making authority and control over the participatory research process. Therefore, when universities and communities join efforts in a CBPR process, roles and responsibilities must be respectfully discussed and thoughtfully designed. As Israel et al. (2003) further suggested, not everyone can be involved in all parts of the research at all times. Nevertheless, Hall's (1975) tenet that a participatory 'research process should be of some immediate and direct benefit to a community and not merely the basis for an academic paper' (p. 28) rings true to this day.

Although we recognise that 'one course may not fully equip a person to undertake [CBPR],...such learning experiences... can put learners on a trajectory for continuing to deepen their understanding of [CBPR]' (Etmanski et al., 2014, pp 9–10). This deepening understanding not only includes practice tools, techniques, strategies, and methods, it also includes understanding values rooted in the potential for individual and collective transformation. As such, to teach the normative principles of CBPR throughout this course, we drew primarily from Transformative Learning Theory (TLT). This will be further discussed below.

Grounding in a Transformative Pedagogy

In the decades since Jack Mezirow (1994) began writing about transformative learning, authors have proposed ways to categorise different approaches to transformative learning (Dirkx, 1998b; Kucukaydin and Cranton, 2012). Dirkx (1998b) presented transformative learning as (i) political liberation and freedom from oppression through consciousness-raising; (ii) perspective transformation through critical reflection; (iii) meaning-making of life experiences through development and growth; and (iv) emotional-spiritual self-knowledge through symbolism to promote conscious individuation (pp 2–8). Kucukaydin and Cranton (2012, p. 44) summarised these same four streams as Freire's (2003) emancipatory approach, Mezirow's (1991) rational approach, Daloz's (1999) developmental approach, and Boyd's (1989) extrarational [emotional-spiritual] approach. These approaches to TLT are not incommensurate: As Dirkx (1998a) asked us to consider, how might learning 'be envisioned in a way that we also foster transformation of ourselves and the world in which we live?' (para 2). Following from this question, the digital field school described here and the overarching graduate program in which it sits contribute to all four aspects of transformation: individual and collective, rational, emotional, and spiritual.

The definition of TLT as 'an orientation which holds that the way learners interpret and reinterpret their sense experience is central to making meaning and hence learning' (Mezirow, 1994, p. 222), is useful for the Global Leadership Digital Field School as well. Students are not only receiving new knowledge but are also evaluating their past beliefs and perspectives through critical thinking, dialogue and links to theory. The learning objectives of the course encourage deepening self-knowledge and intersect with both Daloz's developmental approach and, potentially, Boyd's extrarational approach – should students be on a spiritual journey or open to seeing healing connections through symbolism. Moreover, Yorks and Kasl (2006) defined TLT as 'a wholistic change in how a person both affectively experiences and conceptually frames his or her experience of the world when pursuing learning that is personally developmental, socially controversial, or requires personal or social healing' (pp 45–46). Recognising the diversity and autonomy of each student, we acknowledge that different levels of development and/or healing might take place at any point throughout a graduate program, whether during this activity or beyond it. In addition, we sent each student a sensory package of Indian foods, spices, teas, incense, flowers and materials, which was intended to bring a little bit of India into their homes, thereby engaging multiple senses and enriching the holistic learning experience.

As an educational experience designed to promote transformative learning (Stevens-Long et al., 2012), through the field school we sought to enhance students' capacities to critically and reflexively explore new knowledge, theory and perspectives. It further sought to enhance awareness of privilege, power and intersectionality. Here privilege refers to the advantage an individual has due to their belonging to a particular group or categorisation, which is often socially constructed. In the forms of mobilisations studied in this course, power can be exercised by seeking change through the refusal of the status quo (Krause, 2022). Intersectionality refers to the interconnections of categorisations, whether gender, race, class, religion, sexual orientation, and many others, which often shape an individual's experience socially (Crenshaw, 1991).

Pedagogical Activities

This was a three-credit, elective course offered at a graduate level. Since we were not able to travel due to the pandemic, we had a rather small number of students in this particular offering (six students total). At RRU, each credit represents approximately 33 hours of student effort. Given that this course normally includes a two-week, in country experience, the course was also shorter than most other graduate level courses and was offered over seven weeks. Students were responsible for approximately 10 to 12 hours of asynchronous interactions and readings per week, with approximately four hours of synchronous meetings with PRIA facilitators and community members in weeks 2 to 6. The course included three assignments:

- An individual multi-media presentation (e.g., a narrated PowerPoint) on the topic of empowering women in leadership;
- A team multi-media presentation expanding students' understanding of leadership building in urban poor communities and youth leadership development for safety of girls and women in public places in Indian context; and
- An individual final reflection paper of up to 3,000 words summarising key lessons learned.

Students were also assessed based on their participation and contributions throughout the course.

To implement the Global Leadership Digital Field School, we invited students to:

- Engage with background resources;
- Participate in a synchronous (i.e., real-time) digital interaction with community leaders in India;
- Have a follow-up conversation with facilitators from PRIA;
- Continue making meaning from the site visit through online discussion forums;
- Generate individual and group assignments; and

- Consolidate mutual learning through closing conversations as well as ongoing discussions and practice beyond the course.

The learning journey for each site visit can be represented as follows:

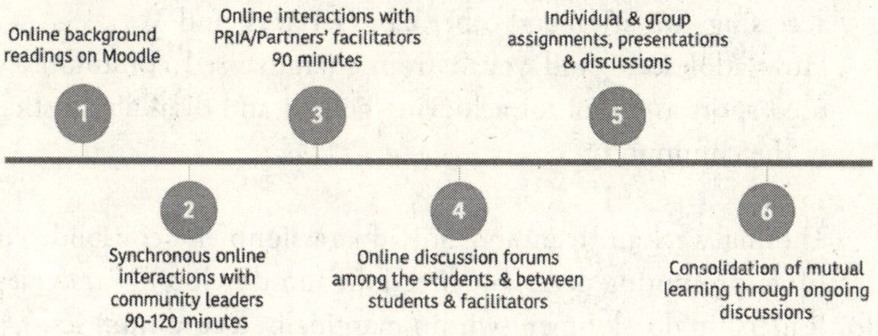

Figure 7.1 The Learning Journey

We cycled through this learning journey multiple times for each of the site visits in weeks 2 through 6, and introductory/closing activities in weeks 1 and 7. The first week focused on developing an appreciation of Indian cultural diversity and an overview of the governance system to situate the leadership development efforts with the marginalised communities in context. Additionally, it provided an overview of PRIA's learning approach and theory of change focused on empowering marginalised people through leadership development, with a short introduction to participatory research as a consciousness-raising and emancipatory approach as practised by PRIA. This introductory week enhanced students' awareness of the complexity and fluidity of culture, while also laying the foundation for the content to be addressed.

The subsequent five weeks supported students in delving deeper into CBPR through site visits that addressed:

- Leadership and organisation-building by women domestic workers towards prevention of sexual harassment in the workplace;

- The role of women elected representatives to make the local governance institutions gender-inclusive;
- The mobilisation and leadership development of people who have limited economic resources residing in urban informal settlements and engaged in informal economic activities, for accessing sanitation and other basic services; and
- How adolescent and youth from marginalised communities used sport as a tool for achieving gender and disability justice in the community.

The final week and team and individual assignments consolidated learning, promoting personal reflection, and developing strategies for leadership development within marginalised communities.

Table 7.1 Summary of Content of Digital CBPR Course

Week 1: *Introduction and Overview*
Week 2: *Strengthening Women's Leadership in Local Governance*
Week 3: *Dignity of Labour: Building Leadership of Women Domestic Workers*
Week 4: *Building Leadership in Civil Society with Urban Informal Residents*
Week 5: *Youth Leadership for the Safety of Girls and Women in Public Spaces: Kadam Badhate Chalo (Stride Your Steps) Campaign*
Week 6: *Youth Leadership in Sport for Development*
Week 7: *Systematisation of Learning: Leadership from Below*

The following section provides an example of the cycle of learning for one week during which there was a site visit. This unit is further described in a blog post (see Royal Roads University, 2021).

Table 7.2 Example of Activities Focused on Strengthening Women's Leadership in Local Governance

Steps and name	Activity details	Time needed	Purpose
Step 1: Preparation	Individual online activity via an online Learning Management System (LMS) (we used Moodle). Students reviewed literature related to women's political empowerment and participation in local governance in India and posted any initial questions in the Moodle discussion forum. Resources were published in established journals or documents produced by the partner organisations in the form of project reports, working papers, audio-visual stories mostly explaining the intervention methods as well as stories of change in the community.	(Monday) One full day given; students had access to readings throughout the whole seven weeks	These background readings gave the students adequate information about the context and actors involved in various community-led interventions and the roles that partner organisations played.

Steps and name	Activity details	Time needed	Purpose
Step 2: Briefing with site contact person	Full class, synchronous (i.e., real-time) online presentation via a video conferencing technology (we used Zoom). The organiser of this site visit gave a presentation on the local climate, key community challenges, and constitutional amendments that reserve seats for women at various levels of government.	(Tuesday) 20 minutes	To provide students with a real-time summary of the context in which elected female leaders were working.
Step 3: Site visit with female community leaders	Interactive, full class synchronous online interactions with female elected politicians via Zoom. Semi-structured format. Translated to English by a facilitator in India. Community leaders were briefed about	(Tuesday) 90 minutes Tip: Ensure time is clear to and appropriate for participants in different time zones.	To deepen understanding of women's leadership in India. Listening to the voices of community leaders – the challenges they faced in demanding rights and entitlements

Steps and name	Activity details	Time needed	Purpose
	the purpose of the interactions prior to the actual interactions with the learners. This helped them organise and share their experience, thoughts and reflections in a systematic manner, leaving space for emergent content as well. Students and RRU faculty members also actively asked questions and sought additional information from the community leaders. Facilitators from the partner organisations not only played the role of an interpreter but also added useful narratives and explanations to help students to understand the context better.		as equal citizens, their mobilisation against this denial from authorities, and the strategies to hold the authorities accountable – all these narratives provided an emotive learning experience for each learner, aligning with extra-rational aspects of Transformative Learning Theory. The opportunity for leaders to ask questions of the Canadian students promoted mutual learning and solidarity.

Steps and name	Activity details	Time needed	Purpose
Step 4: Synchronous meaning-making	Full class, synchronous, online conversation via Zoom. One day following the site visit, a facilitator with expertise in this topic expanded on the nuances that couldn't be explained in the moment.	(Wednesday) 90 minutes	To support students in deepening their understanding of the topic and reflection on similarities and differences with their own experiences. Students could seek additional explanations as well as to draw lessons from the experience. The time gap between these two interactions helped the learner to process the experience and distil out key lessons.
Step 5: Asynchronous meaning-making	Individual and group, online via Moodle. Exchanges of ideas and reflections on the experience continued regularly through	Thursday through Sunday	The longer time frame allowed for integration of learning, preparation for the following

Steps and name	Activity details	Time needed	Purpose
	an online discussion forum both among the learners and between the learners and the facilitators. Students reflected back on key lessons learned throughout the week and commented on one another's reflections.		week, and space to work on individual and team assignments.

For the first and second assignments, students made presentations reflecting on their individual and collective learning. Learning was supported by the design of the weekly interactions, whereby students had a lecture through different scholarly perspectives, planned digital excursions, and the ability to ask questions to community partners and participants. On a subsequent day, they had another opportunity to engage with PRIA scholars to go deeper into the learnings through question-and-answer periods. The discussion with faculty members and facilitators followed by each presentation helped deepen the understanding of partner organisations' theory of change, methods of interventions, and results in terms of community empowerment.

Though designed as part of a Master's of Global Leadership, the digital field school in its entirety or elements of it could be adapted according to different course objectives or instructor intentions in a range of disciplines and contexts, whether internationally or locally focused. For example, instructors teaching about Indigenous governance, community development, adult literacy, political change, etc., might invite groups with which they have a prior relationship to become digital guests in their online or in-person classrooms. As mentioned above, we stress the importance of having a trusting relationship, contacts in the community organisation, preparations for both the students and the guests, and follow-up discussion to support individual and collective meaning-making. Foundational to the success of our experience was the prior relationship between the two institutions. With a good measure of trust and goodwill already in place, we were able to navigate challenges, misunderstandings, and deadlines with grace, generosity and good humor. It also helped that members of the academic institution understood the scope of the community partner's work and trusted that the site visits they selected would offer rich learning.

Opportunities for learning the values inherent to CBPR emerged, for example, through the immersion in the challenges expressed by the domestic workers, youth soccer players, adolescents doing community work, and the work of various community activists. Students expressed that they appreciated meeting women and girls through the weeks and across units to learn about how they creatively mitigated their struggles and the context-related perspectives they shared. Among the community, stories narrated by, for example, powerful women demonstrated how they joined together to create change. Through such examples, students gained critical insight into how these women learned to adapt and change, individually and collectively, through self-awareness and self-management. As another example, through the excursion into urban informal communities, students were introduced to grassroots activism from below. In addition, Indian youth spoke directly to the Canadian students about their activism, outlining the participatory methodology and approach to including marginalised voices and connecting youth to stakeholders, such as Tribal (Indigenous) leaders, teachers and other community activists to develop and communicate solutions. The facilitators in India coordinated the excursions and the meetings with community partners and provided lessons about the challenges. Through such interactions, students enhanced their capacity to develop supportive, reciprocal and productive relationships with people of different backgrounds.

Moreover, students who had not previously traveled to India were exposed to a new country and cultures different from their own, with glimpses into the life experiences, daily joys and struggles, and successful community organising strategies of people from a range of demographics (according to sex/gender, urban/rural, age, and more).

Recommendations for Future Offerings

Through shared reflections, we informally learned from PRIA facilitators that several participants in the host communities in India indicated that they too were impacted through engagement with the Canadian students. For example, both the female politicians and domestic workers indicated that their understanding of the universality of gender discrimination and intimate partner violence was enhanced through conversation with female Canadian students, who identified that they too had shared experiences of oppression, discrimination and violence under patriarchy. Moreover, sharing their experiences with an international (in this case, Canadian) audience provided a global platform for public speaking and the resulting potential for enhanced feelings of empowerment. One group of domestic workers proudly showcased a self-made video that documented their daily commute and routine interactions, for example. Therefore, this course supported a deepening sense of global connection and solidarity among some host community members in India, as well as for the Canadian students and instructors. In greater alignment with CBPR principles, future iterations of this course would do well to shift the gaze from only educating the student–researchers, to place greater emphasis on the benefits to host community members, thereby seeing all participants as mutual learners in the process. Moreover, as discussed at the outset of this chapter, future CBPR courses would do well to experientially reinforce the importance of building relationships based on trust, ethical practice and relational accountability.

Conclusion

This chapter has demonstrated how the content and pedagogical process included in this Global Leadership Digital Field School both drew from and promoted learning about the normative principles of CBPR. Being introduced to a range of community groups with which PRIA works in a participatory way opened new pathways for Canadian students to begin challenging assumptions and critically engaging with the new learning. We recognise that any short-term course, whether online or face-to-face, can only provide background theory, values and principles of CBPR. It is not until people endeavour to put this theory into practice that they truly begin to experientially understand the complexities of developing leadership from the ground up through participatory processes. We hope that this example might help to shape the learning and experiences of future learners endeavouring to understand how participatory research can support leadership development from the ground up and how CBPR can be learned in digital mode for those sceptical of online learning. Whether as researchers or leaders, we hope these students will continue promoting the values of justice, equity, inclusion, empowerment and democracy within their own spheres of influence.

PART 2

INTEGRATING COMMUNITY-BASED PARTICIPATORY RESEARCH IN HIGHER EDUCATION INSTITUTIONS

8

LEARNING COMMUNITY-BASED PARTICIPATORY RESEARCH WITH INDIGENOUS KNOWLEDGE-KEEPERS IN CANADA

CRYSTAL TREMBLAY AND TANYA CLARMONT

Introduction

The Salish Sea Hub was established in 2018 through a collaborative partnership between the University of Victoria, the Victoria Native Friendship Centre (VNFC), and the Victoria Foundation. This initiative aims to build capacities and the co-creation of knowledge that respond to and create action for locally identified issues in alignment with the United Nations Sustainable Development Goals (UN SDGs) and the United Nations Declaration on the Rights of Indigenous Peoples (UNDRIP). Currently led by ten certified mentors from the Knowledge for Change (K4C) Consortium, the hub specialises in training for CBPR, working to expand community–university learning environments and long-lasting relationships with, and impacts in, local communities.

Grounded in Indigenous worldviews and methodologies, the hub is guided by principles of respect, reciprocity, and relational accountability which shape our collaborative approach. By fostering connections and encouraging partnerships, we facilitate community-based and Indigenous-led research training and mentorship, empowering equity-seeking groups – including Indigenous Peoples, youth, elders or seniors, 2SLGBTQ+ people, new Canadians, and those experiencing homelessness. Historically excluded from research processes, these communities are positioned as leaders in the research dialogue, bring valuable lived experience and knowledges, and challenge traditional power dynamics to decolonise knowledge gathering and creation.

In 2019 we launched 'Community-Based Participatory Research: Local Action for the UN SDGs' as an upper-level undergraduate geography course (4th year), which was formalised in the program in 2021 and is offered twice in a year. The course is co-designed and co-taught by the Salish Sea Hub mentors, with support from the Departments Map Shop (and instructor Ken Josephson) and Community-engaged Learning Centre.

This course allows students to actively engage in community-identified research needs, partnering with local community-based organisations. To date, more than 80 students have completed the course, collaborating with 15 community partners on over 25 projects. Many of these initiatives have involved multiple cohorts of students, fostering long-term relationships and continuity throughout several terms. Many of these projects have been identified and stewarded in partnership with the VNFC and the Victoria Foundation.

This chapter describes the ways in which we have intentionally designed the course to be grounded in our guiding principles and reflected in our pedagogy, weaving Indigenous knowledges and methodologies as the foundation for co-learning and reflective practice.

Indigenous Worldviews and Knowledge Systems

It is important to affirm there are more than 700 Indigenous Nations in Canada, sharing over 70 distinct languages and all with a diversity of knowledge systems of language, history, cultural protocols, etc. In this diversity, however, there are overlapping and shared areas of practice and ways of seeing the world. Our course highlights these areas of shared worldview as a foundation to learning more specific Indigenous methodologies and practices once working with a particular group or community.

Our course also stresses the importance of honouring local protocols and the local stewards of the territory above all else. While we are primarily responsible to the stewards of the land, relationships can be cultivated to ensure the necessary work of other groups can be accomplished in a respectful and, if possible, mutually beneficial way with the local nation. We must create the space where outside knowledge sources have value and learn to balance their impacts and uses.

Co-creation, Respect and Collaborative Learning As Normative Principles

Relationship building, reciprocity and mutual respect between students, researchers and community partners are central principles supporting the foundation of our course. These guiding values underpin everything we do and are reflected in the quality of relationships we have with our partners, many of which span years. Students are introduced to these concepts and invited to reflect on and practise bringing these values to life through their partnerships. These principles are essential in the ways we do CBPR, and particularly emphasised in Indigenous methodologies, ethics and research practices.

Our course and student learning experience are guided by principles developed in collaboration with our hub partners:

- Acknowledge, respect and learn from Indigenous ways of knowing and the people on whose lands and waters collaborations will take place
- Collaboration in development of innovative community-driven research and learning
- Commitment to excellence in CBPR process
- Humility and openness to understanding others, being both the learner and the teacher
- Integrity and Honesty in matters related to all areas of collaboration
- Respect for different ways of knowing and being
- Wisdom in having patience and presence in the space of evolving and infinite knowledge
- Principles of community Ownership, Control, Access and Possession (OCAP) inform all hub activities

Students are introduced to the foundations and global movement of CBPR through literature, guest speakers and case studies with an additional focus on Indigenous scholarship and experiential teaching from our partners, mentors, and the Elders and Seniors Advisory Committee at the VNFC. Important works in this area include Wilson's *Research is Ceremony* (2008), Kovach's *Indigenous Methodologies* (2009), Smith's *Decolonizing Methodologies* (2012), Chilisa's *Indigenous Research Methodologies* (2012), Strega and Brown's *Research as Resistance* (2015), and McGregor et al.'s *Indigenous Research* (2018), among many others. These methodologies have profoundly influenced how research is conducted across various communities, emphasising the importance of relationships, reciprocity, community relevance, respect, and accountability. Trust-based relationships must yield positive outcomes for communities and ultimately support the self-determination of Indigenous knowledge systems and ownership.

These teachings are foundational to our course and the principles and values we bring to our partnerships.

Establishing long-term partnerships and continuity (i.e., relationships) between the hub mentors/instructors and community partner organisations and First Nations is vital. Our partnerships go beyond mere transactional interactions; they are built on mutual trust, respect, and shared goals that align with the values and aspirations of the communities involved. Nurturing relationship-building is not just an ideal; it is a fundamental component of effective CBPR and central to our values and work together.

Promoting Sustainable Development and Indigenous Rights through Community-Based Participatory Research

Modeled from the MTP, the course addresses the pressing challenges facing people and the planet by promoting new ways of understanding and collaboration through locally contextualised and co-produced knowledge. Students are introduced to the theory and practice of CBPR, focusing on community-identified research needs that align with the UN SDGs. These 17 global goals, adopted by over 170 nations in 2015, target critical issues such as climate action, health and well-being, gender equality, sustainable cities and promoting peace.

Students learn how CBPR approaches can be a pivotal mechanism for including diverse, often excluded, knowledges into community-identified solutions. The course also covers essential concepts including knowledge democracy, anti-oppressive frameworks and Indigenous methodologies through literature study, case analyses, presentations from community partners, and self-location and self-reflection on one's social identity.

Our course also introduces students to and supports CBPR

projects in alignment with the UNDRIP. The declaration was adopted by the United Nations General Assembly in 2007 as an international instrument designed to protect the rights of Indigenous Peoples worldwide. The 21 articles outlined in the declaration emphasise the importance of Indigenous Peoples' participation in decision-making processes affecting their lives and communities, and it reinforces their rights to freely pursue their economic, social and cultural development.

Our course looks to the UN SDGs and UNDRIP as foundational frameworks and our collective work seeks to advance and shines a light on the tremendous value in CBPR approaches in realising these goals at local scales. Their connections are emphasised in our course, and we encourage our students to reflect on how to meaningfully apply these principles into their projects and relationships. Some of these key learnings include:

- *Strong focus on relationships* between students and partner Indigenous communities/organisations, ensuring research initiatives are guided by the communities' priorities and knowledge systems.
- *Value Indigenous methodologies and knowledge systems.* Students and partners blend community teachings into the research process to encourage a deeper appreciation for and strengthening of partner cultural identities and worldviews.
- *Mutually beneficial partnerships.* Reciprocal relationships ensure the research process benefits all. Students receive an enriched learning environment and research produced is meaningful and impactful for community partners.
- *Changemaking outcomes* that illuminate viable pathways into new existences and empowers the community's self-determination.

We invest in relationships and collective work that supports and uplifts Indigenous Peoples and equity seeking groups in our local communities. Through these partnerships we facilitate evidence producing research gathered from the community's own experiences and knowledge, thus contributing to social justice and equity as called for in UNDRIP. In close collaboration with our partners, we often produce knowledge products, advocacy tools and engagement opportunities that encourage positive action beyond final research papers. Students often are invited to continue working with projects and partners after the class has completed, another testament to the value of these strong relationship-based partnerships.

Pedagogy and Co-learning Approaches from Our Classroom

As with many of the K4C hubs, our founding mentors undertook the MTP training together in 2018 as a cohort, which provided the space and support to co-design the course curriculum together. It enabled a thoughtful and meaningful co-design process, bringing in important elements of both theoretical and experiential learning grounded in local cultural contexts. To date, the course has been offered five times with small cohorts up to 25 of students or terms (13 weeks, approximately 40 hours face-to-face and 25 hours practical experiential learning). Since its inception, the course has been co-taught by the hub mentors through mentoring, offering guest lectures and case studies on specific topics, and has included an immersive module led by co-author Tanya Clarmont and staff at VNFC.

As part of our course, we have integrated several Indigenous methods of teaching and learning that enhance the relevance and effectiveness of the learning while ensuring a strong connection to local communities. These methods not only strengthen partnerships but actively involve Elders and knowledge holders in the educational process, ensuring learning is grounded in cultural context and community knowledge. Our pedagogy and co-learning approach is informed by several key teachings, including the First Peoples Principles of Learning (BC Ministry of Education), and Indigenous pedagogies (see list of resources).

Learning with Elders

One of the most impactful strategies has been the inclusion of Elders in our classroom. Elders bring invaluable traditional knowledge and perspectives that enrich the students' understanding of research processes and community engagement. In workshops and community sessions led by Elders, students learn about Indigenous worldviews, methodologies and the significance of storytelling in knowledge transmission. For example, an Elder might lead a session on the importance of specific local plant species or traditional food sources, incorporating ecological knowledge with personal narratives highlighting their cultural significance.

Students also learn to recognise some knowledge as sacred and only shared with permission and/or in certain situations. Projects involving the identification of cultural sites through community mapping for example, or stories shared with our class are not all meant to be published in research reports and public presentations, and therefore provides students with ethical research practice and relational accountability.

Storytelling as a fundamental tool in learning

Storytelling is central to learning within Indigenous pedagogy and serves as a powerful tool in our CBPR course. Students are encouraged to share their own stories and listen to the experiences of community members, including Elders. This practice not only fosters rapport and trust but also creates a framework for understanding complex social and environmental issues through narrative. Students have discovered how stories provide essential context for research data, fostering empathy and making the research process more relatable and impactful.

Practices of Storytelling in Our Class

Circle: Whenever possible, we sit in a circle during class and when visiting community partners for field-based learning. This accessible and powerful teaching method embodies principles of Indigenous methodologies, such as reciprocal co-learning and the cyclical nature of knowledge generation and exchange. It also creates a shared learning space amongst the group with every participant contributing their words and no one person leading.

Value Life Experience: We encourage students and partners to share their personal gifts and skills with the class and within their projects. We intentionally design projects to allow for flexibility, enabling students to contribute in diverse ways, and we always promote artistic and experiential methods of learning. Creating space for sharing enhances understanding and respect for each other's differences.

Embrace Diverse Perspectives: In our learning environment, we emphasise there are no wrong or right answers. This approach encourages open dialogue and values the rich tapestry of perspectives each participant brings to discussions.

The value of humility

The most common fear among people wanting to work with Indigenous people is the fear of making a mistake. It can be immobilising. We help our students understand they likely will make a mistake, and that is to be expected. They are learners in Indigenous spaces and learners make mistakes. They are encouraged to embrace their humility and accept the limitations of what they know but be brave and open to learning more. In all situations, you can find yourself the learner or the teacher, and humility keeps us open to that possibility.

Learning with an open heart and mind

We recognise and appreciate learning is a journey of time, requiring patience and humility throughout the process. As foundational principles of CBPR and Indigenous approaches, we encourage a way of learning free from agendas or pre-set expectations when collaborating with partners. This practice of patience and emergent learning are essential qualities of an engaged and ethical scholar. This also means a willingness to embrace new ideas without preconceived notions or biases and encourages emotional connections and being empathetic towards others' experiences and perspectives.

Learning is reflective, experiential, and relational

Our learning process is focused on connectedness, reciprocal relationships, and fostering a sense of place. Field trips and hands-on experiences in the local environment are integral to this journey. These activities often involve collaboration with Indigenous community members who share their traditional practices and associated ecological knowledge. For instance, students may participate in ecological restoration, enabling them to witness the application of Indigenous knowledge and understand its relevance in contemporary research.

Our course is designed to guide students through the CBPR process. Although the timeframe is relatively short, students engage in meaningful partnerships by stepping into different chapters of a longer-term research program, sometimes spanning years. For example, a research project may take one or two years to complete, with different cohorts supporting various stages. A fall cohort, when the project is just beginning, might help craft the research questions and instruments, passing this work to the next cohort in the spring term, who would facilitate the subsequent phases.

Assignments, including ethics considerations, engaging the class in research methods, and final projects, are designed to apply course principles to real settings, emphasising group collaboration alongside individual reflective learning. Central to CBPR are the principles of reciprocity and relational accountability, underscoring the importance of creating value for community partners throughout the learning process.

Learning is about understanding one's identity

Fostering an environment where students feel encouraged to share their backgrounds and experiences is crucial in creating a respectful and inclusive learning atmosphere. There are several ways that we support engagement in class and encourage students to appreciate their origins and the diverse perspectives they bring to the classroom. Also, Indigenous partners are bringing their cultural and personal selves to this work every time and the more a student can reciprocate the offering the deeper their mutual appreciation can grow and strengthen the work.

Our course includes *structured peer-to-peer discussion sessions* (such as the 'tell me a story game') where students can engage in meaningful conversations about their experiences. These discussions might be facilitated by prompting students to ask each other questions about their backgrounds, traditions and values. By sharing in a smaller, supportive group, students often feel more comfortable opening up and appreciating the diverse perspectives within their cohort.

We emphasise the importance of *understanding local Indigenous histories* and the broader context of our own backgrounds. This includes discussions on the history of the land on which the university is situated, stories of local Indigenous Peoples, and how these narratives intersect with students' own experiences. By linking personal identities to the community's history, students can gain a richer understanding of their place in that context. Students have opportunity to learn from Indigenous leaders and Elders in the class, who participate as guest lecturers.

Conclusion

The teaching practices shared above have helped to cultivate a sense of responsibility among students to honour and uplift Indigenous knowledges and perspectives in our research efforts. Our course is designed to not only address pressing sustainable development challenges but it also actively works to embrace diverse knowledge systems. By cultivating strong relationships with partners and valuing Indigenous methodologies, we hope to empower students to engage meaningfully with their communities while acknowledging their own identities and backgrounds.

Through storytelling, experiential learning and reflective practices, as described above, students enhance their understanding of research and develop the skills necessary for ethical, impactful partnerships. Our commitment to promoting the UN SDGs and the UNDRIP serves as a foundation for our work, ensuring students contribute to meaningful changes in their local contexts.

Ultimately, this course aims to inspire a generation of scholars who are not only informed about the complexities of community engagement but are also passionate advocates for human rights, social justice and equity. As we continue to learn and grow, we remain dedicated to fostering learning environments that value patience, humility, and the wisdom offered by Indigenous Peoples.

9

COMMUNITY ENGAGEMENT AND COMMUNITY-BASED PARTICIPATORY RESEARCH IN SOUTH AFRICA

RENÉ OOSTHUIZEN

Introduction

This chapter delves into the pedagogical strategies and content used to teach engaged research incorporating CBPR at Rhodes University, South Africa. With community engagement central to the university's mission, this chapter highlights the normative principles guiding the approach, the specific content addressing these principles and the CBPR pedagogical methods employed to teach it effectively. The chapter explores how the UNESCO Chair's Mentor Training Program (MTP) has shaped community engagement with CBPR at Rhodes University, highlighting its impact on fostering inclusive knowledge creation and promoting transformative research outcomes. Drawing on my experience as the Knowledge for Change (K4C) Academic Lead at the university and as the institutional Engaged Research Coordinator, I offer insights into the practical application of CBPR principles, pedagogies and methodologies, reflecting on the successes and challenges encountered.

Rhodes University Community Engagement Division and K4C Hub

The South African Southern K4C Hub* joined the Knowledge for Change (K4C) Consortium in 2020, with the training of three Rhodes University Community Engagement (RUCE) academics (Dr Bezerra, Ms Nqowana, and me), and one community partner (Ms Canca) from the Learning Trust Organisation. The K4C Hub at the university aims to decolonise knowledge production and promote the co-creation of knowledge through CBPR.

Following the MTP training, this team of three academics and one community partner piloted a short course on CBPR Engaged Research for academics and postgraduate students at the end of 2021. This course, funded by the South African Department of Higher Education (DHET) University Capacity and Development Programme, was designed to advance inter/transdisciplinary research and community engagement. Till date, the course has been offered seven times since it was officially launched in 2022, with diverse participation from various departments and organisations.

Normative Principles and Pedagogical Approach in Teaching Community-Based Participatory Research

The pedagogical approach to teaching CBPR at the RUCE Division is underpinned by several normative principles that guide its implementation.† The pedagogical approach includes:

(i) *Reciprocity and Mutual Benefit*

CBPR at Rhodes University strongly emphasizes reciprocity, ensuring that both researchers and community partners benefit from the collaborative research process. This principle

---

* https://www.ru.ac.za/communityengagement/engagedresearch/knowledgeforchangesouthernhub/#d.en.294852

† https://www.ru.ac.za/communityengagement/knowledgewheel/ Accessed April 20, 2024.

challenges traditional research paradigms by promoting an equitable exchange of knowledge and resources.

(ii) *Equity and Social Justice*
Central to teaching CBPR is the principle of equity and social justice. Recognising historical and systemic inequities, CBPR catalyses empowerment and social change. CBPR projects at the RUCE division actively work to amplify marginalized voices and address power differentials within research partnerships.

(iii) *Collaborative Knowledge Creation*
CBPR underscores the importance of collaborative knowledge creation, where researchers and community members co-produce knowledge throughout the research process. This approach values community expertise and lived experiences, ensuring that research outcomes are contextually relevant and practically applicable.

Key principles include:

(i) *Participatory learning*: Encouraging active participation and co-learning among researchers and community members (Lepore et al., 2021).

(ii) *Collaborative approaches*: Emphasising the importance of collaboration at every stage of the research process (Horowitz et al., 2009).

(iii) *Inclusivity*: Ensuring diverse voices, particularly those from marginalised communities, are heard and integrated (Burke et al., 2013).

(iv) *Transformative impact*: Aiming for research outcomes that lead to meaningful change and community empowerment (Rubin et al., 2012).

Incorporating Pedagogical Approach and Principles in the Course

The K4C hub at the university was instrumental in developing a university accredited five-week short course on CBPR Engaged Research.* It was first launched in 2022. The course has been successfully offered seven times since its launch. The DHET University Capacity Development Programme supports the course to fund the attendance of Rhodes University staff and postgraduate students.

The course is open to academic staff and all postgraduate students, regardless of the subject they are studying. The course is not compulsory for postgraduate students. Most students who have attended the course have chosen to do so voluntarily to ensure that the community's voice is incorporated into their research and to facilitate collaboration with communities. This integration is achieved through the principles and methods taught in the CBPR Engaged Research course, which students then apply to their specific research projects after consulting with their research supervisors.

The course offered in Semester 1 (March to April) and Semester 2 (July to August), in 2022, attracted a diverse group of participants. It included eight academic staff, two support staff, two postgraduate students, and two community development practitioners. Participants were from various departments, such as journalism, and organisations, such as the Institute for the Study of the Englishes of Africa (ISEA), the Rhodes University Mathematics Education Project (RUMEP), Rhodes University Community Engagement (RUCE), and the Ubunye Foundation. The programme's transdisciplinary approach was further

* https://www.ru.ac.za/communityengagement/knowledgewheel/__Accessed April 20, 2024.

highlighted by the inclusion of 14 academics from the University of Zululand, who completed the course in person, in June 2022.

The course in 2023 saw 24 participants across Semesters 1 and 2, representing a wide array of fields. Specialisations included zoology and entomology, grounds and garden (quantity surveying specialisation), journalism, isiXhosa primary and early childhood education, biotechnology, statistics, human kinetics and ergonomics, psychology, environmental science, mathematics, biochemistry, and microbiology. Organisations like Ubunye Foundation, Registrar's division, Rhodes Music Radio, RU Water Research Institute, South African Institute for Aquatic Biodiversity (SAIAB), Centre for Biological Control, and Inkululeko also nominated participants. This diversity underscored the programme's inclusive and collaborative ethos, fostering an environment where participants from various backgrounds could engage and learn from each other.

In the first semester of 2024, nine participants from journalism and media studies, information systems, economics, the Centre for Critical Studies in Sexualities and Reproduction, the Office of the Deputy Vice-Chancellor for Research and Innovation, the Centre for Biological Control, and ISEA attended the course. With ten participants already signed up for the Semester 2 course, the Rhodes University K4C Hub continues to grow, reflecting its commitment to fostering community-engaged research and interdisciplinary learning. There have also been inquiries from other South African universities for the course to be offered to their institutions.

The course currently offered does not carry any credits. Rhodes University has received accreditation from the South African Council on Higher Education (SA CHE) to offer a Postgraduate Diploma in Community Engagement (PGDip in CE), which includes the CBPR module as one of its key components. This

PGDip in CE, which will be launched in 2025, will be credit-bearing. The CBPR module will be a 30-credit bearing module in this Diploma program. The Diploma will be registered as a 120 credit honours level (level 8) course on the South African Higher Education Qualifications Framework (HEQSF).

Course Overview, Strategies and Accreditation

The short course on CBPR Engaged Research offered by RUCE Division introduces participants to CBPR, emphasising collaboration and active community involvement throughout the research process (Horowitz et al., 2009). Engaged research entails active partnerships with communities across all stages of the research process, from identifying problems and collecting data to analysing findings and co-creating knowledge (Holliman, 2017). It integrates community perspectives, local knowledge, and everyday experiences, enhancing social relevance, inclusivity, and impact.* Recognising and appreciating diverse forms of knowledge, including community wisdom, is central to engaged research (Tembo et al., 2021).

The course begins with Module 1, which focuses on conceptualising engaged research and CBPR. Participants learn about the significance of engaged research, the role of community engagement in research and the rationale for adopting CBPR methodologies. Module 2 provides an overview of the theoretical frameworks, principles and approaches that underpin CBPR. In this module, participants explore the development of participatory research, core principles of CBPR, practical strategies for working with communities on participatory projects and establishing research partnerships. Module 3 delves into CBPR methods for co-learning and collaborative research with communities. This

* http://www.sun.ac.za/si/en-za/Pages/Sub-menu.aspx Accessed March 24, 2024.

module provides participants with practical tools and techniques for implementing CBPR in their research, exploring various engaged research methods. Module 4 identifies and discusses the challenges of conducting CBPR and explores strategies to overcome these obstacles. Participants engage in critical discussions about real-world issues they may encounter in CBPR projects and how to navigate them effectively. Ethical considerations are the focus of Module 5. Participants examine the ethical dimensions of engaged research, reflect on power dynamics and biases, and discuss the responsibilities of researchers when working with communities. For the final assignment, participants must write a CBPR proposal or research paper detailing how they will incorporate CBPR methodologies into their research. This assignment allows participants to apply the concepts and methods learned throughout the course to a research project relevant to their field.

The course structure includes detailed online self-study components, where participants work through pre-recorded lectures, readings, class exercises and weekly individual assignments and presentations. These assignments serve as building blocks for the final research proposal or paper. The first week introduces the course and covers Modules 1 and 2. Subsequent weeks focus on one module each, with live plenary discussions every Friday.

Each module concludes with an activity for formative assessment, ensuring participants engage deeply with the content. Weekly activities, including module readings, class activities in pairs, individual assignments and presentations reinforce learning. For example, participants engage in class exercises presented orally in pairs and in individual assignments, applying theoretical knowledge related to the module focus area. Participants engage with pre-recorded lectures, readings and online activities at their own pace, followed by weekly plenary discussions that facilitate in-depth exploration, reflection, and peer interaction.

Pedagogical strategies

The course emphasises active learning, participatory methods, and experiential activities. Participants engage in critical dialogues, group discussions, case studies, and collaborative problem-solving exercises.

- *Active learning*: Includes engaging participants in critical dialogues, group discussions, and problem-solving exercises. For example, in Module 3, participants explore CBPR methods by addressing a current community issue through class pairs, group discussions, and collaborative problem-solving activities.
- *Experiential activities*: Includes incorporating case studies and group discussions to facilitate real-world application of CBPR principles. For instance, in the module 'Challenges in CBPR', participants identify challenges they might encounter and how to mitigate and navigate common challenges in CBPR.
- *Reflective practices*: Involves encouraging participants to maintain reflective journals, documenting their thoughts and experiences throughout the course. Reflective practices are particularly emphasised in Module 5, where ethical considerations in CBPR are discussed, prompting participants to reflect on their own ethical stances.
- *Collaborative learning*: Facilitated through fostering a learning environment where participants learn from each other's experiences and perspectives through group discussions and peer feedback. During the plenary discussions every Friday participants share insights and feedback.
- *Formative assessment*: Each module has associated activities for formative assessment at the end of each week. These activities include class exercises in pairs, individual assignments and presentations that serve as building blocks for the final assignment.

Through these strategies, the CBPR course ensures that participants integrate community voices into their research and collaborate effectively with communities, applying CBPR methodologies to their specific research projects.

Course accreditation and certification

The university's Institutional Research, Planning and Quality Promotion (IRPQP) Division conducts an annual evaluation and accreditation of the CBPR course.* This process involves a comprehensive review of the course, which is submitted by the course coordinator along with detailed evaluation and data analysis. The course is reviewed and submitted for evaluation and accreditation annually. This ensures that the course maintains high standards and continues to meet the needs of its participants.

Upon completing all course requirements, including assessments and a final project, participants receive an accredited short-course certificate from Rhodes University. This certification acknowledges participants' proficiency in CBPR methodologies and commitment to ethical and socially responsive research practices.

Integration of Community-Based Participatory Research in Teaching and Research

Academics and postgraduate students who have completed the CBPR Engaged Research short course at Rhodes University have leveraged their training to integrate CBPR principles into their teaching and research methodologies. This section explores three exemplary initiatives that highlight the transformative effects of CBPR in enhancing educational and research practices and community engagement.

---

* https://www.ru.ac.za/institutionalplanningunit/shortcourses/; https://www.ru.ac.za/teachingandlearning/chertl/

Mathematics Winter School: A community-based participatory research approach to enhancing mathematical education

One academic from the Department of Statistics successfully completed the course in 2022. Upon completion of the course, she initiated the Winter School.* The Mathematics Winter School employs a CBPR approach to address challenges in mathematical education. The academic lead, a professor in the department, collaborated closely with local teachers to identify and address specific challenges faced in mathematics education within the Makhanda community.† The initiative benefits learners by enhancing their mathematical skills, strengthening community ties and promoting academic excellence within the community.

The Winter School focuses on Statistics, Probability and Financial Mathematics, aiming to support Grade 12 learners' proficiency in these critical areas. The project facilitates knowledge exchange and professional development opportunities for educators by fostering a supportive network involving local school teachers and university lecturers working collaboratively. This collaborative approach ensures that the community's knowledge and experiences are integrated into the educational process, enriching the learning environment for all participants.

Initially involving a few schools, the project expanded rapidly, encompassing numerous non-fee-paying schools by 2023. The Winter School academic lead secured external funding for 2024 from the South African National Research Foundation, which has ensured the project's continued growth and sustainability. Additionally, the Winter School is supported internally by the

* https://www.ru.ac.za/statistics/latestnews/winterschool.html

† https://www.ru.ac.za/statistics/latestnews/rhodesuniversitysmathematicswinterschoolprogrammeempowerslocallearners.html

university through the Community Engaged Learning Fund. Future initiatives include enhancing communication platforms to improve collaboration and information dissemination among participating schools and stakeholders. This ongoing commitment underscores Rhodes University's dedication to addressing educational challenges and promoting excellence in mathematical education through CBPR principles.

Transforming formative assessment practices in mathematics education in Keiskammahoek, Eastern Cape

In Keiskammahoek, Eastern Cape, CBPR has been instrumental in transforming Formative Assessment (FA) practices for mathematics education in grades 4 to 7. This initiative addresses the pressing need for effective FA strategies tailored to the local context, where limited resources and cultural diversity pose significant challenges. Academics who completed the CBPR Engaged Research course at Rhodes University have integrated CBPR principles into their teaching methodologies. These academics have facilitated the development of culturally responsive FA strategies by engaging local stakeholders such as schoolteachers, learners, parents, and community leaders. The implementation of culturally responsive FA strategies involved incorporating local cultural contexts and student experiences into assessment practices. For instance, incorporating storytelling and local examples in mathematics assessments helped students relate better to the content, thereby increasing their engagement and motivation to learn. This was observed through qualitative data where learners expressed more interest in participating actively in class activities designed around FAs.

The CBPR strategies have empowered teachers through continuous professional development, thereby fostering sustainable improvements in mathematics education. Teachers who participated in the CBPR workshops reported that the revised FA strategies enabled them to provide more targeted and timely feedback to students. This improvement was reflected in the qualitative interviews where teachers noted that they were better able to address student misconceptions before they became ingrained. The professional development workshops designed collaboratively with teachers and community members were instrumental in enhancing teachers' pedagogical content knowledge (PCK) specific to FA in mathematics. This improvement was evident in qualitative feedback from teachers who expressed feeling more confident in their ability to implement effective FA practices. The CBPR approach ensured that the FA strategies developed were not only theoretically grounded but also sensitive to the cultural and contextual realities of Keiskammahoek. This contextual relevance was highlighted in the qualitative data, where teachers and community members emphasised the importance of integrating local knowledge and practices into educational strategies.

Qualitative findings also suggested a positive impact on student learning outcomes. Teachers reported noticing improvements in student understanding and performance on formative tasks, indicating that the revised FA practices were contributing to enhanced learning outcomes.

Integrating community-based participatory research in doctoral research on plastic waste management

The integration of CBPR principles into the teaching of community engagement at Rhodes University has significantly influenced the research approach of a Pharmacy PhD student within the Disaster Management and Ethics Research Group. This student's research focuses on evolutionary bioethics in solid waste disaster risk management, explicitly addressing the surge in plastic waste exacerbated by the COVID-19 pandemic in South Africa.

The student is in the second year of her doctoral studies. She has demonstrated a robust commitment to ethical principles, particularly through the active engagement and decision-making involvement of local communities. During the proposal phase of the research, community consultations were conducted where residents, waste management experts, and environmental advocates participated in discussions on plastic waste management. These forums facilitated consensus-building on focusing efforts towards recycling initiatives and reducing single-use plastics, aligning with both community preferences and environmental sustainability goals.

Post-research, the student plans to conduct evaluations to assess the ethical impact of her approach. This will involve feedback sessions with community members to gather their satisfaction with the level of involvement and respect shown during the research process. Anticipated outcomes include a high level of community satisfaction and a sense of ownership over the research outcomes, demonstrating the effectiveness of ethical considerations in fostering trust and collaboration.

Institutional Advancements through the Course

Since its inception in October 2021, the CBPR short course at Rhodes University has made significant strides.

Establishment of the Engaged Research Community of Practice (CoP)

The Rhodes University Engaged Research Community of Practice (CoP) is a pivotal platform for fostering collaborative and ethically engaged research practices among academics, researchers, postdocs and postgraduate students. Launched on 15 March 2022, the CoP has grown to include six members from diverse fields such as journalism and media studies, psychology, economics, and the Water Institute, ensuring interdisciplinary exchange and learning. The CoP's activities promote dialogue and reflection on engaged research experiences, challenges and solutions. In its inaugural year, the CoP organised hybrid roundtable discussions featuring distinguished speakers from South African and Canadian universities. The CoP roundtable at the Rhodes University Community Engagement Symposium in 2023 was a significant component of the event, focusing on the scholarship of engagement at Global South universities. The session included participants from various South African institutions, who discussed the benefits and challenges of engaged scholarship within their contexts. The CoP's planning meeting in January 2024 set the agenda for the upcoming year, focusing on knowledge dissemination through social media platforms and hosting dialogues at community engagement conferences. In 2024, the CoP hosted a conversation as part of the Rhodes University Community Engagement Conference in May 2024. The dialogue on 'Engaged Research Ethics in South African Higher Education Institutions' provided a comprehensive exploration of ethical considerations in academic research with community engagement. Facilitated by experts and practitioners from various universities, the session illuminated the evolving landscape of research ethics, emphasising historical perspectives, current challenges and future directions. Discussions ranged from developing ethical guidelines for engaged research to the practical implications of community involvement in research ethics processes. Panelists shared insights on fostering ethical awareness, transparency and accountability, underscoring the importance of collaborative approaches between academia and communities to ensure research practices that uphold integrity and benefit all stakeholders. The CoP remains committed to advancing engaged research practices and ethical standards at Rhodes University and beyond, emphasising collaboration, inclusivity and impactful community engagement.

Transition in the Human Research Ethics Processes

The integration of CBPR methodologies into the teaching of community engagement at Rhodes University has significantly influenced the institution's human research ethics processes.*

- *Inclusion of a Community Member on the University Ethics Committee (HREC)*: As a direct outcome of promoting CBPR principles through the short course, the University Ethics Committee has adopted a more inclusive approach by including a community member on the committee. This community member is actively involved in a local community-based organisation called the Learning Trust. Her background includes participation in the MTP and being one of the key four team members that developed the initial pilot of the CBPR Engaged Research short course in 2021. This experience equips her with a nuanced understanding of community needs and perspectives, enhancing their role on the University Ethics Committee. This significant stride fosters meaningful collaboration between the university and the communities it serves.

  Incorporating a community member into the University Human Research Ethics Committee marked a significant shift towards inclusive decision-making. While other committee members typically come from academic backgrounds, the community representative has provided invaluable insights into ethical considerations directly affecting local communities. In 2024, her insights were pivotal during the revision of research protocols and policies, especially as it relates to engagement

* https://www.ru.ac.za/researchgateway/ethics/

and collaboration with communities during research processes. Her input ensured that ethical practices were aligned with community values and needs.

Accountability is strengthened by having a community member on the committee. This involvement facilitates greater accountability from the university, ensuring that ethical guidelines reflect the needs and concerns of those directly impacted by the university's actions. The community member's unique viewpoint helps ensure that the committee's decisions align with the broader community's values and interests, fostering transparency, fairness and mutual understanding. This dual accountability strengthens the university's ethical fabric while fostering a more profound sense of responsibility towards the community.

- *Two-tiered Ethics Application Process for Engaged Research*: Rhodes University has implemented a two-tiered ethics application process in response to the emphasis on engaged research taught through the CBPR course. This revised framework supports researchers in engaging more effectively and ethically with communities.

  The first tier, the scoping approval stage, allows researchers to initiate engagement with the community. This stage creates a platform for identifying research issues and formulating solutions that address such problems, emphasising early community involvement in shaping the research agenda and methodology. Researchers apply to the chairperson of the Human Ethics Committee for scoping approval, which is granted for three months. During this stage, researchers engage in discussions and consultations with community members to gain a deeper understanding of their concerns, aspirations, and the potential ethical implications of the research. This collaborative process ensures the research aligns with the focal communities' needs and values, enhancing the study's relevance and moral integrity.

The second tier involves the submission of a formal research proposal informed by the community's input and feedback gathered during the scoping approval stage. This proposal details the research objectives, methodologies, ethical considerations, and the intended impact of the study. The submission stage allows researchers to demonstrate how the research design incorporates community perspectives, protects community interests and ensures ethical conduct throughout the research process. Researchers must articulate how they will address power imbalances, obtain informed consent, protect confidentiality, and adhere to cultural protocols and ethical guidelines.

Workshops and seminars on teaching community engagement with CBPR

In 2022, 2023 and 2024, several workshops and seminars were hosted by the Rhodes University K4C Hub focusing on teaching community engagement with CBPR. A seminar on engaged research was integrated into the knowledge democracy module at the University of Victoria, highlighting the university's role as the South Africa hub of the UNESCO K4C Consortium. Another seminar targeted students enrolled in the Journalism PGDip in the Media and Research Programme. In July 2024, the CBPR Collaborative Discussion gathered academics from various disciplines and community partner organisations to explore collaborative research approaches.

The Centre for Postgraduate Studies facilitated the Engaged Research Seminar, providing a platform for interdisciplinary discussions. Additionally, a session with Master's students of psychology focused on applying CBPR in mental health within primary healthcare settings, fostering interactive and insightful discussions. A support group for Master's, doctoral and postdoctoral participants in engaged research offered seminars throughout the year, enhancing methodologies and providing guidance. Finally, as part of the Oxford–Berlin Research Partnership Evidence-Based Series, a workshop on CBPR for participants from Oxford and Berlin Universities was held, equipping them with practical tools for integrating community-based research principles into their academic work.* Participants found these sessions highly informative, fostering a spirit of cooperation and mutual learning.

Challenges and Limitations in Teaching Community-Based Participatory Research

Despite the initial successes and contributions of the CBPR teaching initiatives at Rhodes University, several challenges have hindered the full realisation of its potential impact and scope.

Limited scale of community engagement

While the CBPR workshop for community partners in August 2022 garnered participation from various community organisations and stakeholders in Makhanda, the subsequent engagement and ongoing collaboration between academia and these entities could be more consistent. The initial enthusiasm and workshop attendance have only sometimes translated into sustained partnerships and active involvement in research projects.

Resource constraints

The effective implementation of CBPR requires significant resources, including funding for sustained community engagement and

---

*The Oxford–Berlin Research Partnership. Skills workshop on community engagement for researchers, March 2024. https://www.berlin-university-alliance.de/commitments/international/oxford/termine/240503-workshop.html

capacity-building initiatives. Limited resources have constrained the expansion and continuity of CBPR projects beyond the initial phases, impacting the depth and breadth of community impact.

Capacity building

Building and maintaining capacity among academic staff and community partners is essential for successful community engagement with CBPR. This includes training in CBPR methodologies, ethical considerations, and navigating cross-cultural collaborations. Continuous professional development opportunities are needed to enhance community engagement and research ethics skills.

Time and commitment

Engaging in CBPR requires substantial time commitments from researchers and community partners. Balancing academic responsibilities with community engagement can be challenging, particularly when considering the need for sustained relationships and iterative research cycles that respect community timelines.

Evaluation and impact assessment

Assessing the impact of community engagement with CBPR principles is complex and multifaceted. Traditional metrics of academic success may only partially capture the transformative effect on communities. Developing robust evaluation frameworks incorporating community-defined outcomes and long-term impacts remains challenging.

Addressing these multifaceted challenges requires a collaborative effort from all stakeholders involved in CBPR initiatives. By acknowledging and actively working to overcome these limitations, Rhodes University can enhance the effectiveness and sustainability of its community-engaged research efforts, fostering meaningful social change and development within the Makhanda community and beyond.

Conclusion

The experience of the K4C hub at Rhodes University to advocate for CBPR pedagogy and principles has clarified the transformative potential of CBPR in enriching academic teaching and research and fostering meaningful community engagement.

Teaching community engagement incorporating CBPR requires a steadfast commitment to transformative learning and collaborative knowledge creation that bridges academia and society. By navigating challenges through fostering ongoing dialogue and investing in capacity-building initiatives, Rhodes University has established a robust framework for this.

Moving forward, a concerted effort to integrate these lessons into pedagogical practices will ensure community engagement with CBPR at Rhodes University remains responsive, impactful, and sustainable in addressing real-world challenges while advancing equitable partnerships.

10

COMMUNITY ENGAGEMENT AND COMMUNITY-BASED PARTICIPATORY RESEARCH IN INDIA

The Experience of Dayalbagh Educational Institute

JYOTI GOGIA

'To educate a man in mind and not in morals is to educate a menace to society.'

– THEODORE ROOSEVELT

Introduction

Attaining economic development has often been at the cost of social development. Inequalities and environmental degradation increase with exploitation of natural resources. The world needs sustainable human progress along with sustainable economic development. Equitable, inclusive, just, and relevant participation of everyone is crucial to accelerate transitions and build a resilient society. Optimal solutions to problems need to be localised and contextualised as 'one size' does not fit all. Establishing strong connections between knowledge sources is crucial for sustainable and inclusive development. Involving local members in sharing knowledge, technology, techniques and skills to evolve creative global and local solutions is now more relevant than ever.

Education can play an important role – in developing the body, mind, and soul of a human being, and unlocking the full potential of every individual to create a fair and just society. '*Sa vidya ya vimuktaye*' ('Education is that which liberates') is an ancient dictum from India that stands the test of time (Ayesha Nadeem et al., 2017). The United Nations Sustainable Development Goals (SDGs) on education emphasises the need to ensure 'inclusive and equitable quality education' and to promote 'lifelong learning opportunities for all' (Babbar and Johannsdottir, 2024). This requires a holistic educational approach that integrates philosophical principles and pedagogical methods to address the needs of diverse learners, establish connections, and foster wholeness between parts in a person's life or relationships, considering life experiences and cultural backgrounds and known as well as unknown aspects of life (Mahmoudi et al., 2012). In addition to imparting knowledge, education should instil in learners the values of integrity, critical thinking, empathy, and kindness (Government of India, 2020).

India's New Education Policy (NEP) 2020 recognises the pivotal role of the academic community in societal progress and sustainable development. Higher education institutions can play a vital role by conducting locally relevant research to address community needs (UGC, 2022). Educational institutions have the potential to generate opportunities for students from diverse backgrounds, enabling them to bring the benefits of higher education back to their communities. These institutions can also tap into the knowledge nurtured within communities to enrich their educational programmes (Tandon, 2014). Therefore, pedagogy must evolve that is more experimental, holistic, integrated, inquiry-driven, discovery-oriented, learner-centred, discussion-based, and flexible.

The Dayalbagh Educational Institute (DEI) offers an innovative and unique educational approach to foster a better world order by creating 'Total Quality Persons' or 'Super Persons'. A comprehensive focus on community engagement is an essential component of the education system at DEI. Community engagement and community-based participatory research (CBPR) at DEI are focused on fostering collaboration with all stakeholders to bring about meaningful and lasting change. DEI's innovative model is an ideal blueprint to learn how community engagement can be integrated in higher education to bridge the gap between theoretical knowledge and real-world application by actively involving the community.

Role of Community Engagement

> '*Community engagement refers to the initiatives and processes through which the expertise of the higher education institution in the areas of teaching and research are applied to address issues relevant to its community*' (HEQC, 2004).

In its simplest form, community engagement involves the participation of a group of people in strategies and processes sensitive to community context for advancing well-being, collective transformation and overall sustainable development rather than individual upliftment. Hence, seamless integration, collaboration and resource coordination are paramount and foundations of community engagement efforts (Thompson et al., 1990).

Community engagement can also be seen as a continuum of community involvement, aiming to bring about a lasting impact on people's attitudes and behaviours. It requires a set of principles, such as inclusion, respect for diversity, collaboration and shared purpose, adaptability, transparency and trust, and sustained engagement, that respects the rights of community members.

Trust is one of the fundamental tenets of maintaining long-term sustainable commitments in community engagement processes.

Community engagement should be an integral part of the learning and teaching process, rather than just an optional add-on. To be an inherent part of higher education's objectives, university-community linkages must be integrated into making and sharing knowledge, teaching, research and practice. By fostering stronger connections between higher education institutions and the community, the goal is to actively integrate the unique needs and perspectives of the community into the educational process to ensure that education remains pertinent and responsive to the needs of society (Government of India, 2011).

The DEI Educational Policy and Societal Development

The DEI was founded in 1917 by Sir Anand Sarup to set up a co-educational middle school, the Radhasoami Educational Institute (REI). In 1973, DEI was established as a registered body to bring all educational institutes of Dayalbagh under one umbrella. In May 1981, the Government of India recognised DEI (comprising DEI Women's Training College, DEI REI Degree College, and DEI Engineering College) as a Deemed University under Section 3 of the UGC Act (DEI, 2019). The Institute is located amidst the tranquil environs of Dayalbagh, a self-contained colony renowned for its serene environment and secular establishment, in which its inhabitants lead an active, disciplined, and cooperative community life, conforming to the high spiritual ideals of their faith.

The Government of India's NEP was formulated in 1986. Well before this policy, in 1975, DEI had formulated an innovative and comprehensive educational policy. The architect of this policy was Prof. Makund Behari Lal Sahab, an outstanding academician and educationist. The DEI Education Policy is rooted in Indian culture, philosophy, and spirituality. It follows a systems approach integrating social and environmental systems with formal education systems (DEI, 2019). Significant pedagogical values, rigorous research, and direct community involvement cultivate students' understanding of the connections between academic learning, broader public life and their roles as global citizens.

The Institute significantly contributes to societal development in two ways:

1) Through its quality and value-based education system by developing 'Total Quality Persons' or 'Super Persons' who act as powerful agents of social transformation. At DEI, education serves as a pedagogical tool that effectively balances the three Hs: Hand (Hard work), Heart (Emotions), and Head (Wisdom).
2) Through the 'Sigma Six Q-V-A (Quality-Values-Attributes)' way of sustainable living (Figure 10.1). It focuses on direct community engagement and social responsibility in six key areas, viz. agriculture and dairy, education and healthcare, air quality, water quality, innovation and human values, with emphasis on the empowerment of women and the underprivileged (DEI, 2019).

The practice of values such as duty, beauty, humility, loyalty, justice, courage, temperance, and wisdom provide the much-needed inner dimensions for sustainability (Satsangi and Dhir, 2024). A person learns to carry out his/her 'duty' with all sense of 'beauty', 'humility', and 'loyalty' in the DEI educational environment. Co-concurrent human values like 'courage', 'temperance', and 'wisdom' go hand-in-hand with the value of 'justice'. It goes without saying that to stay firmly planted on the path of sustainable development, a person's human character must be shaped by integrating these principles from the formative

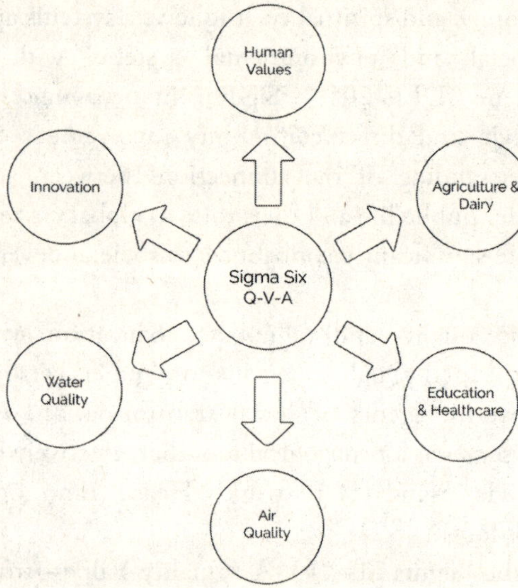

Figure10.1 Sigma Six Q-V-A Model of Dayalbagh Way of Life
Source: Author's compilation adapted from DEI, 2019

years of life, something which the education system at DEI works very hard to achieve. The foundation of community life is the instillation of human values, which influences every facet of social interaction and individual behaviour. The educational system at DEI fosters a stronger capacity for intuitive consciousness and moral and spiritual advancements which can direct the best course in life by making ethical choices based on social, economic, and environmental facets of sustainability.

Interpretive Structural Model at DEI

During his tenure as the Director of DEI, Prof. P.S. Satsangi utilised concepts from applied systems engineering to analyse the relationship between DEI's Education Policy, the educational system at DEI and DEI's organisational elements. He identified 93 elements – spread over the aims and objects of DEI (30 elements), the educational system (33 elements), and DEI's organisation (30 elements) – to develop a hierarchical structure known as the Interpretive Structural Model (Figure 10.2). This model illustrates how elements of DEI's organisational policy are integrated to form an educational system that aligns with the organisation's aims and objectives, ultimately resulting in the development of the Complete Man. This conforms to the concept of Total Quality

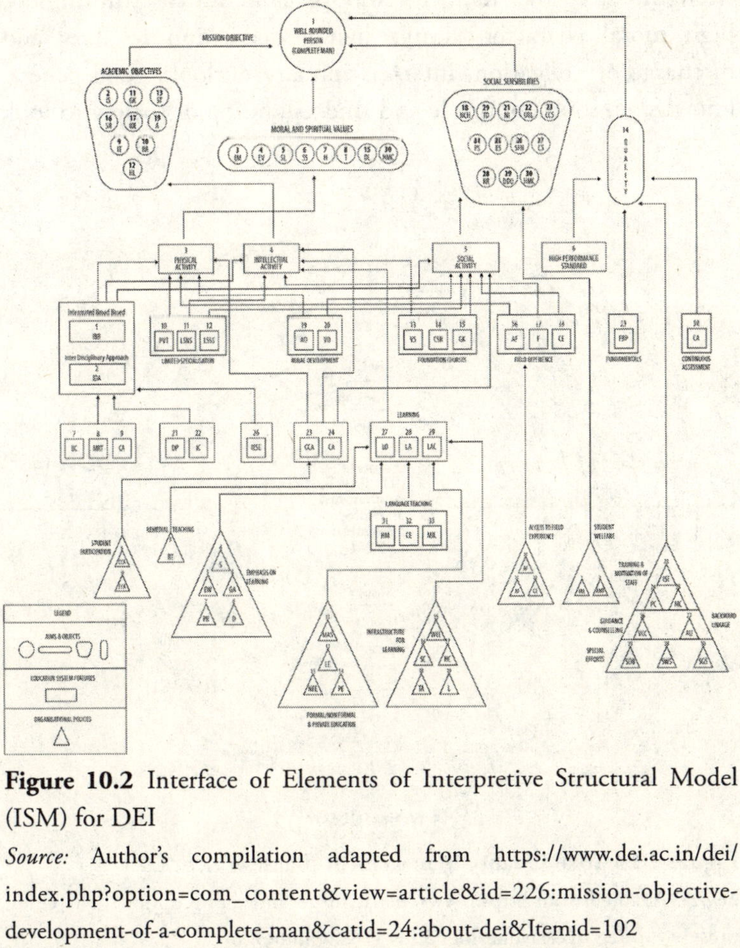

Figure 10.2 Interface of Elements of Interpretive Structural Model (ISM) for DEI

Source: Author's compilation adapted from https://www.dei.ac.in/dei/index.php?option=com_content&view=article&id=226:mission-objective-development-of-a-complete-man&catid=24:about-dei&Itemid=102

Management (TQM) (Figure 10.3) propped firmly on the four pillars of creativity, excellence, initiative and innovation. The system is geared to transform India into a knowledge society and, beyond, to a wisdom society surcharged by the spirit of ultimate consciousness (Satsangi and Dhir, 2024).

The vision and mission of DEI encapsulate its commitment to fostering a human being whose hallmarks are intellectual strength, scientific temper, emotional maturity, truthfulness, high moral character, simple living, dedication to duty and discharge of obligation, inter-disciplinary outlook, good general knowledge, sound aptitude and understanding of society to look

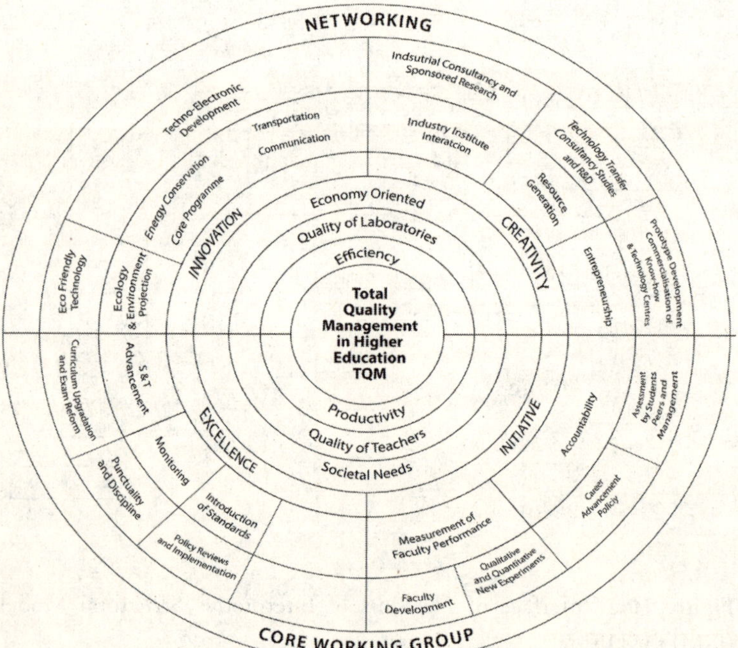

Figure 10.3 Total Quality Management Framework at DEI

Source: Adapted from https://www.dei.ac.in/dei/index.php?option=com_content&view=category&layout=blog&id=51&Itemid=326

at the deeper purpose of life through a high order thought process (DEI, 2020a). It proposes a model that believes in 'excellence with social relevance', imparting 'value-based and quality education' to reach the last, the least, the lowest and the lost, contributing to the nation and community by empowering marginalised groups, women and children, and building the economy through research and frugal innovation anchored in the principle of achieving more with less (Satsangi and Dhir, 2024).

The DEI Education Model

The DEI education model is designed to support students in reaching the highest level of Maslow's hierarchy of needs (Figure 10.4). It aims to foster self-governance and advanced critical thinking skills. This approach focuses on imparting practical, lifelong skills extending beyond traditional academics and preparing students for success in all aspects of life. Additionally, the model encourages customisation and personalisation, fostering a circular economy of soul and spirit through selfless service, community engagement and serving those in greatest need. By emphasising innovation, value addition and deep thinking, the model aims to contribute to developing a society grounded in wisdom, empathy and understanding. Furthermore, it advocates for the principle of minimalism, empowering students to achieve more with less. The DEI education model presented in Figure 10.5 encompasses various dimensions of development, outlining the trajectory from inner growth to global leadership.

Community Engagement at DEI

Community engagement in its real sense is a two-way partnership that benefits everybody involved. The successful collaboration between educational institutions and communities relies on reciprocal support. Both parties must actively engage themselves in the development process.

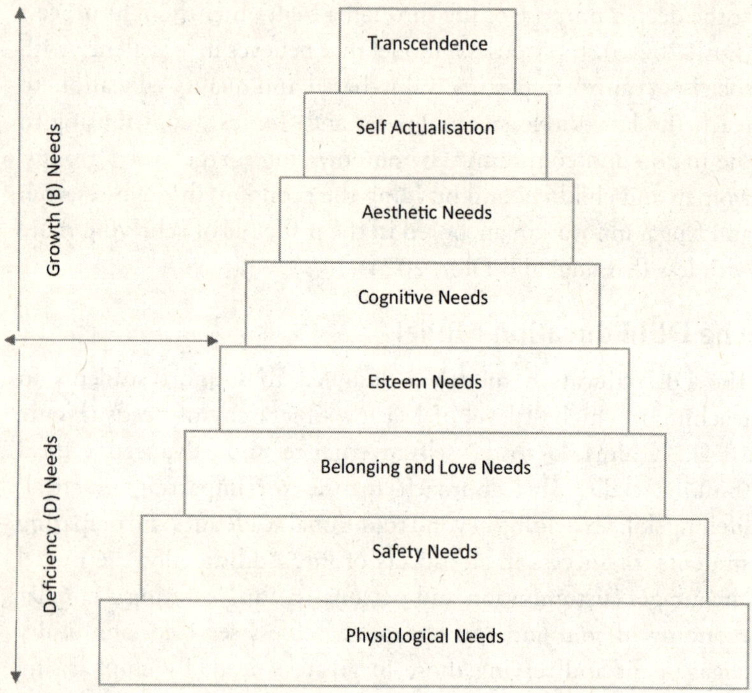

Figure 10.4 Maslow's Hierarchy of Needs – Extended

Community engagement is an intrinsic feature at DEI. The institute provides an environment for all stakeholders to get involved in community engagement programmes, leveraging the distinctive strengths of each community member. CBPR has been inter-twined into the community engagement programmes at DEI to actively engage all stakeholders in a collaborative and equitable research process.

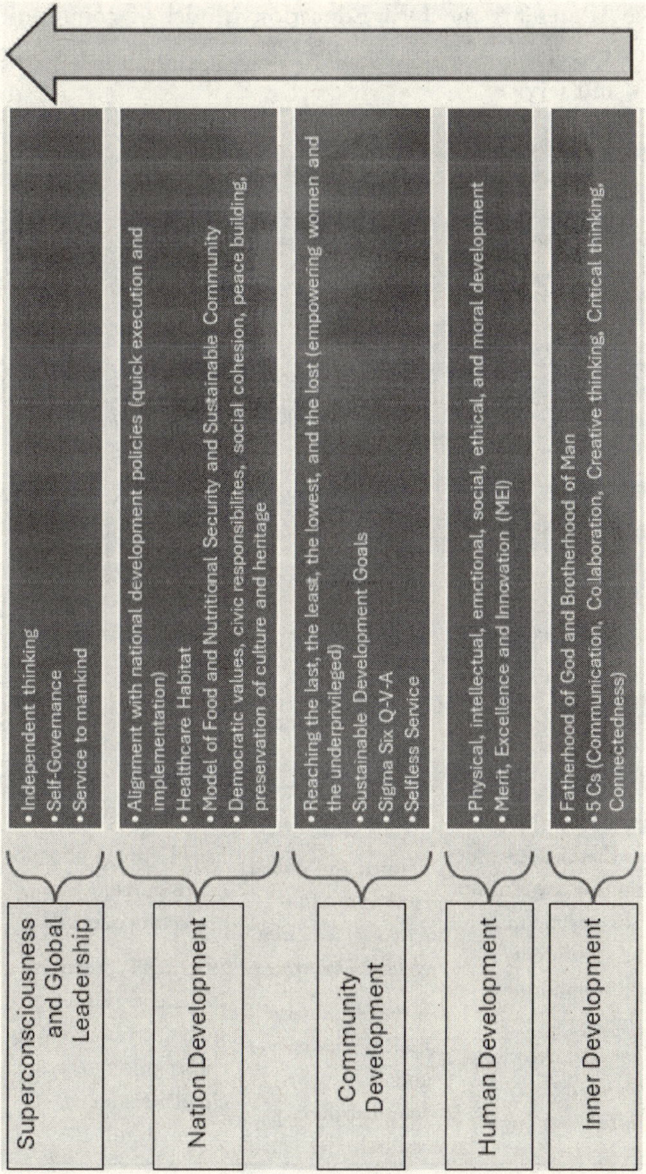

Figure 10.5 The DEI Education Model

Source: Adapted from the presentation of Prof. P.K. Kalra, Senior Director, DEI

Table 1 presents the DEI Education Model of community engagement and CBPR across three facets: teaching–learning, research, and service.

Table 10.1 DEI Education Model of Community Engagement and CBPR

Community engaged teaching–learning	**Community-based participatory research**	**Community service**
University Support to Communities		
Affordable and accessible education *(Reaching the last, the least, the lowest, and the lost)* Community engagement for all disciplines (Theory) (*NSS, core courses, environmental studies)* Vocational and skill courses, adult education (Life-long learning) Teaching and learning strategies (Service learning, co-op training, externship, internship, practicum, experiential, student-exchange programmes, multi-languages) School for children of neighbouring communities	Accessing local knowledge and issues Frugal innovation *(Quantum Jugaad)* Optimal technology interventions for social welfare Socially relevant research, consultations and counselling Trained and skilled faculty and staff *(Access to local and global expertise)* Interdisciplinary, multidisciplinary and transdisciplinary research	Serving society *(Reaching the last, the least, the lowest, and the lost)* Community engagement for all disciplines (Experiential) *(NSS, core courses, environmental studies)* Need-based programmes for rural, tribal and underprivileged (women), life-long learning Establishment of nano/micro start-ups and marketing network Sustainable practices (Solar energy, mist sprays, resource conservation, recycling, circular economy, minimalism)

Community engaged teaching–learning	Community-based participatory research	Community service
Community Support to the University		
Advisory Committee on Education (a non-statutory body serving as a think-tank)		
Research Advisory Committee on Agriculture		
Honorary teaching/ administrative support		
Students/alumnus support		
Manpower (skilled and unskilled)		
Vast agricultural area with a variety of crops/medicinal plants		
Gaushala (access to different livestock)		
Charitable hospital		
Target population		
Collaborations		
Local		
National		
Global		
The success of the DEI collaborations relies on the sharing of resources – land, labour, capital, entrepreneurs (administrators and advisors), and responsibilities		

Source: Author

The teaching and learning, research and service functions of the DEI Education Model places considerable emphasis on community engagement. It is a mainstreamed, and not a separate, activity. Therefore, it is not limited to a select few but for everyone. Students do not just offer their services to outside communities but need to learn from them by becoming part of the community. DEI regularly engages in community outreach activities in the rural areas of Agra district as well as in different locations across the country, including Noida, Gurugram, Chennai, Bengaluru, Mumbai, New Delhi, MTV Puram, Rajaborari, Murar, and Timarni (DEI, 2019).

Community engaged teaching-learning

The nature of engagement extends beyond exchanging information and knowledge to joint endeavours and decision-making, ultimately leading to shared leadership. DEI's approach to community engaged education surpasses conventional practices by fostering meaningful connections between academic stakeholders and non-academic organisations.

The educational framework at DEI has taken the notion of 'maternity to eternity' as its gospel and strives to cultivate children with exceptional (superhuman) qualities by integrating an individual's physical, intellectual, emotional, and ethical development (Dua et al., 2023; Bhatnagar, 2023; Gautam and Kumar, 2023). It starts in the third week of the Superman Evolutionary Scheme, a program started in January 2017. It is an innovative concept where infants and children participate in congregational prayers, selfless service (*seva*) in fields and healthcare exercises every day at the agroecological-cum-precision farming sites twice a day (before and after school) along with a parent or caregiver. Children are engaged in learning – arithmetic, language, computer skills, self-defence – in the lap of nature and participate in cultural activities like yoga. The 'Dayalbagh Way of Life' combines Eastern simplicity, culture and beliefs with Western scientific temper and educational excellence.

DEI and Dayalbagh associated schools, spanning from primary to intermediate levels, are situated in different states across India (Uttar Pradesh, Uttarakhand, Bihar, Punjab, Madhya Pradesh, Andhra Pradesh, Tamil Nadu, and Delhi). These schools are operated entirely by voluntary teaching and administrative staff, guided by the principle of serving humanity selflessly. To bring education to remote areas, interns who are unable to physically visit these locations, utilise a specially designed system called SCOTLS (Student Centric Online Teaching Learning System) to connect with rural students. This digital pedagogy aims to empower rural areas through digital education initiatives and address the shortage of teachers in these regions. It also benefits the interns by providing them exposure to digital teaching, learning and evaluation practices. Interactive digital pedagogy has improved students' performance and enhanced technological competence (Ahuja and Yadav, 2019). DEI also provides quality education through Information and Communication Technology (ICT) via its extensive network of 100 learning centres and six off-campuses in India (DEI, 2019). These initiatives aim to advance social inclusion and accessibility to education.

The Faculty of Education at DEI runs the train-the-teacher programs facilitated by its M.Ed. students to enhance the skills of teachers and improve quality of education in schools. Through these programs, M.Ed. students visit remote schools in Rajaborari and Timarni (Madhya Pradesh), collaborating with rural teachers to help them upgrade their teaching techniques. They focus on creating resource plans, lesson plans, and audio-visual teaching aids, and organise workshops and demonstration lessons tailored to the specific needs of the teachers, particularly in spoken English (DEI, 2019).

A Massive Open Online Course (MOOC) 'Community Engagement and Social Responsibility',* prepared by DEI under the Unnat Bharat Abhiyan, is available on the University Grants Commission's SWAYAM platform since February 2023. DEI is the host university of this course for all learners across the globe.

Experiential education offers immersive, hands-on learning opportunities that connect theoretical knowledge with real-world experience. Core courses such as the National Service Scheme (NSS), General Knowledge and Current Affairs, Rural

* https://onlinecourses.swayam2.ac.in/ugc23_ge04/preview

Development, Agricultural Operations, Environmental Studies, Comparative Studies of Religion (secular education system), and Cultural Education and Co-Curricular Activities (cultural and literary activities, games and sports) facilitate DEI students to understand and learn their societal roles without caste, religious and cultural biases. All undergraduate, diploma and certificate students are required to take these credit-based core courses.

Skilling is developed in phases (Figure 10.6) and is seamlessly integrated into mainstream education through age-appropriate activities (Dua et al., 2023). Skill-based courses in DEI help increase employability and empower people economically and socially (Sharma et al., 2021). Skilling at DEI starts early, with activities like tinkering, living and mobile labs for school children. Senior students can pursue different vocations through modular programs alongside their regular courses. They learn skills such as carpentry, spinning, weaving, leather work, smithy, moulding, gardening, printing and tailoring. Textile, block printing, stitching, food processing, and handicrafts are also taught, especially for empowering community girls and women. DEI serves as a laboratory for field work and experimentation. It is the country's first community college to produce students with vocational diplomas in automobile and information technology. DEI has been certified as the best 'Solar Skill Training Institute nationwide' and won the Championship Trophy at the National Solar Skill Competition in 2017. It is home to skilling centres like the Centre for Applied Rural Technology (CART) and Deen Dayal Upadhyay Kaushal Kendra (DDUKK) (DEI, 2019).

Lifelong learning theory and community-engaged pedagogy embrace co-learning rooted in a deep respect for the prior knowledge and experiences that community partners bring to the conversation around community-engaged activities. Adult learners share their experiences and build on personal self-direction that

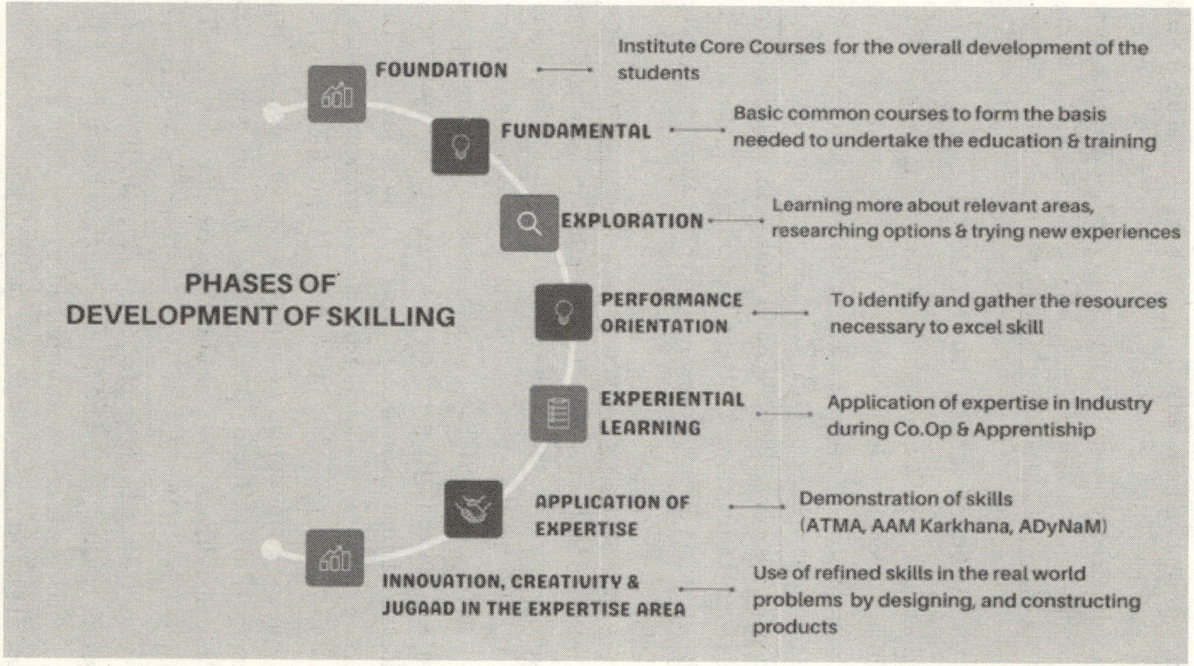

Figure 10.6 Phases of Development of Skilling at DEI

Source: Adapted from the presentation of Prof. P.K. Kalra, Senior Director, DEI

recognises theoretical knowledge must be relevant to real life. DEI's lifelong learning and extension activities run by faculty members and students create opportunities for individuals to enhance their employability and promote social equity, ultimately working towards an inclusive and equitable society.

Community-based participatory research

Research with the CBPR approach assists in assessing and resolving problems of society by bringing their perspectives to the forefront. As a result of strong, constructive interconnectedness with the community, researchers at DEI have access to local issues and challenges. They can easily collect and analyse insights based on local needs and aspirations. DEI supports enhancing overall well-being by including diverse knowledges and promoting community participation.

DEI has created an environment that fosters creative ideas from young students on socially relevant problems and facilitates the transformation of these 'idea quanta' into frugal or jugaad solutions. This harnessing of small, frugal innovations is called 'Quantum Jugaad'. DEI has established the Quantum Jugaad Incubation Centre (QJIC) to help student entrepreneurs assess their ideas and turn them into successful business models. The centre promotes creative thinking and an entrepreneurial mindset to transform innovative ideas into marketable products. This has resulted in the establishment of numerous student-operated, on-campus enterprises. The purpose of these enterprises is not to create revenue-driven ventures, but value creation that benefits the marginalised (DEI, 2019). There are some great examples of innovative ideas being implemented. They include a sensor network for tracking cattle and monitoring their health for a local dairy, a smart solar energy control and management system, a low-cost 3D printer, a solar-operated van for transportation, and battery-operated carts for moving about within the campus.

DEI partnered with BSNL, a government telecommunications company, to customise technology to connect the main campus with the rest of the world. It facilitates establishing last-mile mobile connectivity in villages to facilitate e-education, telemedicine and e-commerce in remote rural and tribal areas. In DEI's ICT centres and in the tribal village belt in Rajaborari and Timarni in Harda District of Madhya Pradesh, instructors are sharing their expertise and e-content. This technology intervention has provided schoolchildren in remote villages with exposure to science at practically no cost (DEI, 2020b). Access to technology has empowered tribal women to create self-help groups and set up sustainable nano-enterprises through frugal innovation and low-cost inputs. These women are receiving online training and marketing their products on the internet.

Atal Tinkering Labs have been set up in DEI schools to provide a creative workspace for young students to bring their ideas to life through hands-on, 'do-it-yourself' projects. These labs aim to nurture innovation, skills, creativity, critical thinking, design thinking, social and cross-cultural collaboration, and ethical leadership. The goal is to empower students to develop innovative solutions for complex problems and contribute to India's journey towards a knowledge-based economy.

DEI emphasises high-quality research that cuts across various disciplines and directly addresses the pressing needs of society, the nation and the global community. This includes fostering interdisciplinary, multidisciplinary and transdisciplinary research that is highly relevant and impactful. DEI has identified nine emerging research areas: agriculture, entrepreneurship, classical studies, digital life, nature and mathematics, esoteric art and science, sustainability, thinkism, and maintenance networks. These areas are being actively researched to define the role of humans in an era dominated by super-intelligent machines on a global scale. This involves transcending traditional boundaries of departments and faculties and establishing multidisciplinary research divisions to integrate diverse expertise from the sciences, humanities, technology and management fields.

DEI has set up the Centre for Consciousness Studies, which supports research across various disciplines such as botany, zoology, chemistry, physics, computer science, mathematics, psychology, management, languages (English/Hindi/Sanskrit), theology, commerce, education, engineering and medical science. Research encompasses areas of neuro-theology and Eastern philosophy, neuro-aesthetics, psycholinguistics, esoteric art and science, indigenous knowledge systems, and sustainability across different dimensions. The primary focus of the research has been on creating tailored methods, processes or technologies suitable for Indian society, aiming to be cost-effective and inclusive across all social strata to improve their quality of life.

DEI boasts a sophisticated array of research platforms (Figure 10.7) that actively demonstrates the practical application of socially relevant research in various fields:

- Agroecology-cum-precision farming for humans, plants, and animals – biodiversity parks, social forestry, organic farming, dairy cattle
- Air, water, soil quality and conservation – misting and spraying, river water filtration, soil testing, rainwater harvesting, sewage treatment plant
- Virtuous virtual communication – e-education, e-skilling, telemedicine, i-connect (industry-connect), r-connect (rural and tribal connect)
- Energy – e-vehicles, smart microgrid, solar energy, solar thermal cooking system
- Neighbouring communities – healthcare, Yamuna bank development, use of *jalkumbhi* (water hyacinth)

- Safety and security – camera monitoring systems, fencing of agricultural land field camps, Radio Frequency Identification (RFID), Unique Identifier (UID), Rapid Action Force (RAF), self-defence training for women and children
- Sustainable healthcare habitat – balanced diet and nutrition, eco-friendly bamboo structures (classrooms and creche), integrated health care system (AYUSH), yoga, meditation
- Technologies – additive manufacturing, drones, technology assistance for logistics
- Waste management and recycling – recycling biomass, circular economy, revival of barren land, biogas plant

Numerous research initiatives have resulted in the successful registration of several patents.

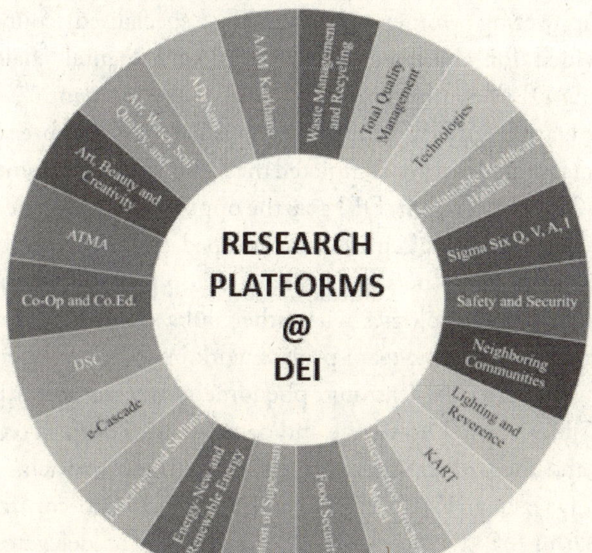

Figure 10.7 Research Platforms at DEI

Source: Adapted from the presentation of Prof. P.K. Kalra, Senior Director, DEI

DEI's community-based, multi-component interventions reinforce the well-being of people within a defined local community. It collaborates with multiple stakeholders in fulfilling its goals, including women, community members, government and non-government agencies, and nonprofit organisations. DEI is addressing need-based issues and trying to provide frugal and flexible solutions to various challenges. Need-based interventions are effective strategies to empower people to achieve their desired goals.

The community members benefit from a comprehensive range of support services including expert advice, consultations and training in areas such as agriculture, dairy farming, hygiene, healthcare, education, business development, livelihood improvement and security measures, with a particular emphasis on empowering women. Additionally, specialised counselling is provided for children with physical and mental challenges, reflecting DEI's commitment to inclusive development.

The Dayalbagh K4C Hub was established in 2023. Three faculty members from DEI have completed the MTP. Having become a part of the K4C Consortium, DEI gets the opportunity to connect with the global standards of curriculum and pedagogy to train the next generation of researchers in CBPR, and also gets the opportunity to share its methodologies with other hubs. This includes DEI's experiences of effective team project work in community-engaged learning, experiential learning, phenomenon-based education for responsible action, knowledge and competencies beyond technical detail, and the Collaborate-Converse-Converge approach.

The Dayalbagh K4C Hub is a thriving centre for co-construction and sharing of knowledge. In 2024, a group of delegates from Mizan K4C Hub, Universiti Sains Islam Malaysia (USIM), International Youth Centre (IYC) Malaysia, School of Education at the University of Glasgow in Scotland, and Participatory

Research in Asia (PRIA) visited the Dayalbagh K4C Hub. This visit facilitated bidirectional knowledge exchange of ideas on community engagement initiatives, which is essential to support the growth of the hub.

Community-engaged services

The commitment to reach 'the last, the least, the lowest, and the lost' is reinforced through various social service–based programmes. To provide easy access to healthcare facilities, and empower young women, the underprivileged and the underserved, a weekly free integrated medical and rural development camp is organised by DEI in collaboration with Saran Ashram Hospital, Dayalbagh (Satsangi and Dhir, 2024). Dedicated staff and students, along with multi-specialty physicians, radiologists, eye specialists, child specialists, physiotherapists, gynaecologists and surgeons, offer their services at the camps. In addition to offering medical care, the camps also function as a hub for providing counselling services related to education, employment and agricultural methods. They also offer vocational training programmes. The camps host various child development initiatives, including the 'Hole in the Wall' programme which focuses on teaching basic computer and language skills. Additionally, the camps provide physical training and recreational facilities for children. This unique working model of community engagement creates infinite opportunities through the three Es, i.e., Education, Employability, and Entrepreneurship (ibid.). Millets-based foods, fruits, milk and protein nutritional supplements are given to children, which enhance overall health (Panwar et al., 2023).

To build strong families, communities and nations, it is crucial to prioritise women's education and empowerment. DEI faculty and students are involved in providing training and support to help women form and sustain self-help groups. The goal is to make women self-reliant and improve their social status by assisting them with production, obtaining raw materials and marketing their produce. Self-help groups have been formed in communities neighbouring Dayalbagh and at Rajaborari. The Institute also conducts surveys in neighbouring villages to assess their needs and then offers various skill building programmes (sewing, embroidery, handicraft, textile, block printing, tie and dye, pottery, etc.).

The synthesis of mainstream education and entrepreneurship has led to the 'Earn while Learn' (Earn→Learn→Earn) programme at DEI through on-campus enterprises in dairy, food processing, automobiles, apparel design, etc. These programmes provide students with a feasible method to fund their education (DEI, 2019) without imposing financial strain on their parents. As a result, economic disparities are mitigated, and students are less likely to drop out of the university due to financial challenges, addressing a significant issue within the higher education system.

DEI supports the skilling of rural women and youth through ATMA (Apparel and Toy Manufacturing Association), ADyNam (Agro and Dairy Nano Processing of Multiproducts) and AAM (Automotive and Multi-skill) *karkhana*s (garages). The women and youth are supported to set up nano enterprises after completing their training. This training model is called the Rural Economic Zone (REZ) to Special Economic Zone (SEZ) to Internationalisation Model (Dua et al., 2023). The products made by these enterprises are sold locally and globally through DEI centres and community centres.

DEI presents the best example of protecting India's heritage and culture. People learn the intricate art of weaving, connecting threads of tradition with contemporary designs. By providing a platform for participants to learn craft skills, they are empowered to preserve and pass on these traditional forms of knowledge, fostering a sense of pride. The crop residue–based handicraft extension activities illuminate the intersection of creativity, tradition and community. The lab-cum-research centre at DEI functions with the intent of 'humanising technology' not 'technology technisizing humans'. In the words of Dr M.B. Lal Sahab, DEI's founder (DEI, 2019):

> *We should try to see that the modern trends become only supplements and not substitutes of our basic concepts of education. We do not like to put the clock back but would certainly do well to introduce a more human and realistic approach to education to meet the present day needs of society.*

The entire Dayalbagh community has benefited from the Institute's organic farm products, biodiversity parks, sewage, water and air treatment facilities, and sustainability practices. DEI also assists the district administration in cleaning the River Yamuna at Vaikunthdham (Swargdham), Poiya Ghat, Agra. Different departments at DEI collaborate with local citizens, government officers and other stakeholders to carry out these sustainability actions. DEI in collaboration with the Society for Preservation of Healthy Environment and Ecology and Heritage of Agra (SPHEEHA) and Nagar Panchayat, Dayalbagh, has initiated significant steps to protect the environment and ecology of Dayalbagh.

Community support to the University

DEI's linkage with the community is not one-sided but bidirectional which nurtures the democratic idea of community engagement. The co-learning process also enhances the strength of CBPR by making theory more relevant to practice. The Institute benefits from various forms of community support.

The Advisory Committee on Education (ACE), a non-statutory body that serves as a think-tank, is an innovative approach that provides visionary guidance to achieve excellence with relevance in education. It consists of eminent academicians, educationists and alumni of DEI. The advice given by ACE is considered by the statutory bodies of the University (Dua et al., 2023). A nomination process helps select individuals to become members of the ACE. Individuals who uphold similar ideologies and core values are nominated.

The Scientific Committee on Agriculture at DEI comprises stakeholders from the Institute and the community to get theoretical and practical ideas regarding agricultural and dairy-related issues to frame strategies for agriculture and dairy development. Individuals with advanced knowledge of agriculture are nominated for membership to the committee.

The Institute receives skilled and unskilled manpower and services from the community. The university's faculty and staff, including individuals in senior administrative roles like the Director (Vice-Chancellor), Registrar and Treasurer offer their expertise as honorary services. It is common for retired faculty members to continue contributing to the institution through roles such as emeritus, adjunct or visiting faculty. The Institute enjoys robust support from students and alumni. Recently, the DEI Alumni Connect 2024 brought together a diverse group of former students. This gathering was not just a simple reunion; it was a powerful demonstration of the alumni's commitment to preserving the environment and taking responsibility for the health of the Yamuna. The event symbolised their shared dedication to environmental consciousness and the rejuvenation of this important natural resource.

The Dayalbagh community provides DEI an opportunity to resolve complex issues in a real-world setting. Several programmes are implemented collaboratively with community stakeholders. Stakeholders are fully engaged and share a sense of social responsibility, fostering a spirit of brotherhood. The Dayalbagh community generously provides the university with various resources, including agricultural land and dairy cattle such as cows, buffaloes, goats, and camels for research experiments. Recently, there have been experiments conducted on mixing milk for improving health outcomes.

Collaborations

Internationally, DEI collaborates with institutions to expand its global presence and share expertise from its targeted research. DEI has signed several Memorandums of Understanding (MoUs) and pacts for collaborations (locally, nationally, and internationally) with communities, universities, research centres, industries, corporates, ministries, and non-governmental organisations that support the integration of indigenous and scientific knowledge and promote knowledge mobilisation. Some of the collaborations are with (DEI, 2019):

- National Dairy Research Institute, Karnal, India
- Tata Institute of Fundamental Research, Mumbai, India
- Indian Institute of Science, Bengaluru, India
- Indian Institute of Technology (Delhi, Kanpur, Mumbai and Chennai)
- Indian Institute of Management (Ahmedabad and Indore)
- Ministry of Textiles, Government of India
- Northern India Textile Research Association (NITRA), Ghaziabad, India
- Maruti Suzuki India Ltd., Gurugram, India
- University of Maryland, College Park, United States
- University of Waterloo, Canada
- Michigan State University, United States
- DEI–Seneca (Canada) Collaboration
- DEI–Stanford–DBT Collaboration

- International Centre for Genetic Engineering and Biotechnology, New Delhi, India
- Society for Preservation of Healthy Environment and Ecology and Heritage of Agra (SPHEEHA), India

Collaborations with communities support faculty and researchers by providing insights into social interconnections, local culture and lifestyle. Such collaboration enables the development of solutions that are not only effective but also culturally appropriate, reflecting a deep understanding of a community's unique needs and challenges.

Conclusion

The DEI Education Policy focuses on bringing academic excellence along with holistic development. It follows a systems approach that integrates social and environmental systems with the formal system of education (DEI, 2019) to help create a culturally and linguistically consistent environment for community-based experiential learning. The educational approach at DEI is centred around fostering a culture of academic learning and societal values. This approach equips individuals with academic knowledge and catalyses a significant shift in their belief systems, awareness, and sense of responsibility towards society. The result is the cultivation of global leaders who embody the ethos and principles of the Dayalbagh way of life.

DEI is dedicated to embracing **D**iversity, **E**quity, and **I**nclusion to ensure that all individuals are supported and included, regardless of background or identity. Mahatma Gandhi's *Antyodaya* philosophy stresses the importance of actively supporting and uplifting the most marginalised members of society. DEI, through its community-based initiatives, is creating paths for self-sustenance and meaningful participation of communities.

The success of DEI's community-engaged programmes is due to the collaborative sharing of resources and responsibilities among all stakeholders. This cooperative effort helps to build trust and encourages long-term commitments. This approach leverages existing strengths and achieves a harmonious blend of research and action, benefiting scientific progress and the community.

The words of two former Indian presidents who visited DEI reflect the institution's commitment to community-engaged education as a model for the rest of the country and the world (DEI, 2019):

> *The Dayalbagh institution in my opinion is a unique one. Everybody is made to work, is given the lesson of dignity of labour, and made to feel that not only work is dignified but work is also worship. I am quite sure that this institution will become a model for the rest of the country to follow. In fact, it should be the endeavour of the Government to take children from other parts to come and stay here for a week, so they may imbibe the spirit and learn from the kind of disciplined life that exists here.*
>
> – HONOURABLE SHRI R. VENKATARAMAN, Former President of India, on his visit to DEI on 16 March 1992

> *What makes a university great is the quality of education. DEI is exemplified by this statement, in letter and spirit. We have a roadmap for India becoming an economically developed nation by the year 2020. Fundamental to this is education with a value-based system. I am glad that DEI is promoting education with a value-based system.*
>
> – HONOURABLE DR A.P.J. ABDUL KALAM, Former President of India, on his visit to DEI in 2011

Acknowledgements

The author would like to extend sincere gratitude to Prof. Prem Kumar Kalra, Senior Director at Dayalbagh Educational Institute for his invaluable support, ideas, suggestions, and insightful feedback that have greatly contributed to this chapter. Additionally, heartfelt thanks are extended to Prof. J.K. Verma, Head, Department of English Studies at DEI for his assistance in refining ideas and editing the content.

11

SERVICE LEARNING AND COMMUNITY-BASED PARTICIPATORY RESEARCH IN INDIA

The Experience of Christ University

SHARON VALARMATHI

Introduction

Higher education should involve students in an active learning strategy that allows them to apply their classroom learning into practice. Their participation and involvement in hands-on learning should help them gain meaningful experiences. Active learning has been proven to help students improve their performance, allowing them to internalise it in contrast with rote memorisation (Haidet et al., 2014; McKeachie, 1999). Active learning has numerous benefits, particularly in developing 21st-century skills in students (Tantia et al., 2024). They gain from interactions, improve their understanding and take ownership of their learning (Suresh et al., 2022; Reinschmidt et al., 2019). Their experiences are enriched when their academic content is applied in real-time.

Making education creative and participative is a daunting

task for faculty members. Service learning is an active learning strategy that is beneficial to both students and the community. It is an organised experience which involves community–academia partnerships for reciprocal learning (Stewart and Wubbena, 2015). The nexus of academics and service helps students develop their academic and personal lives in connection with communities (Stanton et al., 1999; Blundo, 2000).

Christ University in Bangalore, India encourages students to apply their domain knowledge to address community concerns through service learning courses and projects. The CBPR approach is used to sensitise pupils in how to engage ethically with communities. Each identified community project must be approved by the course mentor, and students undergo orientation and training before starting their service learning projects. Students are graded based on community needs assessment strategy, group reflection, process of community engagement, and submission of final reports.

Service Learning and Community-Based Participatory Research

Service learning is a process of organically integrating course content with community engagement, incorporating intentional learning goals and service goals. It gained momentum in the 19th century, with various researchers and practitioners viewing the educational experience through active experimentation and reflection as vital for lifelong learning and student development (Hatcher and Bringle, 1997; Kendall, 1990). Sigmon and Ramsey (1979) defined service learning as an educational enrichment experience through community intervention. Furco (1996) viewed service learning as a balanced approach to experiential education, where the service provider and service recipient have equal focus.

Over the past 50 years, service learning has emerged as a

transformative process based on participatory education. An experiential approach, it connects students to the real world (Valarmathi et al., 2024). It is also an andragogy in which students can identify community problems and work on them to provide updated solutions (Tantia et al., 2024). Andragogy is a student-centric learning approach where students take an active role and ownership of, and accountability for, their learning. The learning and motivation to learn is intrinsic and self-directed. Service learning andragogy witnesses students' active participation with regular feedback from the community, teachers and peers. It allows students to reflect on their experiences at every stage of their community engagement, gain a deeper understanding of course material, and develop social responsibility (Resch and Schrittesser, 2023). Through service learning and meaningful societal engagement, community issues are addressed with worthwhile solutions (Valarmathi et al., 2024).

Community-based participatory research (CBPR) is an approach in which research is conducted in partnership with community members whose issues are identified and studied. It offers a new outlook on traditional research (Tandon, 2002). CBPR emphasises the relationship between researchers and participants. CBPR is not research *about* the community but research *with* the community (Krishnan et al., 2020; Bush et al., 2017). It emphasises co-learning and co-creation of knowledge. In CBPR, community members are not merely receivers of services but share their indigenous knowledge, from which the researcher can also gain insights. This approach recognises community members as competent partners in addressing issues concerning them (Krishnan et al., 2020). Collaborative engagement empowers participants to get involved, engage in and take ownership of the research (Marcus et al., 2011), though the degree of involvement may vary based on the research. The knowledge produced through

CBPR is authentic and democratised for social change. Actions are initiated to change the underlying identified problems with the community's resources.

Community-based participatory research and service learning are valuable approaches to coaching students in addressing community issues. Both approaches are unique, but also have many commonalities (Blundo, 2000). Service learning attempts to make curricular connections to community engagement by mapping learning goals with service goals, while CBPR aligns service goals with gaining new knowledge and insights from the community.

Service learning draws from CBPR's principles to make it an effective learning and engagement strategy. Using participatory research tools strengthens the way students are involved in community interventions. Otherwise, service learning would be purely academic research and pedagogy (Blundo, 2000). The blend of service learning, an experiential learning tool, and CBPR's principles make it more rigorous and meaningful for students and the community. Similarly, CBPR practice requires academic continuity and long-term project sustainability. Students can follow up batch after batch through the service learning projects being undertaken.

Service learning and CBPR have structured processes to achieve the desired outcomes. Both are grounded in ethics and equality; they are not arbitrary or unorganised. Both aim to address community needs or issues which do not emerge from a review of past literature but are immediate concerns that need to be discussed through personal interaction. How the issue is addressed can be scientific and can originate with a community survey. This process requires frequent interaction between the community and the students. The consent of community members is essential for both CBPR and service learning. It also builds a connection between the university and the neighbouring communities. Many partnerships may emerge as a result of such interaction.

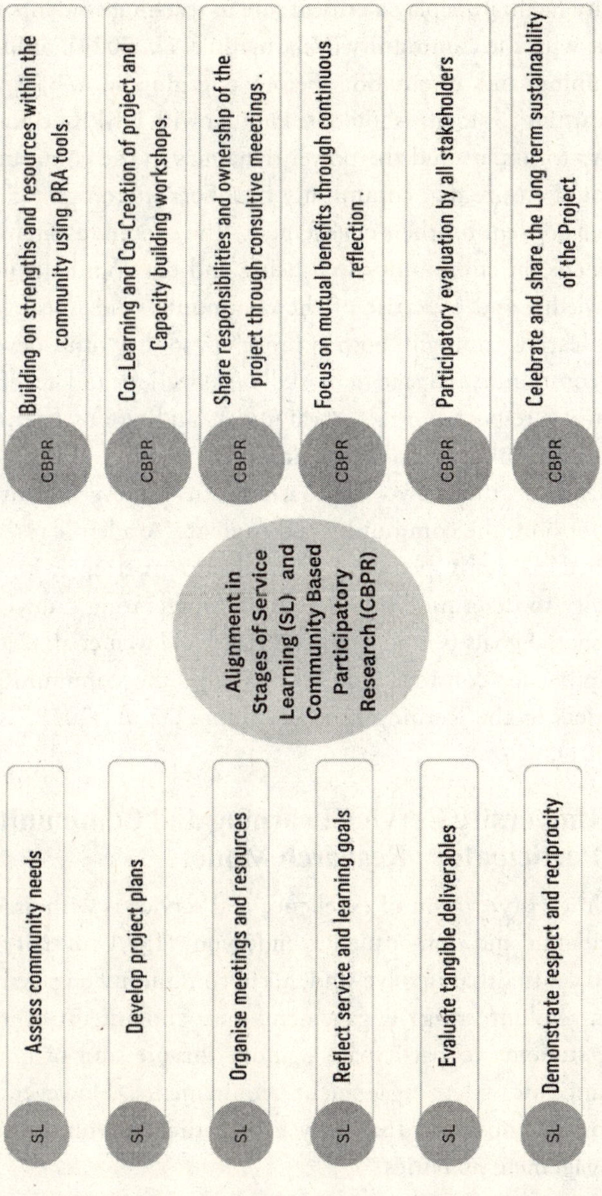

Figure 11.1 Nexus of Service Learning and CBPR Approach at Christ University

Source: Author

Faculty facilitators play a critical role in teaching students how to engage with the community (Valarmathi et al., 2024). Students need training and orientation before engaging in CBPR and service learning. Students should be familiar with CBPR principles and ethics to understand the power dynamics in the community. They should ensure that community members are recognised and have given consent for their engagement. The chosen research area should focus on community well-being and development, using the knowledge and expertise of the community and researchers. Students learn by doing in both approaches, so they must develop specific community engagement skills. Reflection and feedback help cultivate respect and reciprocal understanding in students so that they can connect with the community.

A blend of these two approaches can achieve maximum benefits for both the community and students. Academic research is enriched as both pedagogies involve partnering with the community to determine their needs and integrating knowledge to meet shared goals (Gimpel et al., 2018; DeHaven et al., 2011). Both approaches consider and acknowledge the community as stakeholders in the learning process (Gimpel et al., 2018; Israel et al., 2001).

Christ University Service Learning and Community-Based Participatory Research Model

Christ University's vision of excellence and service is witnessed in every academic and non-academic endeavour. The University has dedicated centres that involve students in community engagement practices. Volunteering engagements are non-credit-bearing, allowing students to participate without the pressure of graded performance or strict engagement requirements. However, the institution has observed that only a few students volunteer for social engagement activities.

The University embraced service learning with a United Board Grant in 2016, familiarising all members with its concept and implementation. It offers a platform for students to embrace social responsibility and develop civic awareness through experiential societal learning.

With overwhelming support from faculty and students, the Centre for Service Learning was established in 2022 to facilitate training, assessment, and implementation strategies. Executive members of the Centre underwent the MTP in 2022, fostering the emergence of a model that embraces both service learning and CBPR. The Centre for Service Learning offers micro-credential courses on service learning and CBPR.

Currently, service learning is a mandatory two-credit requirement for undergraduate courses, ensuring students' participation and completion as part of their graduation requirements. Fifteen departments offer service learning courses within their respective disciplines. Departments have the flexibility to design and implement their courses after approval by the Centre's advisory board. In one academic year, over 1,000 students participate in service learning courses at the university. All students in the third or fourth semester of undergraduate programs participate in semester-long group service learning projects.

A service learning project is meaningful only when community members are involved and supported in the reciprocal learning process, where the community and students are equal beneficiaries (Sigmon,1979). The course design at Christ University is carefully crafted to ensure there is equal balance between service and learning, and constant involvement of all stakeholders to maximise results.

The institution has designed phases of student engagement for service learning projects in a unique model called ADORED. ADORED stands for:

Assess – Community Needs
Develop – Project Plans
Organise – Meetings and Resources for Operationalising the Plan
Reflect – Service and Learning Goals
Evaluate – Tangible Deliverables
Demonstrate – Respect and Reciprocity

The ADORED model enhances students' understanding of their roles and active involvement in community interventions, meeting both academic and community requirements. It focuses on the process and progress of attaining the outcome rather than merely attaining the goals.

There are several phases in completing the service learning project under the ADORED model – investigating community needs, planning and preparing to address the identified needs, executing the desired plan, reflecting on the service and learning goals, and demonstrating the results with community partners through celebration.

In the first phase of the ADORED model, students identify a suitable and feasible community and consider the community members' willingness to collaborate for a new project. Students are also encouraged to follow up on a project initiated by a previous batch to ensure sustainability and long-term association with the community.

In this phase, students need to learn about the community with whom they will engage. They document community resources and the skills they possess to address issues. CBPR principles of building on the strength of the community are noted while surveying it. Using Participatory Rural Appraisal (PRA) tools like transect walks and community resource mapping for a comprehensive understanding of the community is essential. The

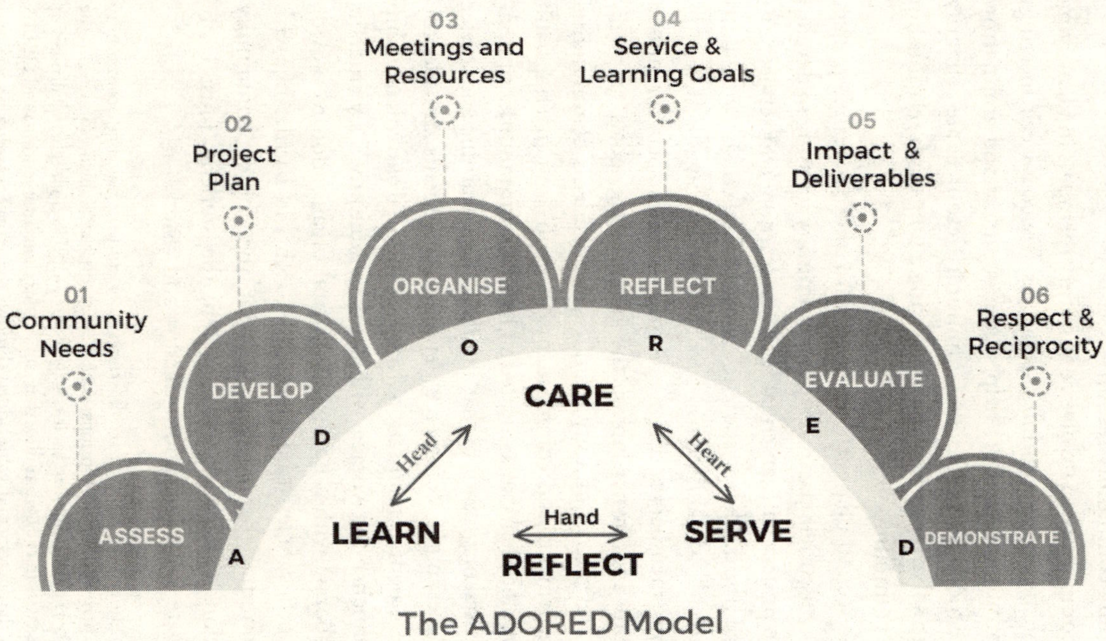

Figure 11.2 The ADORED Model at Christ University: Service Learning Phases

Source: Author

Plus Minus Delta chart*, another popular tool in PRA, is also used for mapping community resources.

It is compulsory to involve community members in identifying the problems and determining priorities. Twice-a-week meetings with community members help students understand and narrow down the root causes of issues. Community resources are primarily utilised to solve these problems. Ensuring a long-term relationship with the community is also essential.

In the second phase, students co-learn and co-create a project plan. They use their classroom and community learning to develop a suitable project with an equal focus on learning and service.

In the third phase, students schedule meetings with non-governmental organisations, civil society organisations or community members to design and implement the plan for mutual partnership and ownership of the project. The goals are well-defined, and the community members and students communicate their engagements and commitments through joint meetings and discussions. Students are educated to identify communities or non-governmental organisations that align with their learning and service goals. For example, commerce department students can identify non-governmental organisations focusing on social entrepreneurship or microfinance for women within the community. Law students will collaborate with a non-governmental organisation to provide legal aid or awareness camps on citizen rights in partnership with the community. Before working with the chosen community organisations/civil society organisation, the students must verify and evaluate the organisation's mission and vision.

*The Plus Minus and Delta chart illustrates how students can map community responses across three dimensions: PLUS identifies available resources in the community that can enhance their engagement; MINUS highlights challenges or deficiencies within the community that can hinder their intervention; and DELTA represents the incremental value added through the service learning project that will benefit both students and the community.

The next phase is reflection, an ongoing act in a service learning project. Students are trained to maintain a journal of their weekly engagements and activities. The mid-reflection phase helps students analyse if they have deviated from the original plan and to strategise or modify their actions to bring meaningful connections with the course content to meet the project's goals (Chika-James et al., 2022).

The fifth phase is evaluation. Involving all stakeholders (peer mentors, faculty facilitators, and community partners) in assessing the project's process and progress is crucial. The participatory evaluation method measures the project's deliverables and activities. Students evaluate their service learning projects through peer evaluations and a community feedback system. Faculty members assess students' engagements based on tangible deliverables and impact analyses compiled by the students. Community partners are also involved in assessment through viva voce examinations, where they identify tangible deliverables and provide feedback on the benefits to the community. Students are evaluated not only on the outcomes but also on the process of interaction with the community. They also need to share the project's sustainability plans.

The service learning project is concluded by demonstration. Students hand over the project to the subsequent student cohort. They disseminate vital information about the project to ensure its sustainability.

Finally, the students are invited to celebrate the project's success by sharing and disseminating their service learning projects. Students share their experiences and learning at the Service Learning Day Celebration held at the culmination of the academic semester. Community partners are invited to this celebration and share their experiences of participating in the project.

Service learning project reports are maintained by respective faculty mentors in the digital repository of the institution. Sharing project performance helps all stakeholders understand the gap in the implementation of service learning projects and take corrective measures in the curriculum or service engagement hours.

Students must seek and consult community members' involvement at every stage to clearly define project goals (Moore and Donaldson, 2022). Before proceeding with the survey or community mapping, learners must sign an undertaking about the ethical considerations for undertaking a service learning project (Juliana et al., 2022). Students take accountability for their actions and behaviour in the community. They respect community members' privacy by seeking consent before taking pictures or gathering information. Students engage respectfully with the community and actively learn from their experiences. When discussing solutions, they collaborate with community members, offering alternatives without imposing suggestions or opinions. There is no exchange of money or private information involved. Students share their findings with the community and celebrate achievements together. Furthermore, they raise community concerns to local authorities for necessary attention. This approach ensures that the students' actions are not only academically rigorous but also ethically grounded, exemplifying integration of service learning protocols with CBPR ethics into the model.

Reflection is a crucial element in the process, without which learnings and service goals are incomplete. Students reflect in class and post community engagement hours on how to apply their knowledge to the community's identified needs. Students are asked to reflect before, during and after the project. Continuous reflection helps students identify gaps in their learning goals and allows them to correct any misconceptions and myths about community knowledge and culture. They learn from interacting and observing rich, indigenous community knowledge (Cowden et al., 2013).

The Pottery Town Initiative: A Service Learning Project

Pottery Town is a settlement of skilled pottery artisans in Bangalore with a history dating back to the British colonial period. The community has thrived by crafting earthenware, though the shift to alternative materials has posed significant challenges. Artisans often encounter low turnover periods due to ineffective product marketing strategies. The community has also received notice from the government to relocate due to construction of the metro in Bangalore. Despite these challenges, a few families make a living through this traditional craft. They remain loyal to their art creations, love their work, and want to continue to showcase their skills and preserve this rich heritage. The community's existence is at stake, and now they need to establish themselves in a new location, learn to innovate, build a new customer base, and meet changing customer demands.

A group of students from Christ University's School of Commerce identified Pottery Town as a community in need. They designed a project to apply their marketing skills and learned the art of making pottery from the potters themselves. They also invited interested students from other departments to join a pottery design workshop and create visibility for the artisans via social media.* This initiative has been a long-term service learning project, with each cohort of students handing over their reports to a subsequent batch.

As part of the service learning project, students set up an online forum for the artisans to showcase their products for online customers. They also researched new earthenware products, e.g., kitchen utensils, plates and teacups for personal use and to generate

*Instagram page: was https://www.instagram.com/pottery_town_bengaluru/?igsh=bmQ4NDU0cXBydndq

additional income for the community. Students trained the community in using online platforms for promoting the artisans' products and provided education on financial literacy. Artisans were aided in understanding marketing dynamics and creating new portfolios for their businesses. The students also helped connect the community with other businesses in the earthenware sector, facilitating bulk orders and securing raw material supplies.

This service learning project equally focused on community well-being and student learning, fostering a mutually beneficial relationship. Students have utilised their marketing knowledge and social media tools to serve a community in need. Students have also understood the hard work of artisans and the benefits of using earthenware. Several of them have switched to using earthenware in their daily lives. The artisans, reassured and encouraged, have willingly shared their expertise, passing on skills to the younger generation while learning new marketing skills and increasing their income.

Conclusion

Christ University has embedded CBPR principles in the implementation of its service learning projects. Creative and art-based reflection techniques learned during the MTP have been passed on to students participating in the service learning courses and projects. These methods have enriched students' learning experiences by encouraging them to not merely reflect on their learning and service activities but also to creatively express their interactions with the community. This creative reflection has enabled students to document and share their experiences in innovative ways, fostering a deeper connection and understanding between students and community members.

The MTP mentors, after undergoing the training, have made significant changes in their teaching methods and pedagogy.

They have adopted more participatory and inclusive approaches, ensuring that students are active collaborators in the learning process. This shift has made the service learning program at the University more dynamic and impactful, benefiting both students and the community.

Christ University has created space for students to learn new things through collaboration with many organisations that support students to undertake community engagement. The university has initiated several community development projects aimed at empowering communities and improving their livelihoods. It organises periodic visits to these communities, allowing students to interact and learn from them. This enriches their academic learning and allows them to be partners in community living. Students also develop essential skills such as communication, problem-solving, observation, peer learning and interpersonal interactions.

In summary, the integration of CBPR principles, learnt through the MTP program, has not only enhanced the university's existing service learning program, but has also facilitated the personal and academic growth of teachers and students.

12

STRATEGIES FOR TEACHING COMMUNITY-BASED PARTICIPATORY RESEARCH FOR PEACE IN COLOMBIA

IRMA ALICIA FLORES-HINOJOS AND LUISA FERNANDA GONZÁLEZ PINEDA

Introduction

The Colombia IAPaz K4C Hub was founded in 2018 as part of the K4C Consortium of the UNESCO Chair in Community-Based Research and Social Responsibility in Higher Education. The hub is a partnership between the Cañon de Combeima Women's Association, located in the department of Tolima, and certified K4C mentors from two higher education institutions: the University of Los Andes, situated in Bogotá, the Capital District of Colombia, and the University of Ibagué, based in the city of Ibagué in the department of Tolima. The coordination of the hub is at the University of Los Andes, thereby leveraging the academic and administrative resources of this institution. The academic and administrative structures of the university involved in the hub's processes and the CBPR training courses include the Vice-Presidency of Research and Creation, the Faculty of Education and the Office of Continuing Education.

According to a study by Colombia's National Center for Historical Memory, the civil conflict in Colombia has resulted in up to 2,20,000 deaths, 25,000 disappearances, and 5.7 million displaced persons over the past half-century. A peace process and an agreement between the government and the leaders of the Revolutionary Armed Forces of Colombia (FARC), the country's largest insurgent group, halted the violence in 2016. The peace process faces many challenges, including widespread public concern that the peace deal offers too much leniency to perpetrators of violence. But the deal's backers are hopeful that the early phases of demobilisation, which are already underway, will lead to a sustainable peace.

This is the context in which Colombia IAPaz Hub decided to focus its work on peacebuilding since its inception and is a space that favours dialogue and exchange of knowledge between different groups, communities and institutions at the local and regional levels. It promotes reflection, participation and action as well as training in CBPR for the new generation of participatory researchers. It also provides support in research processes and the dissemination of results for social transformation to achieve peace in the country.

The hub has tried to work with communities historically affected by the armed conflict in different regions of Colombia. As a group, we reflected on what actions are necessary to build peace and what actors should be involved. We collectively discovered that to build peace it is necessary to work together with different actors such as communities, demobilised insurgents, military forces, and armed conflict victims to re-establish trust in each other and find new ways for more compassionate interactions, conflict resolution, and developing social-emotional skills that allow us to connect with others.

Responding to the political and social context of the country, the Colombia IAPaz Hub has oriented its training courses, workshops and research actions to fulfil SGD 16, which has the purpose 'to promote peaceful and inclusive societies for sustainable development, provide access to justice for all and build effective, accountable and inclusive institutions at all levels' (Nacional Unidas, 2018).

The Colombia IAPaz Hub has offered the course 'Strategies for Community-Based Participatory Research' since 2022. The course is part of the continuing education strategy of the university, which has allowed students from different parts of the country and Latin America to participate. The program is aimed at professionals from various disciplines (science, humanities, social sciences, education), especially those involved in community research.

The first offering of the course was in the 2022–10 semester. It has continually been offered in the 2023–20 and 2024–10 semesters, and students have also been enrolled for the 2024–20 semester. Three cohorts of researchers have been trained and 15 to 25 students have participated in each semester.

The course is facilitated by two permanent K4C mentors, supplemented by other mentors and guest experts. It is a four-module course which lasts two months. The classes are held in biweekly sessions of two hours each in synchronous virtual mode.

Building Community-Based Participatory Research Competencies for Peace

The hub uses three important epistemological sources to provide theoretical and methodological CBPR related content in its trainings. First is the approach and tradition of Participatory Action Research (PAR) developed in Colombia by Colombian academics and activists such as Orlando Fals Borda, Lola Cendales, Victor Negret, and Normando Suarez, among others. Second, is the approach and theory of popular education, based on the experiences of Paulo Freire, Carlos Rodrigues Brandao, Anton de Shutter, Francisco Vio Grossi, Oscar Jara, and Boaventura de Sousa Santos, among others. Third are the approaches for the democratisation of knowledge, open science and the ethics of CBPR learnt during the MTP conducted by the UNESCO Chair in Community Based Research and Social Responsibility in Higher Education.

Courses, workshops and research projects raise awareness among trainees about the capabilities of human beings to peacefully transform conflict situations (Muñoz and Jiménez, 2015). In particular, we aim to develop competencies that privilege emotional intelligence, active listening, self-reflection and the search for social justice from an ethical and solidarity perspective based on the principles of imperfect peace (Muñoz and Jiménez, 2015). We understand imperfect peace as a process in continuous construction and resignification, 'which humanizes us, allows us to identify ourselves with our conflictive conditions of existence, those of our allies and those of our adversaries, and opens up real possibilities of thought and action' (Muñoz and Jiménez, 2015, p. 51). Thus, the formative perspective of the hub's courses and workshops focuses on creating competencies in students that (i) facilitate the development of a critical conscience, (ii) fosters non-violent forms of coexistence and (iii) promotes the empowerment of communities by respecting and building real possibilities for reflection and action. In this way, the training of new community-based participatory researchers for peace will strengthen the social fabric through inclusive, participatory and representative decision-making in their contexts, thus responding to the needs of communities and institutions involved in the co-construction of peacebuilding.

Theoretical and Pedagogical Strategies

In 2023, the Ministry of Science, Technology, and Innovation developed an action initiative called the Science for Peace Mission (PIIOM Misión Ciencia para la Paz, 2023). The mission seeks to create and consolidate science and peace ecosystems in Colombia that close territorial gaps and integrate the well-being of all Colombians. This goal will be achieved through Science, Technology, and Innovation (ST&I) initiatives with a restorative approach and a focus on social, economic, and environmental justice.

The hub's course 'Strategies for Community-Based Participatory Research' was (re)aligned with the strategic objectives established by the Ministry (PIIOM Misión Ciencia para la Paz, 2023), which include:

1. *Strengthen territorial governance for the sustainability of peace*: Promote governance structures that foster sustainable peace in affected regions.
2. *Recognise and recover ancestral knowledge for integral justice*: Value and reintroduce ancestral knowledge as a basis for environmental, social, and economic justice.
3. *Promote the production and social appropriation of new knowledge*: Encourage the creation and use of new knowledge, technologies and innovations guaranteeing human rights.
4. *Promote new citizenship and a culture of peace*: Encourage active citizenship and a culture of peace that contribute to the reconstruction of the social fabric in various regions and territories in Colombia.

The ecosystem approach of the Science for Peace Mission has been taken up in the design of the course. Approached from a systemic perspective, ecosystems serve as a methodological framework for analysing and understanding complex scenarios and environments. Using CBPR, the course articulates mechanisms and spaces for ecosystems between actors in a specific territory, designed to address the problems and effects of the war in that region. This articulation includes:

1. The delimitation and understanding of actors: Identifying and understanding the dynamics and relationships between actors within a given space.
2. The search for spaces and dialogue: In the face of common problems and objectives, identifying the ecosystems that can participate in the solution.
3. Developing strategies for intervention and collective action.

The course is based on Vygotsky's pedagogical approaches (1981) which state that learning is conditioned by the society in which we are born and developed. From this sociocultural perspective, learning is achieved through the interaction between a facilitator of the process (the teacher), the students, and the sociocultural context in which learning is implemented.

Anchoring courses in social reality allows students to understand the practical meaning of theory. By applying their knowledge in practice, they acquire more pragmatic, valuable, and lasting learning. This student-centered method (as distinct from teacher-centered content) challenges them to assume learning autonomously in real contexts; at the same time, it is coherent with the constructivist perspective, is based on knowledge of the context, and contributes to the development of skills for living in a complex and changing environment (Lou and MacGregor, 2004).

The course design is based on three fundamental pedagogical strategies. These are:

1. The Flipped Classroom Method
2. Collaborative Learning
3. Project-based Learning

The Flipped Classroom Method

This method changes the traditional learning dynamic by requiring students to interact with course materials, such as lectures or readings, outside of class time, usually through online platforms. This strategy allows students to progress at their own pace and choose their learning location, thus promoting flexibility in the learning process (Schmidt and Ralph, 2016). In Brightspace, the learning platform for the course, students have access to theoretical material, videos and other virtual resources that correspond to each session. Supported by a set of reflective questions designed specifically for each session, they are expected to use these materials to prepare for each class. This allows students to come to the session prepared to construct meaningful learning with their peers.

Collaborative Learning

This approach is based on Johnson et al. (1998), who define it as a carefully designed system of interactions that organises and induces reciprocal influence among the team members. It develops through a gradual process in which each person feels mutually committed to the learning of others, generating a positive interdependence that serves as a scaffolding for their learning. This principle of collaborative learning also contributes to the formation of the processes that students will have to develop when they implement the CBPR research proposal in partnership with the communities.

Project-Based Learning

This approach allows us to guide the research process that students will co-design with their community partners. From this perspective, students research, create, learn, apply what they have learnt to a real life situation, share their experiences with others, reflect continuously, and analyze the results of their decisions and actions. Students learn to co-construct and work as a team with their community partners to solve the problem (among several options) they wish to address. From this perspective, all those involved in the research process generate learnings to solve a problem that interests and affects them.

Course Structure

The course material is structured around three main axes:

1. *Theoretical-epistemological*: Focuses on the principles and foundations of CBPR, PAR, action research, and other participatory methodologies.
2. *Methodological*: Explores various research methods useful for working with communities, emphasising arts-based methods.
3. *Practical*: At the beginning of the course, participants are expected to have a relationship with a community that will be their community partner and with whom they will co-develop the research.

The peace theme is transversal and is interwoven in the different topics addressed in each session.

Table 12.1 Structure of the CBPR Course Offered by Colombia IAPaz Hub

Module Content	Sessions
Module I • Theoretical foundations and conditions for working under PRA principles • Peace as the main objective	Session 1. Course introduction and participant's presentation
	Session 2. History and development of the PAR and CBPR approach.
	Session 3. Epistemological and methodological differences between traditional research approach and PAR/CBPR approaches.
	Session 4. PAR/CBPR approaches

Module Content	Sessions
Module II • Building bonds with the community • Ethics and power relations in co-constructing a participatory research process	Session 5. Introduction to the field study design
	Session 6. Building bonds with the community. Ethics and power relations in the co-construction of a participatory research process.
	Session 7. Understanding the context and the needs of the community to raise the problem; the SDG approach.
	Session 8. Imperfect peace approach and co-construction paths with communities under the principles of SDG16.
	Session 9. Ethics and power relations in the construction of knowledge in PAR/CBPR for peace.
Module III • Collect, analyze and socialise knowledge in a participatory way	Session 10. Data collection and knowledge production methods. Art-based methods approach.
	Session 11. Data collection and knowledge production methods. Art-based methods approach.
	Session 12. Data collection and knowledge production methods. Art-based methods approach.
	Session 13. Socialisation of fieldwork proposals.
Module IV • Presenting the field work and the co-construction of change	Session 14. Exposition of fieldwork proposals.

The processes, content, educational resources and activities in the different sessions include:

- The incorporation of multiple modes of research which encourages a variety of research approaches and methods that enrich the understanding of social problems and actions through practice.
- The promotion of community work skills which enables students to critically address identified needs within the community and reflect on how they can engage and involve themselves.
- An orientation towards research ethics and values from ethical research practices and with a strong connection to the values of the contexts.
- The development of a solid understanding of power dynamics and the importance of alliances in the research and educational context.

Use of Technology

The course has been adapted to the virtual mode and is taught through the Brightspace platform of the University of Los Andes. The design and implementation of the course using Virtual Learning Environment (VLE) has been enriched by:

- Padlet, Canva, Mentimeter, and other apps. These simulate a classroom in the virtual world and allow the development of educational processes based on new dynamics, such as access to content on demand. In addition, they provide specific spaces for discussion and answering individual questions on shared topics. These applications have proven to be crucial, as they facilitate interaction and active learning among participants.
- Discussion forums guided by questions related to the theme of the session, in which students participate by presenting their points of view as well as their understanding of the concepts.

This facilitates active participation and interaction among students.

- Field diaries as an essential component for individual reflection. These journals allow students to reflect individually on the topics covered in class and consolidate their fieldwork proposals. This component has also been fundamental for the personal and academic development of the students, as it fosters a deeper and more applied understanding of the content.

Due to the short duration of the course, sessions are conducted synchronously twice a week. Collaborative activities that put the principles and methodologies into practice are undertaken in each session. This dynamic allows students to acquire competencies in using community research strategies and applying them when working with their chosen community partners.

Examples of the Use of Pedagogical Strategies

The following are examples of how the pedagogical strategies are used in the course.

Flipped classroom

- Has been used in session on methods of data collection and knowledge production.
- Students learn data collection methods in PAR, which aim to build knowledge through the collective understanding of reality in different social processes. We move away from a technical or operational use of methods to open up a range of possibilities for collecting information, where methods and techniques can be used for negotiation with communities, self-diagnosis, design and implementation of actions, and critical reflection that emerges from the process.
- To prepare students for the sessions, readings and videos in

Spanish focused on PAR and CBPR are used. This theoretical preparation provides students with a solid conceptual framework to then apply in their case study, in which they explore how PAR and CBPR can be used to address specific issues within local communities.

Readings:

- Francés, F., Alaminos, A., Penalva-Verdú, C., and Santacreu, Ó. (2015). Participatory research: methods and techniques. Pydlos ediciones. Chapter 6. participatory research techniques for social creativity (pp 83–148).
- Cunha, M. and Mantilla, R. (2015). Thematic sociodrama: a research method. Revista Brasileira de Psicodrama, 23(1), 14–22.
- Romero, (2010). The sociogram.
- A tool: Talking Card

Videos:

- Sociodrama: https://www.youtube.com/watch?v=qyBBipI2K1w
- Sociogram: https://www.youtube.com/watch?v=wtqfzxXqLP8
- Talking maps: https://www.youtube.com/watch?v=yR6OCywY1kw

- Pre-session activity: Based on the readings and videos, students are asked to reflect on the following questions.
  - How would I use one or more of these methods in my context?
  - For which of the research phases?

Collaborative learning

- In Session 1 (Introduction to the course and presentations of the participants), students individually make a brief personal presentation that includes a photo, their name, name of the

institution or organisation to which they belong, and the location where they work professionally with communities. For this session, we use Padlet, an online platform that allows the creation of interactive digital 'walls' where the students can add various types of content, such as text, images, links, attachments and videos. These walls are collaborative, allowing multiple users to contribute and edit content in real time. Students use the Padlet presentation to answer the following questions:
  - What motivated me to take this course?
  - What do I know about the PAR perspective?
  - Am I involved in a research project?
  - What is the context in which I will carry out my fieldwork?
  - What is the problem I want to address in this community?
- In Session 3 (History and development of community-based participatory research), students work in groups to construct a graphical representation of the historical development of PAR based on the assigned readings. They use tools such as concept maps, timelines, infographics, or collages. Additionally, each student incorporates into the graphical representation a personal moment marking when they first encountered the PRA proposal in their personal history.

Project-based learning

- Students have the autonomy to choose topics of interest and design their field projects. These are both individual and group projects. Students have presented a variety of case studies that address diverse issues and community contexts in Colombia, such as:
  - Culinary traditions in Palestina (Huila)
  - People from the Afro-Colombian community council Cocomacia

- Meeting of communities of the Atrato River (Chocó)
- Analysis of library books in the framework of the Reading Party program through an intersectional framework of gender, race, and class
- Recovery of urban vegetable gardens as environmental classrooms in Ciudad Bolivar
- Participatory process with children and adolescents around the archaeological park of Usme
- Reflection on the meaning of participation in the search for missing persons
- Transformation in the exercise of citizenship

Guest speakers

- Guest speakers such as university professors and K4C mentors are invited to present their experiences in engaging with community partners.
- In Session 6 (Building bonds with the community), the guest speaker emphasized how to initiate the PAR/CBPR process in the community to identify the problem/need.
- In Session 11, guest speakers presented different strategies for knowledge dissemination at various levels, such as the community itself, local and regional decisions, as well as public policy formulation. The focus was on understanding practices to effectively and meaningfully communicate findings obtained through the research process.

Key Lessons

Through its pedagogical design oriented to action and community collaboration, the course 'Strategies for Community-Based Participatory Research' has promoted an effective integration between theory and practice, contributing to social transformation and sustainable development of Colombia. It has enabled students to develop a reflective, critical and autonomous role in their learning and become committed to the processes of peaceful transformation. It has also contributed to the continuous training of the members of the Colombia IAPaz Hub. Nonetheless, significant challenges remain in teaching the course.

The full virtual mode of the course makes it impossible to facilitate face-to-face knowledge sharing among students, which is critical for collaborative learning and reflection. This limitation can affect the depth and breadth of academic and practical discussions.

The sustainability of community engagement is also a major challenge. Ensuring that the relationships built during the course endure and continue to benefit communities requires specific strategies, such as long-term planning and active participation of community members in decisions and activities.

In terms of archiving project proposals, it is critical to establish an organised and accessible system to ensure that proposals are available to different cohorts of students. This facilitates continuity and allows new generations of students to build on previous work, fostering innovation and the continued development of community initiatives. Resources to create and maintain a useable archive are limited.

Power dynamics play an important role in project implementation. How power relationships are managed within teams and between students and communities can influence the effectiveness and ethics of participatory research.

Students face challenges in ensuring adherence to sound ethical principles. Practicing these ethics can be complicated by the dynamic and complex nature of community interactions and the research process, but it is critical to ensure respect and integrity in all stages of the research.

13

TRANSFORMING INSTITUTIONAL CULTURE

Mainstreaming Community-Based Participatory Research in Unibagué-Colombia

MÓNICA DEL PILAR ÁLVAREZ AND IRMA ALICIA FLORES-HINOJOS

Introduction

The University of Ibagué is located in the capital city of the department of Tolima in the Andean region of Colombia. The department of Tolima occupies an important place in national history due to its politics and its trajectory during the armed conflict. Tolima is one of the territories that experienced great violence due to constant clashes between insurgent groups. Consequently, this region nowadays is projected as the perfect location for the construction of peace and regional development (Navarro Barros and Uribe Sarmiento, 2019).

The University of Ibagué is a private higher education institution, founded in 1980 by a group of business and civic leaders of the Tolima region. The university provides a consolidated education for the region, as it has assumed as its main mission a commitment to regional development by generating social change that promotes inclusive and participatory strategies (Parra and Álvarez, 2020). The university recognises the historical linkages of Tolima, seeking to discover and learn collectively with other territories.

As a result of a process of reflection and dialogue with its entire community, the Institution presented a proposal in 2021 for the re-signification of its 'being' and 'acting' inspired by the *Necessary University* model. This model refers to a style of university organisation open to change; one that faces the new challenges of a globalised society and assumes leadership that is mobilised by knowledge. Although structurally unequal, this model aims to result in building a hopeful youth with a global vision, and active and critical perspectives. Sustainable human development is another major objective of this model, as it continuously reinterprets the meaning of its classic functions within global and regional perspectives (Orozco and Reyes Alvarado, 2021).

With the creation of the Necessary University mission at the University of Ibagué, the training of professionals with the ability to address complex problems in different areas of human activity, with a critical and constructive attitude and spirit of service, has become central. The mission aspires for professionals to have a growing commitment to the generation of new knowledge, as this significantly contributes to the improvement of quality of life and social equity (Tünnermann Bernheim, 2007). In this regard, one of the forces of change identified by the University of Ibagué in its re-signification process is the emergence of new ways of knowledge production from a transdisciplinary perspective which is in dialogue with different cultures of knowledge. This process, while creating new perspectives for the future, remains embedded in its history (Orozco and Reyes Alvarado, 2021).

Thus, the University of Ibagué recognises itself as an extended learning community in which students, professors and actors of the territories participate and commit themselves to the flourishing of collective capacities for social change, regional development and peacebuilding. The region, then, is not just a geographical coordinate where the institution is located, but a vital part of the identity of the university, the site for collaboration, dialogue, and construction of the public good with mutual care. With this in view, the Institutional Educational Project at the University of Ibagué assumes education as a process that transcends the individual and must necessarily dialogue with the concrete needs of society with a critical sense of service (Araujo, 2013).

Professors at the University of Ibagué are recognised as integral companions in a student's learning process. They lead the design of meaningful teaching–learning experiences and manage participatory research projects. Professors guide the research in ways that celebrate and stimulate different methods of knowledge production with diverse communities and groups. Thus, the research led by the professors at the University of Ibagué is relevant for creating a dialogue with local issues, is oriented to social transformation and leads to the expansion of possibilities for mobilisation and collective action.

As part of its comprehensive commitment to the region, in 2011, the University of Ibagué created the 'Peace and Region Semester'.* As a strategy, this course aims to provide students with an experience of citizenship training, through the creation of collective and contextual capacities within the territories. Each academic year, interdisciplinary teams of students from the faculties of engineering, humanities, economics, natural sciences, and law in their last semester of study spend four months in local organisations in municipalities in south-central Colombia.

---

*For more information on the Peace and Region Semester, please consult Chapter 12 (pp 232–255) in Lepore et al. (2024). The chapter is authored by Irma Flores, Luisa Fernanda González, Andrés Astaiza and Daniel Lopera. https://brill.com/display/book/9789004687769/BP000023.xml

In this period, they participate in projects that address regional issues, contribute to peacebuilding, and promote a dynamic of cooperative work between the university and the territories.

In this background, the University of Ibagué, in 2022, designed the training program 'Capacity Building for Community-Based Participatory Research in the Necessary University'. The program is offered in collaboration with the UNESCO Chair in Community-Based Research and Social Responsibility in Higher Education and the Colombia IAPaz Hub. The design draws on the learning and experiences of the MTP, as well as the CBPR/PAR course led by Hub Colombia. The following sections present the purpose, scope and methodology of this training program.

Purpose: The 'Flourishing' of Capabilities

The word 'flourishing' comes from the Latin word *florescere* and means to make a plant bloom or refers to a person or an idea that prospers and grows. In the perspective of the human development approach, capabilities refer to substantive opportunities, also real freedoms to lead the kind of life that people value; hence, capabilities relate to the ways of being and doing that people consider desirable for a dignified life (Sen, 1999). Although the original theoretical development of capabilities defines them from an individual perspective, the communitarian approach proposes a collective view of capabilities, so that they respond to being and doing that are achieved socially because of collective action (Ibrahim, 2006).

As a consequence, the blossoming of capabilities for CBPR is oriented both to the individual and the collective development of being and doing with a new sensitivity and understanding of the ways of producing and mobilising knowledge. Moreover, this is done by working with the community from authentically participatory and dialogical experiences, focused on the collective blossoming in the territories. Therefore, we speak of a training program and not a course, because it is recognised that the learning process of the CBPR approach is only the beginning of a path of reflection-action for participants to become ambassadors of this methodology in the role they occupy in the Necessary University. From this perspective, their role as ambassadors is to weave bridges between the functions of teaching, research and service, and recognise research as a critical and creative path with openness to the epistemological diversity of the territories and with ethical and social commitment.

Scope of the Program

The training program is aimed at professors, regional advisors, unit coordinators and community partners that are involved in achieving the mission of the university and have a direct link with the community. The training of these educational actors enables dialogue based on different experiences, the construction of common meanings regarding authentic participation, and the co-production of knowledge to influence territorial agendas. The program design is oriented for each mentor to appropriate the historical, conceptual and methodological elements of CBPR, framing their experiences and trajectories in a regional university committed to the flourishing of capabilities for wellbeing and peace building.

The program is based on three fundamental premises: (i) the problematisation of the regional context as a condition for the production of knowledge, and pedagogical and transdisciplinary action; (ii) the collaborative production of knowledge in the territories as a political instance for social transformation; and (iii) CBPR as a reference to strengthen the pedagogical model and local impact of the Peace and Region Semester, with the perspective of expanding the learning community in the region.

In the 2023 cohort, 21 mentors were trained, including nine full-time professors from the university and 12 regional advisors from the Peace and Region Semester. A total of 11 case studies were developed and will be compiled into a book that is expected to consolidate local reference resources for teaching and learning CBPR at the University of Ibagué. The case studies were developed in collaboration with diverse community partners, from aqueducts and environmental recuperators to women's associations and youth collectives who also joined the residencies (that are part of the program) to share their experiences of knowledge mobilisation.

A total of 23 mentors participated in the 2024 cohort; 20 of them are full-time professors and three are territorial allies of the Peace and Region Semester. The university considers it important to promote a new generation of researchers from local communities in each cohort. It is hoped this will allow these local communities to recognise and value their knowledge and life trajectories in their own historical and epistemological frameworks. It allows for the possibility of local communities participating in a fair and equal dialogue with academics who are trained in a new sensibility and research praxis. The 2024 cohort will also publish a book of the case studies and collective learning produced in the CBPR process.

Methodology of the Program

The training methodology of the program recognises that education as a social and political fact is not neutral, and that it embodies in its practice ideological interests and discourses that, by being in a territory with historical and cultural particularities, acquires its own identity (Brennan, 2008). In this way, the program recognises that pedagogy is transformative when it challenges the reproduction of dominant values and introduces new topics and terms of conversation that were previously on the margins or systematically produced as invisible within the social structure

(Star and Strauss, 1999). Based on this perspective, the teaching–learning of CBPR is presented as a transformative experience, with a methodological design that combines autonomous online learning with experiential learning through the development of a case study in alliance with a community partner. To organically link these two elements, reflection on the co-production of knowledge and the possibilities raised by the Necessary University are the main drivers of the process.

The teaching–learning combines autonomous online learning for 42 weeks provided through the institutional e-education platform. It also includes synchronous online sessions to deepen thematic knowledge and collective mentoring of case studies, which is conducted in parallel with the classes. Additionally, there are two on-site residencies (one at the beginning and one at the end of the program), each lasting one week, led by the facilitator team.

The first residency of the year takes place in the first month of the training and includes a visit to one of the case study* sites of a mentor from the previous cohort, with the purpose of allowing the participants to see the experience which they have to undertake during their learning period. For this purpose, a tool called *sentiobservation* guide has been designed. The mentors are invited to visit the field as an experience of discovery and encounter based on two moments. The first is an exercise to connect with the emotions, sensations and ideas that are awakened by the field

* For example, in the first residency of the 2024 cohort, the field trip took place in the village of La Chamba in the municipality of Guamo Tolima. There, Natalia Ramirez and Carlos Barrios, mentors of the 2023 cohort, together with the youth collective Guardianes de la Chamba, presented their case study in which they asked themselves: How can the community 'ArteSanar' La Chamba through new artistic manifestations be led by young people? In this context, the term 'ArteSanar' was coined by the community to symbolise the reconstruction and strengthening of the social fabric through art.

visit and the dialogue with community partners through a body mapping exercise linked to the senses. Second, the guide suggests a series of questions for conversation and reflection that lead mentors to inquire about the way trusting relationships have been built and maintained and the aspects that have been decisive in the co-production of knowledge.

The design of the on-site residencies recognises CBPR as a collective and creative construction inspired by respect, diversity, mutual support, unity, and cooperation in all its dimensions. Thus, the learning activities in the residencies include spaces for the dialogue of knowledge, the exchange of information among mentors regarding the progress of their case studies, and the recognition of knowledge production experiences led by communities in the region. The vital character of research becomes evident as a dynamic process that transforms over time, and as an organic fabric created by several hands, one that is configured as a collective expression of a way of being, doing, and understanding in the specific context of this territory.

Researching with the community and cultivating relationships of collaboration and trust among community researchers implies a conscious effort to create research linked with the territory and nature, as well as the ability to express this alliance through the care of life, the care of ties, the care of the fabric, and care of the territory. Therefore, residencies have been included in the training process as acts of joy and enjoyment, for the possibility of meeting, of reconciling that knowledge and research is not as something that happens behind a desk in the coldness of an identity that calls itself academic, but one that is born and recreated in the warmth of the world of life.

The contents of the training sessions are organised in 21 units, of which ten are oriented to topics directly related to the epistemological and methodological foundations of CBPR; three to individual reflection and self-evaluation on the learning process and the development of the case study; four to the construction of proposals to integrate CBPR in the curricular design of the university and the definition of strategies for integrating the principles of this approach in teaching and extension; and four units dedicated entirely to collective mentoring around the case studies. Each unit lasts two weeks and includes readings, discussion forums, orientations in the case study and synchronous meetings for collective mentoring.

It is important to mention that the advancement of the case studies occurs in parallel with the learning in the thematic units in such a way that meaningful learning is privileged through experiential learning. The literature shows that experiential learning for adults is meaningful to the extent that it stimulates the ability to put into context what is learned through their own experience, which allows them to deepen concepts and questions that would hardly emerge in an eminently theoretical process where only cognitive processes are involved (Sisselman-Borgia and Torino, 2017). In the same sense, the development of the case study allows mentors to search for their identity as community researchers, that is, the discovery of who they are as facilitators and co-researchers participating in a collaborative experience of knowledge production.

Another important aspect of the training is for mentors to reflect on strategies that would allow them to create opportunities and conditions for other actors in the wider community to learn about the CBPR approach as an essential part of the flourishing of collective capacities. Thus, they should explore creative ways to inspire students, other teachers and actors in the region to recognise themselves as agents in processes of co-production of socially engaged knowledge that reclaims diverse cultures.

Upon completion of the training, each mentor needs to take up their strategies and build his or her action plan as an ambassador of CBPR in the Necessary University. This implies a conscious effort to elaborate and re-elaborate the current ways of thinking and make sense of their understanding of research and the differences that exist between researching with others and researching for others (Dirkx, 2012). It is not a matter of renouncing the interests or forms of research that were already known, but of broadening the view of the different ways in which knowledge manifests itself, and the diversity of paths that can be followed to produce research from collaborative experiences that subvert, in many ways, the individualism and selfishness that characterises today's society.

The training program 'Capacity Building for Community-Based Participatory Research in the Necessary University' has made its place in the University of Ibagué and in the region. It has promoted research as part of its social responsibility, configured to lifelong learning, linked to the identity, worldview and shared interests of the region. Through this training program, the Necessary University has materialised as open to the new social demands of the region, is related to greater inclusion and permanence in discussions in the public sphere and has enriched the field of experiences and knowledge for dialogue, citizen advocacy and new modes of production and social use of knowledge that give rise to mobilisation and participation of different actors. This CBPR training is building a collective, transformative leadership of the communities and the university to achieve territorial public agendas.

Key Lessons

Community-based participatory research teaching and learning provides unique opportunities to model alliances and collaborative processes, as well as to incorporate non-traditional learning strategies for the development of skills and attitudes that awaken greater commitment, motivation and reflection of the teaching content in higher education institutions. In addition, by promoting collective learning among academics and community actors, it enables an explicit debate on the power dynamics that exist between universities and communities, which in other contexts would only be addressed superficially. The following paragraphs present some reflections, based on the experience of the University of Ibagué's training program, that may be useful when designing teaching–learning experiences on CBPR.

One of the first aspects to consider is that the process should provide sufficient time for critical discussion that transforms the two views that often prevail in the academy about the community. The first view sees the community from a romantic perspective in which it is considered a reality of unalterable perfection and harmony, endowed with a certain passivity and attitude of expectation towards the university. The second view associates the community with the marginal and vulnerable, discarding any relationship of proximity and ignoring the diverse capacities and powers immersed in it.

Therefore, before addressing the critical principles of CBPR, it is necessary that the training include content aimed at broadening and problematising the conceptions of the community and recognising the importance of a participatory understanding of the context and the experience of the actors who inhabit it, since each community is also defined in terms of its context and history (Rosenthal et al., 2009). Those who are part of the training should understand the community as a fabric of trusting and caring relationships around referents of meaning and belonging that facilitate the construction of agreements and collective decision making, for the community is not exempt from tensions or imbalances in power relations (Stoddart, 2007).

A broad view of the community makes possible an essential shift in the way of critically reading the context as part of the process of co-production of knowledge. Often, academics strive to understand the community and its territory based on its needs and problems, biasing the ways in which relationships are established. Reading communities from the recognition of their capacities, strengths, interests and opportunities, is a learning process that should also be explicitly promoted in CBPR training processes. Along the same lines, the importance of identifying actions and strategies that have been previously devised and explored by the community to transform its context should be emphasised.

It is common in academia to assume that research is a path oriented to the repetition of models and theories, whose rigor is subject to the fact that the social world fits into a category or the thinking of a researcher from the academy. For this reason, an aspect that is essential within CBPR training is to lead participants to recognise research as a creative act with a life of its own. It calls for collaborative work and the discovery of collective power, which, in turn, invites the possibilities of dreaming by the community and the recovery of the power of knowing and transforming.

This implies providing sufficient space for reflection so that participants can shed the idea of research as an aseptic experience where emotions have no place. From the development of a case study, or the recognition of others' experiences, participants must achieve an openness to CBPR as an experience that involves all senses and emotions, and where rigor and validity are configured in terms of transparency, the richness of dialogue, and the methodological depth with which participation emerges. This must be accompanied by an autonomous process of theoretical and conceptual revision that allows understanding of the historical and epistemological roots of the approach, as well as its contributions to open science and the democratisation of knowledge.

It is useful to promote scenarios to collectively identify challenges that may be common to those who participate in the training, encouraging the listening of reflections and good practices as an iterative process. In other words, the dialogue of knowledge about the challenges and possible alternatives for action is not something that occurs at a specific moment in the process but is a space that remains open throughout the training.

One of the most common challenges identified in the training for the 2023 cohort related to building and maintaining relationships with community partners. Building trusting relationships that involve transparency, commitment and the ability to recognise the expertise that all co-investigators, both academic and community, can bring to the case study takes time and requires willingness and perseverance. Faced with this common challenge, spaces for exchange were generated in which the mentors themselves raised recommendations and new questions to be considered in a long-term agenda for CBPR to expand its roots in the Necessary University.

Along with a deep understanding of the community context, extending CBPR's roots in the university is only possible if the teaching of CBPR adapts and dialogues with the context of institutional challenges and with the relationships that have already been woven with the communities. Thus, the training must provide a meaningful experience in which issues about knowledge production that were not previously evident are highlighted and prepare academics to collaborate with others in this process. Hence, it is essential to incorporate learning activities that stimulate their skills for communication, collaboration, empathy and agreement building.

Committing to CBPR training represents great challenges, especially because it requires a commitment to action and collective learning in diverse contexts where cooperation is not always easy. It is necessary to remain hopeful, remembering that promoting values such as collaboration, trust and solidarity in the co-production of knowledge is revolutionary when we inhabit a society that seems to prefer individualism, competition and personal gain. Moving forward with this revolution is at once our duty, commitment, passion and inspiration.

14

RECONNECTING HIGHER EDUCATION WITH SOCIETY

The Experience of the University Grants Commission in Building Community-Based Participatory Research Capacity in India

DIKSHA RAJPUT AND ANSHUMAN KAROL

The purpose of the education system is to develop a good human being capable of rational thought and action, possessing compassion and empathy, courage and resilience, scientific temper and creative imagination, with sound ethical moorings and values. It aims at producing engaged, productive, and contributing citizens for building an equitable, inclusive, and plural society as envisaged by our Constitution.

– India's National Education Policy 2020, p. 5

Historical Background

The educational landscape in India has been shaped by numerous historical events, policies and reforms. Post-independence, India sought to establish a robust higher education system that could cater to its diverse and vast population. The Radhakrishnan Commission (1948–49) and the Kothari Commission (1964–66) laid the groundwork for educational reforms aimed at improving the quality and accessibility of education in India. The National Policy on Education (NPE) 1968 and the subsequent NPE 1986 were significant milestones in this journey, emphasising the importance of inclusivity, access and quality in education.

Despite these efforts, the Indian education system continued to face challenges, including disparities in access and quality, relevance, and a lack of emphasis on critical thinking and practical skills. The need for a comprehensive overhaul became increasingly evident in the 21st century, as India sought to position itself as a global leader in innovation and economic development.

The National Education Policy (NEP) 2020 emerged as a response to these challenges. It represents a paradigm shift in the Indian education system, focusing on holistic, flexible, multidisciplinary education suited to the needs of the 21st century, aimed at bringing out the unique capabilities of each student. The policy envisions an education system rooted in Indian ethos that contributes directly to transforming India into an equitable and vibrant knowledge society by providing high-quality education to all.

National Education Policy and Unnat Bharat Abhiyan

The NEP 2020 is guided by several normative principles aimed at creating a more equitable, inclusive, and sustainable future for India. Central to these principles is the idea of holistic and multidisciplinary education, which seeks to break down the silos of specialised education and foster a broader understanding and skill set among students. This approach is designed to cultivate critical thinking, creativity and problem-solving abilities, preparing students to tackle the complex challenges of the modern world.

Inclusivity is another cornerstone of the NEP. The policy emphasises the importance of providing equitable access to education for all sections of society, particularly the historically marginalised and disadvantaged groups. This includes measures such as the establishment of special education zones, scholarships and support systems to ensure that every student can receive a quality education, irrespective of their socio-economic background.

Sustainability is also a key focus of the NEP. The policy highlights the importance of integrating environmental education into the curriculum to foster a sense of responsibility and stewardship towards the planet among students. This is in line with the global Sustainable Development Goals (SDGs) and India's commitment to environmental sustainability.

Complementing the NEP, the Unnat Bharat Abhiyan (UBA) aims to bring transformational change in rural development processes by leveraging knowledge institutions to help build the architecture of an inclusive India. Launched in 2014, UBA 1.0 envisioned transforming rural India by promoting eco-friendly technologies, decentralisation and the utilisation of local resources, reflecting Mahatma Gandhi's vision of self-sufficient villages. The program was designed to promote knowledge sharing, participatory approaches and resource convergence to address challenges like inequality, climate change, and urban migration. Suitable rural clusters were selected for eco-friendly and sustainable development, by conducting village assessments, reorienting academic curricula to rural needs and implementing science and technology interventions. UBA operates through a structured coordination system involving the Ministry of Education, Indian Institute of Technology (IIT) Delhi (as the National Coordinating Institute), and regional and participating institutions.

By fostering a closer relationship between educational institutions and rural communities, UBA aims to ensure that the benefits of academic knowledge and research are not confined within the walls of institutions but are extended to address the real-world challenges faced by rural populations. The UBA emphasises collaboration among educational institutions, implementation agencies and grassroots stakeholders. This collaboration is intended to drive sustainable development, enhance rural livelihoods and contribute to the overall socio-economic development of the country. NEP's mission aligns with UBA's emphasis on community engagement and social responsibility.

Guidelines on Fostering Social Responsibility and Community Engagement in Higher Education Institutions

The University Grants Commission (UGC) of India has played a pivotal role in shaping the higher education landscape in the country. UGC's Quality Mandate initiative was launched in 2018, with the all-encompassing priority to improve teaching–learning and innovative skills, critical thinking, inclusiveness, employability, learning outcomes curriculum framework, gender sensitisation, social connect, sustainable development competitiveness, and skill development of students in the tertiary education system in India. Linking the Quality Mandate's focus on improving societal linkages of higher education institutions (HEIs) and enabling students to become socially productivity, UGC set up a Subject Expert Group (SEG) under UBA. The SEG prepared and submitted a report on 'Fostering Social Responsibility and Community Engagement in Higher Education Institutions in India'* in January 2020. The report emphasised the importance of socially relevant courses that will make all students understand India's rural society, the government's rural development schemes, and contribute to the betterment of society and policies. The UGC organised a two-day National Workshop (on 21st and 22nd January 2020

---

*University Grants Commission, *Fostering Social Responsibility & Community Engagement in Higher Educational Institutions in India*, January 2020. https://www.ugc.gov.in/e-book/uba/mobile/index.html

in New Delhi), bringing together various stakeholders (university faculty from across the country, nodal officers under the UBA, representatives from the SEG and the UGC) to discuss the relevance of inculcating the idea of social responsibility in the youth and how to link students with society through socially productive activities during their period of higher education study.

The launch of the NEP 2020 in July 2020 and the post COVID-19 scenario demanded that community engagement be mainstreamed in all teaching–learning, research and service activities of HEIs. In December 2021, UGC framed the 'Guidelines on Fostering Social Responsibility and Community Engagement in Higher Educational Institutions in India 2.0'.* These guidelines included key recommendations of NEP 2020, and called for the capacity building of faculty members as Master Trainers through Regional Centres, and development, and introduction of two-credit courses on CBPR in universities as a fundamental component of academic programs. The guidelines also emphasise the importance of building sustainable partnerships between HEIs and local communities. These partnerships are intended to be mutually beneficial, with communities gaining access to academic resources and expertise, and institutions gaining insights and knowledge from the community that can enhance their research and educational programs.

By promoting CBPR, the UGC aims to bridge the gap between academia and society. HEIs are encouraged to develop curricula that include community engagement and engage actively with local communities, leveraging their academic and research capabilities to address local challenges. This not only enriches the educational experience of students but also instills in them a sense of civic duty and social responsibility. Further, it ensures that the research conducted within HEIs has a tangible impact on

---

*Vide letter of the Secretary, UGC to all vice-chancellors dated December 23, 2021

society, particularly in addressing the needs of underprivileged and marginalised communities.

The principles outlined in the NEP 2020, initiatives like the UBA, and the UGC's guidelines provide the foundation for energising an education system that is socially responsible and provides solutions to emerging challenges, while staying rooted in the values of equity, inclusivity and sustainability.

Investing in Capacity Building for Implementation of the UGC Guidelines: The Master Trainers Training Program

The NEP 2020 endorsed the recommendations in the UGC Guidelines for Fostering Social Responsibility and Community Engagement in HEIs in India. The NEP states that local knowledge and wisdom of our rural and tribal communities must be valued in undertaking research, and involving local communities in partnership with students and researchers to find innovative local solutions and adaptation of appropriate technology to solve the challenges faced by them.

A well-designed CBPR course that provides opportunities to students for community engagement is only possible if teachers and professors at HEIs are equipped to develop, teach, implement and integrate into various disciplines and curricula the two-credit course on CBPR as outlined in the UGC guidelines.

The UGC proposed that Master Trainers be trained in CBPR methodology, with a three-fold objective:

a) To understand the framework of UGC/UBA guidelines on Fostering Social Responsibility and Community Engagement.
b) To understand the principles and methodology of CBPR underlying field-based learning.
c) To strengthen competencies in use of various methods of CBPR through field practice.

Seven Regional Centres that would act as the extended arms of the UGC in developing a larger outreach of the Master Training program were identified. These Centres are: (i) the Dayalbagh Educational Institute in Agra, Uttar Pradesh; (ii) Kurukshetra University in Kurukshetra, Haryana; (iii) National Law University in Bhopal, Madhya Pradesh; (iv) Gandhigram Rural Institute in Dindigul, Tamil Nadu; (v) Central University of Odisha in Koraput, Odisha; (vi) Tezpur University in Tezpur, Assam; and (vii) Rashtrasant Tukdoji Maharaj University in Nagpur, Maharashtra. Further, Subject Expert Groups (SEG) were also formed to work on bringing curricular reforms at the undergraduate and postgraduate levels to integrate the concept of social responsibility and community engagement into the curriculum rather than placing it as a standalone activity.

Each batch of selected Master Trainers would undergo residential training at the Regional Centres before they started developing and teaching the CBPR course.* The training would be led by a team of UGC appointed experts in CBPR.†

In 2022, UGC provided financial assistance to the Regional Centres for conducting capacity building programs in CBPR for faculty in India's HEIs.

---

*The two-credit course on Community Engagement and Social Responsibility is coordinated by Dayalbagh Educational Institute, Agra, on the SWAYAM Portal of the Ministry of Education, Government of India. This is a multidisciplinary elective course of 10 weeks duration for undergraduate and postgraduate students. The course is divided into 10 modules (online class/lecture of 1 hour duration and 3 hours of field work for each module). (https://onlinecourses.swayam2.ac.in/ugc23_ge04/preview)

† Dr Rajesh Tandon, Founder-President, PRIA and UNESCO Co-Chair in Community Based Research and Social Responsibility in Higher Education was a Member of the UGC Expert Group for preparing the Guidelines. He spearheaded the Master Trainers Training Program across the seven Regional Centres during 2022.

Table 14.1 Structure of UGC Master Trainers Training Program

Day	Session I	Session II	Session III	Session IV	Session V
Day 1	Inaugural Session	Introductory Session with Master Trainers	Understanding the Principles of CBPR and UGC's Two-Credit Course Content and Structure	Understanding Local Realities (Transect Walk and Social Mapping)	Field Visits
Day 2	Recap and Presentations and Debriefing of Field Visit and Community Engagement	Field Visit – Institutional Mapping	Debriefing of Community Engagement		
Day 3	Recap and Presentations and Debriefing of the Field Visit	Understanding Language and Culture as a form of Knowledge	Learning CBPR Method – Venn Diagram and Experiential Learning	Recommendations on Assessment and Next Steps	Valedictory Session

Structure and Pedagogy of Master Trainers Training Program

Batches of university teachers were identified to participate in the 'Master Trainers Training Program on Capacity Building of Faculty for Community-Based Participatory Research'.

The program was designed as an intensive three-day residential training for each batch of 30–40 Master Trainers. The trainings were conducted in 2022.

This structure ensures a comprehensive approach to building capacities of faculty in CBPR, offering both foundational knowledge in theoretical sessions followed by practical experience. Theoretical sessions were focused on understanding CBPR principles, course content, and integrating knowledge forms, while practical sessions involved field visits to facilitate the participants' learning of CBPR methods like transect walks, social mapping, and institutional mapping. The participants were also provided with reading materials on CBPR methodologies, the UGC Guidelines on Fostering Social Responsibility and Community Engagement in HEIs, and a manual on how to replicate the training in their respective institutions.

The pedagogy used to deliver the training was a unique participatory training methodology, pioneered by PRIA as an alternative approach to traditional training. As part of this methodology, learners actively participate in the learning process, contributing their needs, questions, reflections, analyses and strategies.

The participatory training methodology ensures that all aspects of learning, from theoretical understanding to practical application, is part of the participant's learning experience. This approach integrates various elements of education, from cognitive and theoretical understanding to emotional, social and practical development. The goal is to ensure that participants not only grasp the concepts intellectually but also connect emotionally and socially with the communities they will engage with. Diverse methods and interactive sessions like group discussions, field visits and debriefing sessions are used to allow participants to experience real-world scenarios and understand the social dynamics at play in community engagement, thus nurturing both their intellectual and empathetic capacities.

The following criteria were used to create a conducive learning environment for the participants. These were acknowledged by the participants in the feedback received after the training.

Structured, yet flexible training design – The meticulous planning for each session created an atmosphere highly conducive to learning. A structured yet flexible approach allows participants to engage deeply with the material, fostering a rich educational experience. For example, during all the sessions, participants were encouraged to share their own field experiences and challenges. This open discussion not only enriched the learning environment but also allowed participants to learn from each other's practical insights and link them with theoretical underpinnings, thereby deepening their understanding of the subject matter.

Learning by doing – The 'learning by doing' methodology significantly enhanced the workshop's effectiveness. Participants were taken to local communities to practise and test what they had learned in the theoretical sessions. This hands-on approach enabled them to directly apply theoretical knowledge, thereby reinforcing their understanding and retention of the concepts presented. During the field visits, they conducted focus group discussions, transect walks, developed resource maps of the communities, and tried to develop their understanding not just of the issues, but also of the context in which the communities lived, giving the faculty an appreciation and respect for the lived experiences of communities. The opportunity to undertake what they had learnt in the classroom to real-world applications and then critically analyse their experiences enriched the learning process, providing them with firsthand ways in which they could teach students.

The initiative to involve teachers in community activities was found to be useful. When involved in actual community activities, they shift from being merely 'teachers' to active practitioners. The experiential involvement allows them to apply their newly acquired knowledge in real-world contexts, fostering deeper understanding and reflection, and nurtures a sense of social responsibility.

Individual and group activities – Engaging in both individual and group activities encouraged personal accountability and teamwork, promoting a deeper comprehension through collaboration and peer learning.

Comprehensive application strategies are used to ensure that participants can apply what they have learned in a practical, effective, and well-rounded manner. These strategies cover a range of applications, from developing research questions that are community-centered to using various data collection methods that respect and incorporate indigenous knowledge. In the Master Trainers Training Program, this was evident through activities like community mapping exercises, where participants learned how to visually represent community assets, challenges and relationships. While working with communities, it is important to ensure that the chosen research methods are not only scientifically rigorous but also culturally sensitive and respectful.

Engaging with communities – Opportunities to engage with communities enhances the learning experience and connection to the community.

During the training phase, the faculty from academic institutions were given the opportunity to interact and engage with local and grassroots civil society organisations from the regions where the trainings were scheduled. This allowed them to build connections with the organisations, which subsequently will support their community engagement efforts undertaken with students. Civil society organisations play a critical role in maintaining linkages with the community. The established rapport between a local organisation and communities facilitates smoother and more effective fieldwork for students, and the organisation's work ensures continuity of the initiatives undertaken by the students as part of their community-engaged projects. Moreover, civil society organisations provide valuable insights and contextual knowledge, enhancing the teachers' ability to guide students. Before students embark on engaging with communities, orientation sessions in collaboration with civil society organisations prepares them for the practical aspects of their project and research efforts. This preparation includes understanding the local context, cultural nuances and specific challenges in the community. Such preparation will help students navigate the complexities of fieldwork, conduct their research with a better contextual analysis, and ensure that their community engagement is respectful of local dynamics – ultimately making such engagement more impactful and beneficial for the students and the community.

The training program also made teachers aware that students' engagement with the community must be sustained and remain non-extractive. This can be ensured through continued collaboration between academic institutions and the civil society organisations with which they are connected. Engagement must include follow-up visits, ongoing research partnerships, and continuous support for community initiatives from the HEI. Additionally, knowledge sharing can be facilitated through regular workshops, joint publications and longer-term collaborative projects that address community needs.

Achievements and Challenges

The analysis of feedback from participating institutions – private, autonomous, deemed and state universities – reflects the advancements the UGC has made and the challenges it continues to face in promoting social responsibility and community engagement of HEIs in India.

Post the training, many institutions have actively embraced the UGC's guidelines, with the Master Trainers conducting orientation and training sessions for other faculty members from various departments such as public health, commerce, management, engineering, computer science, arts, and sciences, covering both undergraduate and postgraduate levels. The growing momentum behind these programs, with many institutions planning additional training and implementation in the coming years, reflects the strong foundation the UGC has built for the long-term success of community engagement and CBPR in Indian higher education.

Several institutions have already implemented the two-credit course on community engagement as per the UGC guidelines. A few institutions have offered this course on campus and through online platforms like SWAYAM, further expanding reach and accessibility. Student enrolment in the Community Engagement and Social Responsibility MOOC on the SWAYAM platform has increased from 7219 in the January 2023 semester to 12,004 in the July 2024 semester.

The feedback also sheds light on the growing awareness among faculty members regarding the importance of community engagement. HEIs are increasingly recognising the need to integrate community enagement and social responsibility into their core curricula, aligning with the UGC's broader goal of preparing students not only for professional success but also as meaningful contributors in society. Yet, this awareness is still limited, given the vast landscape of HEIs in India.

The feedback also highlights several challenges that need to be addressed to enhance the effectiveness of CBPR in HEIs. Time constraints and financial limitations are the most commonly cited barriers in implementing community engagement activities. HEIs are working to overcome constraints by planning future training sessions and leveraging internal resources. To overcome these challenges, HEIs should seek to allocate dedicated time and resources for CBPR projects and explore funding opportunities from government agencies, non-governmental organisations and private sector partners.

UGC continues to refine its guidelines by developing detailed instructions, providing technical support and facilitating knowledge exchange among institutions.

Ways Forward

The commitment to refining strategies, improving resource mobilisation and enhancing curriculum integration will ensure that the UGC's efforts will continue producing tangible benefits for both educational institutions and society. Future plans are in place for further training sessions in 2024–25, showcasing UGC's sustained commitment to the Master Trainers Training Program.

In the guidelines of the Malaviya Mission Teacher Training Programme (MMTTP) launched in February 2024, CBPR has been included as a theme to be covered in the one-week Short Term Programme/Faculty Development Programme to be conducted by UGC's Malaviya Mission Teacher Training Centers.

The UGC Regulations on Minimum Qualification for Appointment of Teachers and Other Academic Staff in Universities and Colleges and Measures for the Maintenance of Standards in Higher Education 2018, which are in the process of being amended, will count notable contributions by faculty members in community engagement and service, per NEP 2020 recommendations for Career Advancement Scheme (CAS) in HEIs.

The National Assessment and Accreditation Council's (NAAC) binary accreditation, which is underway, also proposes to include community engagement by HEIs as one of the metrics under UBA.

Finally, it is important to continuously evaluate and reflect on the impact of CBPR initiatives. HEIs should implement robust monitoring and evaluation mechanisms to assess the outcomes of community engagement activities and identify areas for improvement. By systematically documenting and sharing best practices, institutions can learn from each other's experiences and collectively advance the field of CBPR.

HEIs should strive to make community engagement an integral part of their academic mission, rather than a peripheral activity. This can be achieved by embedding CBPR into the core curriculum, research agendas and institutional policies. It is essential to foster a culture of collaboration and mutual respect between academic institutions and communities. This requires building long-term partnerships based on trust and shared goals.

The UGC guidelines have been instrumental in promoting the use of CBPR for community engagement and fostering social responsibility in HEIs. By building capacities in CBPR, the UGC has facilitated a more inclusive form of knowledge production that values the lived experiences of communities, making meaningful contributions to the sustainable development of India. Ongoing dialogue between the UGC and HEIs to address logistical and resource-related challenges in embedding CBPR in the teaching and research functions will ensure that all institutions, regardless of size or funding, can participate in this important national initiative.

15

CONCLUSION

Challenges and Future Opportunities in Teaching Community-Based Participatory Research

BUDD HALL AND RAJESH TANDON

Decolonizing knowledge calls for greater recognition of the validity and applicability of diverse sources of knowledge to the exigencies of the present and future. It requires a shift away from seeing indigenous epistemologies as objects to be studied rather than viable approaches to understanding and knowing the world.

– *Reimagining our Futures Together: A New Social Contract for Education*, p. 146

Knowledge is power; knowledge is also a source of power; and, knowledge is an instrument of power and control over others. When one set of knowledge is projected as superior to others, then superior knowledge-holders 'colonise', control, devalue and systematically undermine the knowledge of other communities and societies.

The starting point for such 'colonisation of knowledge' was in Europe with the advent of the voyages of exploration and trade that were undertaken from the Iberian Peninsula. A particular driving force for these endeavours was the peculiar but potent idea of there being one truth. It is this idea that then drives the wars of expansion, colonisation and enslavement in the Americas, Africa, and Asia. Each of these conflicts was accompanied side by side with the destruction and marginalisation of knowledge systems of the cultures which became the victims of the period of colonial expansion. This war on knowledge is referred to as 'epistemicide', ensuring the spread of a particular type of discourse and the perpetuation of a particular type of power relations between the rulers and those they rule (Hall, 2016).

Colonial invasion always destroyed knowledge and its modes of dissemination of local communities. Inca codicils, or Indigenous kingdoms and their spiritual sites of learning or Buddhist monasteries…every invader used this 'weapon' to dehumanise the raided and paint them as inferior in knowledge and capacity. Burning of women as witches in medieval Europe is another manifestation of suppressing women's knowledge and wisdom; similar acts continue in many parts of the world even today. Similar forces continue till date where the 'expert' knowledge of 'high priests' of academia is systematically used to undermine knowledge of tribals, lower castes, women, minorities, people with disability, etc.

Forces perpetuating 'epistemicide' are continuously challenged through alternative ideas and counter-hegemonic coalitions. Contemporary recognition of multiple epistemologies and ecologies of knowledges provides new opportunities to re-balance the academic with the community, bridging knowledge cultures (Lepore et al., 2024). It can be encapsulated by the idea of 'epistemic justice', or simply as 'knowledge democracy'.

What do we mean by knowledge democracy? It refers to an interrelationship of phenomena. First, it calls for recognition of ecologies of knowledge and cognitive justice such as organic, spiritual, and land-based systems, frameworks arising from our social movements, and the knowledge of the marginalised or excluded everywhere. Second, it affirms that knowledge is both created and represented in multiple forms including text, image, numbers, story, music, drama, poetry, ceremony, meditation, and more. Third, and fundamental to our thinking about knowledge democracy, is understanding that knowledge is a powerful tool for acting in social movements and elsewhere to deepen democracy and to struggle for a fairer and healthier world. We think of this as knowledge activism. And finally, knowledge democracy is about a balance between providing open access for the sharing of knowledge so that everyone who needs knowledge has access to it, balanced with the protection of knowledge by groups such as Indigenous Peoples to own and control their own knowledge. It is also about intentionally linking values of justice, fairness, and action to the process of creating and using knowledge. The transformative potential of knowledge production and dissemination through community-based participatory research (CBPR) is at the heart of understanding and deepening a knowledge democracy.

Building Decolonised and Values-Based Capacities in Community-Based Participatory Research: Key Lessons

As we set out in the Introduction to this book, it has not been our intention to offer additional rationales for making use of CBPR for knowledge creation, validation, sharing, and action. This case has been made and accepted widely. Neither have we intended to create a methodological text on how to do CBPR. We remain of the opinion that the way one goes about putting CBPR into practice needs to be reinvented for every context. What we have tried to do, based on our years of experience in training K4C mentors, is to provide insights into how to facilitate the learning of CBPR. We have learned that teaching the values, the theories and the practices of CBPR is challenging. Many of us are trained as discipline or subject matter specialists. We know the details of knowledge of water, population health, civil engineering, sociology, Indigenous studies, and much more. But we may not have had an opportunity to think about the best way to teach an interdisciplinary, values-based, place-based, linguistically, and culturally based approach to the knowledge of lived experience, particularly from and amongst those whose knowledge lies outside mainstream academic knowledge. In this regard, the chapters offered in this book by various members of the K4C consortium, based on their efforts to date, provide some key lessons about teaching and learning CBPR.

I. Lessons for teaching community-based participatory research

- **Remain connected to the five pedagogical principles of the MTP.** These are (i) attention to ethics, (ii) understanding knowledge is power, and power in knowledge work, (iii) use of multiple modes of inquiry, (iv) learn by doing, and (v) paying attention to the skills of facilitating and listening in research. Walter Lepore and Wafa Singh (Chapter 2) describe the rationale behind these pedagogical principles.
- **Use knowledge creation to contribute to countering power imbalances.** It is important to know what kinds of power exist, where that power is exercised, and in what form the power exists. John Gaventa's powercube (in Chapter 3) is a salient way of understanding the different *forms* (visible, invisible, and hidden forms), *levels* (global, national, local, and household levels), and *spaces* (closed, invited, and claimed spaces). Analysing all these dimensions of power in the context in which the learning and research are occurring is critical to the teaching of CBPR.
- **Ethics in CBPR goes beyond the narrow approach.** Institutional ethics review boards in universities, hospitals,

schools, and research organisations are a common and often used 'symbol' of ethical research. Our teaching of ethics in CBPR involves mutual respect, equity/inclusion, democratic participation, active learning, collective action and personal integrity. Sarah Banks' chapter (Chapter 4) shows the importance of using several approaches, such as theatre, thought showers, dilemma cafes, and other arts-based approaches, through which this broad based understanding of ethics can be learnt.

- **Arts-based methods of knowledge gathering extend the power of research.** Over the years of our MTP, arts-based research and knowledge sharing methods have been amongst the most popular part of our curriculum. Arts-based methods allow for the bringing together of cognitive and affective knowledge, creating a means of understanding and sharing deep and complex ideas in a more accessible way. Such methods extend the power of research by working beyond the limitations of positivistic and academic knowledge culture practices. Darlene Clover (in Chapter 5) demonstrated and practised these methods in and beyond K4C, as her chapter explains in depth.
- **Feminist perspectives are important to create empowering learning spaces.** Women's knowledge is often subjugated in economic, political and academic contexts. Adopting a feminist approach to learning CBPR attends to the learning needs of all women. Increasingly, it is also a means of making higher education safe for all genders. Nandita Bhatt's and Tariqa Tandon's experience of working with universities in India and the Commonwealth describes (in Chapter 6) the practice of feminist pedagogy in CBPR training, while also emphasizing the need for 'safe spaces' as sites of respectful learning.
- **CBPR can be learnt effectively through digital-only modes.** Digital learning platforms have proliferated over the past decade and took on special significance during the Covid-19

pandemic. Etmanski et al. have shared some very effective digital learning tools that they have developed (Chapter 7). For international and global learning communities, use of these tools on digital learning platforms is perhaps the only way to provide cost effective opportunities for teaching and learning CBPR.

II. Practices to help institutionalise community-based participatory research

While training in CBPR has been going on for nearly four decades (and PRIA has been a prime global centre for the same), need for institutionalising such learning opportunities has been critical, and not so well-developed. The K4C model of institutionalisation has many innovative features that can be taken forward.

- **Build relationships of trust with communities**. The example of incorporating Indigenous pedagogy (inclusion of Elders, sharing stories, participating in ceremony) in learning CBPR speaks of relational accountability, respect, reciprocity and the honouring of local Indigenous protocols. Protocols are the ways in which Indigenous communities build relationships and trust within their communities and with non-Indigenous people. Institutional mechanisms for such partnerships have been demonstrated in the very model of K4C where each Hub is a partnership between an academic and a practitioner organisation, as illustrated by the Hub at the University of Victoria (Chapter 8).
- **Embed principles of CBPR in community engagement mandates.** In many academic institutions and teaching programs, community engagement has been mandated over the past decade. It is important to embed CBPR principles for respectful mutual learning in those learning/teaching programs of community engagement. Chapters 9 and 10 describe such

innovative practices in their institutions from Africa and Latin America, as they became trained mentors in K4C Hubs. Community engagement movement in academia needs to be careful not to make it one-way teaching shop for communities.

- **Incorporate principles of CBPR in service learning.** Reciprocity, mutual benefit and a focus on equity and social justice in the service and research functions of higher educational institutions create institutions that are holistic. CBPR as a central building block in the service learning (Chapter 11) and community leadership (Chapter 12) learning experiences of students bridges the divide between classroom learning and application of such learning to real life challenges.
- **Adopt a university-wide framework of teaching and research based on CBPR**. Engagement and knowledge democracy are at the heart of the entire university if it wants to foster social responsibility. The University of Ibagué in Colombia calls its vision 'The Necessary University'. To achieve this vision, a structured capacity building program has been put in place, as described in Chapter 13. It is the formal commitment of university leadership that creates a university-wide institutional framework for learning, practising and teaching CBPR by all departments, disciplines and programs.
- **Integrate community engagement and social responsibility in national policy.** The National Education Policy (NEP) in India has committed itself to a vision of engaged learning and research by students and teachers. The University Grants Commission's (UGC) Framework on Fostering Social Responsibility and Community Engagement has created the backbone for furthering this vision through new opportunities to build capacities in CBPR, both for teachers and students. The UGC Master Trainers Training Program is building CBPR capacities in public universities. Such 'flourishing of capacities'

is a combination of on-line teaching, face-to-face reflections, and field work. This model has enormous potential for nation-wide impacts through teaching and learning CBPR.

Looking Forward

This book with contributions from many members of our K4C Consortium is the first time that we have undertaken a global reflection on how best to create learning opportunities for the next generation of community-based participatory researchers. This reflection could not have happened outside of the creation of the K4C global consortium itself. The K4C Consortium is characterised by being decentralised, values-based, inter- or trans-disciplinary, place-based, decolonial, and celebratory of Indigenous knowledge, the epistemic privilege of lived experience of the excluded, and open to the use of creativity and arts to name our world. Our K4C hubs challenge dominant structures of higher education by being formally constructed as partnerships between communities and higher education institutions.

When we (Budd and Rajesh) along with others first launched the International Participatory Research Network in 1978, we were met with ridicule by mainstream academics of the day. But social movements in South Africa, the Philippines, India, and America took it up with enthusiasm as it validated the knowledge being created by the marginalised and excluded majorities around the world. It took the university world until the early 21st century to accept the diverse discourses of participatory research and engaged scholarship as legitimate approaches to knowledge creation. Yet, one still finds within some disciplines or some universities a discomfort with a discourse that emphasises empathy, solidarity and equity as more important than objectivity and distance.

So, we were delighted and affirmed when we read the UNESCO Recommendation on Open Science, the reports of the UNESCO

World Conference on Higher Education, or similar reports by the International Science Council which all support a vision of knowledge democracy, of engagement with communities, of respect for Indigenous and other knowledge systems, and a requirement that research brings benefits to those communities most in need.

The historical trajectories of emergence and practice of foundational perspectives in CBPR have had rich and diverse heritage. In different socio-ecological contexts around the world, participatory research and its future 'avatars' evolved in different ways and vocabularies. The movement of CBPR over the past two decades, as it began to gain credibility in academia, has also been conceptualised and practised in diverse ways. When an idea gains widespread acceptance, it faces risks of losing its moorings. That is why we have been modeling and arguing for teaching and practice of CBPR in a **socially responsible and ethically anchored** manner.

Several streams of theorising, practice and advocacy need to be pursued if such a socially responsible and ethically anchored trajectory of CBPR is to be strengthened in future. These include:

Democratising access to learning CBPR

The recent efforts to decentralise K4C at regional levels are meant to create easier access for new generation of students and practitioners to learn CBPR within the K4C framework. We are delighted that such regional K4C Mentor Training Programs have already begun in East Africa and South-east Asia. As new regional K4C mechanisms move forward in other regions, access to learning and practicing CBPR in this modality must be even more local and context specific. Diversities of languages, socio-ecologies, and societal challenges require national and sub-national structures for teaching CBPR. Capacity for local language training with learning materials in those languages will be essential for expanding access in future.

Investing in community knowledge capacity

Even in the most inclusive K4C hubs, resources for systematisation of community knowledge are administered by academic partners. Resources for participation of community knowledge workers in accessing such CBPR learning opportunities remain scarce worldwide. This reality has restricted the possibility of joint learning of CBPR by academic students and community practitioners. To partially address this challenge, we launched a Community Scholars Fund last year to cover costs of community practitioners in joining MTPs. Much more needs to be done in this regard to overcome the chasm in accessing opportunities for joint learning and practice.

Redesigning research funding protocols

Over the years, newly inspired and trained young researchers have begun to formulate co-construction of research projects to practise CBPR in socially responsible and ethically anchored ways. They face obstacles in accessing research funding, both locally and globally, because the research funding models and protocols are unable to respond to such co-construction approaches. Across the world, national and international research funding agencies continue to apply research funding protocols evolved during a previous era of academic-driven, unilaterally formulated research projects with research questions, methods of data collection and analysis predetermined before consultations with community partners begin. Therefore, we are now supporting efforts to redesign research funding systems and protocols that can include such CBPR-driven projects. In partnership with International Development Research Centre, we launched the DECODE project in 2024 precisely towards this end.

Transforming academic research cultures

As young researchers enter the profession, they begin to learn how tightly controlled and narrowly measured career steps are universally practised in academic research institutes, departments and centres. Conversations about transdisciplinarity, local community and Indigenous knowledge, building mutually respectful societal partnerships are sidelined as the culture emphasises individualism, publications, and conferences with peers. Sharing knowledge products and platforms with community/societal partners and finding new ways of knowledge mobilisation are discouraged. This research culture needs to change if CBPR has to be integrated in everyday research, and principles of Open Science have to be practised. While some movement in this direction is emerging from research funders in the Global North, not much shift is being discussed in the Global South, yet.

Demonstrating impacts on Agenda 2030

Hundreds of local CBPR research studies have been conducted by the MTP mentors. Several local stories of change have already emerged. As a next step, it is important to systematise and articulate systemic impacts of such local research. The promise of K4C contributing to improving positive changes towards achieving Agenda 2030 and climate issues needs to be cumulatively demonstrated. This collective effort will further strengthen the K4C Framework of CBPR training and knowledge democracy.

Lest the above present a picture of a long journey ahead, especially towards institutional reforms in research eco-systems, much progress has already been made. No conversation of research councils or funding agencies or domain networks happens without attention to decolonised, co-construction of knowledge and CBPR. Many K4C hubs have brought forward new leaders in such a knowledge democracy movement from around the world. Investing in this generation of leadership to become global champions of K4C will be particularly critical in the near future. The UNESCO Chair in Community Based Research and Social Responsibility in Higher Education is committed to promoting new Chairs over the next four years in diverse locations with diverse partners to carry forward this agenda of Knowledge for Change.

Neither of us (Budd or Rajesh) imagined how far the participatory research innovation 45 years ago would travel. We did not plan all the steps, though we did seize opportunities as they came about. The response to monocultures of development, science and governance needs to be anchored in the framework of knowledge democracy. Local knowledges, local actors, and local solutions are already making a difference in responding to climate impacts worldwide.

A new vision of the world – equitable, just, and sustainable – can only be built through transformative knowledge movements everywhere.

Hope is infectious, as we have learnt in these five decades. Therefore, we continue hope!

REFERENCES

Chapter 1

Brown, D. and Tandon, R. (1983). Ideology and political economy in inquiry. *The Journal of Applied Behavioral Science*, 19(3), pp 277–294. https://journals.sagepub.com/doi/10.1177/002188638301900306

Canadian Commission for UNESCO (2021). *Indigenous Perspectives on Higher Education*, UNESCO. https://fpcf.ca/files/indigneousperspectiveshighereducation-1.pdf

Chambers, R. (1994). *Paradigm Shifts and the Practice of Participatory Research and Development*, Working Paper 2, Institute of Development Studies (IDS), UK. https://opendocs.ids.ac.uk/articles/report/Paradigm_Shifts_and_the_Practice_of_Participatory_Research_and_Development/26477083?file=48231088

Diaz-Arevalo, J.M. (2022). In search of the ontology of participation in Participatory Action Research: Orlando Fals-Borda's participatory turn, 1977–1980. *Action Research*, 20(4), pp 343–362. https://journals.sagepub.com/doi/10.1177/14767503221103571

Fals-Borda, O. (1998). *People's Participation: Challenges Ahead*. Intermediate Technology Publications, New York, London.

GUNi (2008). *Higher Education: New Challenges and Emerging Roles for Human and Social Development*. Higher Education in the World Report 3. GUNi Series on the Social Commitment of Universities. Global University Network for Innovation (GUNi), Barcelona.

GUNi (2013). *Knowledge, Engagement and Higher Education: Contributing to Social Change*. Higher Education in the World 5. GUNi Series on the Social Commitment of Universities. Global University Network for Innovation (GUNi), Barcelona.

Hall, B. (1975). Participatory research: An approach for change. *Convergence*, 8(2), pp 24–32.

Hall, B. (2005). In from the cold? Reflections on participatory research from 1970–2005. *Convergence,* 38(1), pp 5–24.

https://www.researchgate.net/publication/285085627_In_from_the_cold_Reflections_on_participatory_research_from_1970-2005

Hall, B., Jackson, E., Tandon, R., Fontan, J. and Lall, N. (2013). *Knowledge, Democracy and Action: Community–University Research Partnerships in Global Perspectives*. Manchester University Press.

Hall, B., Tandon, R. and Tremblay, C. (2015). *Strengthening Community–University Research Partnerships: Global Perspectives*. PRIA and University of Victoria.

Hall, B., Tandon, R., Lepore, W. and Singh, W. (2016). *Knowledge and Engagement: Building Capacity for the Next Generation of Community Based Researchers*. PRIA and University of Victoria.

International Commission on the Futures of Education (2022). *Reimagining Our Futures Together: A New Social Contract for Education*, Report on the UNESCO World Higher Education Conference, UNESCO.

Planning Commission (2011). *Report of the Subcommittee on Community Engagement*. Government of India. https://unescochair-cbrsr.org/unesco/pdf/resource/SC_Community_Engagement_Final%20Report_7%20May.pdf

de Sousa Santos, B. (2007). Beyond abyssal thinking: From global lines to ecologies of knowledges. *Revista Critica de Ciencias Sociais*, 30(1).

Tandon, R. (1979). From clarity to anarchy: Participatory research approach (A critique of the methodology of the participatory research approach). Presented at African Region Workshop on Participatory Research, Institute of Development Management, Tanzania.

Tandon, R. (2003). Should participatory research be taught in a university? Keynote address delivered at a seminar on 'Participatory Research Methods', organised by PRIA and University of Mysore at Mysore on September 23, 2003.

UNESCO (2010). *Communique: 2009 World Conference on Higher Education: The New Dynamics of Higher Education and Research for Societal Change and Development*, 5–9 July 2009, UNESCO. https://unesdoc.unesco.org/ark:/48223/pf0000183277

UNESCO (2021). *UNESCO Recommendation on Open Science*. UNESCO. https://www.unesco.org/en/legal-affairs/recommendation-open-science

UNESCO (2022). *Beyond Limits. New Ways to Reinvent Higher Education*. Working document for the World Higher Education Conference. 18–20 May 2022. https://www.whec2022.org/EN/homepage/Roadmap2030

UNESCO (2023). *Knowledge-Driven Actions: Transforming Higher Education for Global Sustainability*, Report prepared by Independent Expert Group on the Universities and the 2030 Agenda, UNESCO. https://unesdoc.unesco.org/ark:/48223/pf0000380519

University of Victoria (2009). *The Funding and Development of Community University Research Partnerships in Canada: Evidence-Based Investment in Knowledge, Engaged Scholarship, Innovation and Action for Canada's Future*. Report on study conducted by Office of Community-Based Research, University of Victoria, Canada.

University of Victoria (2007). Announcement of opening of new Community-Based Research Office. https://www.uvic.ca/news/topics/2007+uvic-opens-new-community-based-research-office+ media-release

Visvanathan, S. (2009). The search for cognitive justice. india-seminar.com. https://www.india-seminar.com/2009/597/597_shiv_visvanathan.htm

Watson, D. (2009). Universities and lifelong learning. In Peter Jarvis (ed.), *The Routledge Handbook of Lifelong Learning* (pp 102–113). Routledge.

Watson, D. (2007). *Managing Civic and Community Engagement – Managing Universities and Colleges: Guides to Good Practice*. McGraw-Hill Education.

Watson, D. and Maddison, E. (2005). *Managing Institutional Self-Study*. Open University Press.

Chapter 2

Cornish, H., Fransman, J. and Newman, K. (2017). *Rethinking Research Partnerships: Discussion Guide and Toolkit: Christian Aid Centre of Excellence for Research, Evidence and Learning*. Christian Aid, Economic and Social Research Council (ESRC) and The Open University. https://www.christianaid.org.uk/sites

Doering, A. (2006). Adventure learning: transformative hybrid online education. *Distance Education*, 27(2), pp 197–215.

Garrison, D.R. (2017). *E-Learning in the 21st Century*. Routledge.

Gaventa, J. and Cornwall, A. (2008). Power and Knowledge. In P. Reason and H. Bradbury (eds), *The Sage Handbook of Action Research: Participative Inquiry and Practice*, 2nd edition, pp 172–189. Sage Publications.

Hall, B.L., Tandon, R. and Tremblay, C. (eds). (2015). *Strengthening Community University Research Partnerships: Global Perspectives*. PRIA/University of Victoria.

Halverson, L.R., Graham, C.R., Spring, K.J. and Drysdale, J.S. (2012). An analysis of high impact scholarship and publication trends in blended learning. *Distance Education*, 33(3), pp 381–413.

Helve, H. (2015). A longitudinal perspective on worldviews, values and identities. *Journal of Religious Education*, 63, pp 95–115. https://doi.org/10.1007/s40839-016-0021-5

Lepore, W., Hall, B.H. and Tandon, R. (2021). The Knowledge for Change Consortium: A decolonising approach to international collaboration in capacity building in community-based participatory research. *Canadian Journal of Development Studies,* 42(3), pp 347–370. https://doi.org/10.1080/02255189.2020.1838887.

Lepore, W., Tandon, R. and Hall, B. (eds) (2024). *Bridging Knowledge Cultures: Rebalancing Power in the Co-Construction of Knowledge*. Brill. https://doi.org/10.1163/9789004687769

MacFarlane, A. and Roche, B. (2018). Blurring the boundaries between researcher and researched, academic and activist. In S. Banks and Brydon-Miller (eds), *Ethics in Participatory Research for Health and Social Well-Being*, pp 56–79. Routledge.

Molosi-France, K., and Dipholo, K. (2022). Community based participatory research: A ladder of opportunity for engaged scholarship in higher education. *Journal of Contemporary Issues in Education*, 17(2), pp 111–122. https://doi.org/10.20355/jcie29514

Palahicky, S., DesBiens, D., Jeffery, K. and Webster, K., (2019). Pedagogical values in online and blended learning environments in higher education. In J. Keengwe (ed.), *Handbook of Research on Blended Learning Pedagogies and Professional Development in Higher Education*, pp 79–101. IGI Global.

Park, P. (2001). Knowledge and participatory research. In P. Reason and H. Bradbury (eds), *The Sage Handbook of Action Research: Participative Inquiry and Practice*, pp 81–90. Sage Publications.

Raes, A., Detienne, L., Windey, I. and Depaepe, F. (2020). A systematic literature review on synchronous hybrid learning: Gaps identified. *Learning Environments Research*, 23(3), pp 269–290. https://doi.org/10.1007/s10984-019-09303-z

Tandon, R. (2005). *Participatory Research: Revisiting the Roots*. Mosaic Books.

Tandon, R., Hall, B.L., Lepore, W. and Singh, W. (eds). (2016). *Knowledge and Engagement: Building Capacity of The Next Generation of Community Based Researchers*. PRIA/University of Victoria.

UNESCO Chair in Community-Based Research and Social Responsibility in Higher Education (2024). *Knowledge for Change (K4C) Global Consortium Report, June 2024*. PRIA.

United Nations. (2011). 'Global is local and local is global,' Secretary-General tells hometown audience. *UN News*. https://rb.gy/1tvcse

Venneri, E. (2020). Reflexivity in adult education: Some theoretical elements for a debate. *International Journal of Social Sciences & Education*, 10(1), pp 38–46.

Wadhwani, D. and Malpani, P. (2023). United Nations Sustainable Goals: Global to local need of the hour. *Social Science Research Network*. http://dx.doi.org/10.2139/ssrn.4426147

Chapter 3

Annan, Kofi Atta (1998). The quotable Kofi Annan: Selections from speeches and statements by the Secretary-General, United Nations Digital Library (un.org).

McGee, Rosie, Pettit, Jethro and Wegner, Fiammetta (2020). 'Learning about power in a Master's for reflective social change practitioners,' in R. McGee and J. Pettit (eds), *Power, empowerment and social change*, Routledge.

Gaventa, J. (2006). Finding the spaces for change: A power analysis, *IDS Bulletin,* 37(6), pp 23–33, doi:%2010.1111/j.1759-5436.2006.tb00320.x

Gaventa, J. (2020). Applying power analysis: Using the 'powercube' to explore forms, levels, and spaces, in R. McGee and J. Pettit (eds), *Power, empowerment and social change*, Routledge.

Gaventa, J. (2021). Linking the prepositions: Using power analysis to inform strategies for social action, *Journal of Political Power,* 14(1), pp 109–130, DOI: 10.1080/2158379X.2021.1878409

Gaventa, J. and Cornwall, Andrea (2006). Challenging the boundaries of the possible: Participation, knowledge and power', *IDS* Bulletin, 37(6), pp 122–128, DOI: 10.1111/j.1759-5436.2006.tb00329.x

Pettit, Jethro (2010). 'Multiple faces of power and learning,' *IDS Bulletin*, 41(3) (May), pp 25–35. https://doi.org/10.1111/j.1759-5436.2010.00134.x

Core background reading (open access)

Gaventa, J. (2006). Finding the spaces for change: A power analysis, *IDS Bulletin,* 37(6), pp 23–33, doi:%2010.1111/j.1759-5436.2006.tb00320.x

Gaventa, J. (2021). Linking the prepositions: Using power analysis to inform strategies for social action, *Journal of Political Power,* 14(1), pp 109–130, DOI: 10.1080/2158379X.2021.1878409

Gaventa, J. and Cornwall, Andrea (2006). Challenging the boundaries of the possible: Participation, knowledge and power', *IDS* Bulletin, 37(6), pp 122–128, DOI: 10.1111/j.1759-5436.2006.tb00329.x

Other key resources on power (open access)

www.powercube.net

DCA Learning Lab, 'Introducing the Power Cube' (animated cartoon) https://vimeo.com/253176500/5a7c832a2b

Pettit, Jethro (2010). 'Multiple faces of power and learning,' *IDS Bulletin*, 41(3) (May), pp 25–35. https://doi.org/10.1111/j.1759-5436.2010.00134.x

Just Associates: MCH3: Power – Concepts for Revisioning Power for Justice, Equality and Peace – JASS (justassociates.org).

Just Associates: A New Weave of Power, People and Politics: The Action Guide for Advocacy and Citizen Participation – JASS (justassociates.org)

Hunjan, Raji and Pettit, Jethro (2011). *Power: A practical guide for facilitating social change*. Collective Wellbeing Carnegie UK. https://carnegieuktrust.org.uk/publications/power-a-practical-guide-for-facilitating-social-change/

Chapter 4

Banks, S., Armstrong, A., et al. (2013). Everyday ethics in community-based participatory research. *Contemporary Social Science*, 8(3), pp 263–277. https://doi.org/10.1080/21582041.2013.769618

Banks, S., Rifkin, F., Davidson, H., Holmes, C. and Moore, N. (2014). *Performing ethics: Using participatory theatre to explore ethical issues in community-based participatory research*. Centre for Social Justice and Community Action, Durham University, UK.

Banks, S. and Brydon-Miller, M. (2019a). Ethics in participatory research. In S. Banks and M. Brydon-Miller (eds), *Ethics in participatory research for health and social well-being: Cases and commentaries* (pp 1–30). Routledge.

Banks, S. and Brydon-Miller, M. (eds) (2019b). *Ethics in participatory research for health and social well-being: Cases and commentaries*. Routledge.

Banks, S. and von Köppen, M. (2021). Ethical issues for practice and research in congregate settings during the Covid-19 pandemic: Cases and commentaries. *Ethics and Social Welfare*, 15(3), pp 328–335. https://doi.org/10.1080/17496535.2021.1961367

Buchanan, J., Collard, L. and Palmer, D. (2019). Koorliny birniny, ni, quoppa katatjin: Respect and ethics in working with Indigenous Australian communities. In S. Banks and P. Westoby (eds), *Ethics, equity and community development* (pp 123–142). The Policy Press.

CSJCA (Centre for Social Justice and Community Action) (2015). *Dilemmas cafés: A guide for facilitators*. Durham University, UK. https://www.durham.ac.uk/media/durham-university/research-/research-centres/social-justice-amp-community-action-centre-for/documents/toolkits-guides-and-case-studies/Dilemmas-Cafe-Briefing.pdf

CSJCA and NCCPE (Centre for Social Justice and Community Action and National Coordinating Centre for Public Engagement). (2022a).

Community-based participatory research: A guide to ethical principles and practice (2nd edn). CSJCA and NCCPE, UK. https://www.durham.ac.uk/media/durham-university/departments-/sociology/Community-Based-Participatory-Research-A-Guide-to-Ethical-Principles,-2nd-edition-(2022)-.pdf

CSJCA and NCCPE (2022b). *Community-based participatory research: A guide to ethical principles and practice (2nd edn), Appendix, toolkits and cases.* CSJCA and NCCPE, UK. https://www.durham.ac.uk/media/durham-university/departments-/sociology/Ethical-guidance,-toolkit-and-cases,-final-version,-Dec-2023.pdf

Egid, B., Roura, M. et al. (2021). 'You want to deal with power while riding on power': global perspectives on power in participatory health research and co-production approaches. *BMJ Global Health*, 6(11), e006978. doi:10.1136/bmjgh-2021-006978

Gyekye, K. (2010) 'African Ethics', *The Stanford Encyclopedia of Philosophy.* https://plato.stanford.edu/archives/fall2011/entries/african-ethics/

Iltis, A and MacKay, D. (eds) (2024), *The Oxford Handbook of Research Ethics.* Oxford University Press.

Narayanan, P., Brear, M., Shabangu, P., Groot, B., van den Eijnde, C. and Banks, S. (2023). Ethical issues in participatory action research on Covid-appropriate behaviour and vaccine hesitancy in India: A case with commentaries. *Ethics and Social Welfare*, 17(2), pp 221–228. https://doi.org/10.1080/17496535.2023.2209363

Tayebi, N. S., von Köppen, M., Plunger, P., Börner, S. and Banks, S. (2023). Researching with care – participatory health research with Afghan women refugees in Germany during the Covid-19 pandemic: A case with commentaries. *Ethics and Social Welfare*, 17(2), pp 229–235. https://doi.org/10.1080/17496535.2023.2209364

Chapter 5

Bagley, C. and Cancienne, M. (eds) (2002). *Dancing the data.* Peter Lang.

Clover, D.E. (2011). Successes and challenges of arts-based participatory methodologies with homeless/street-involved women in Victoria. *Action Research Journal,* 9(1), pp 12–26. http://arj.sagepub.com/content/9/1/12

Clover, D.E. (2005). Sewing stories and acting activism: Women's leadership and learning through drama and craft. *Ephemera: Theory and Politics in Organization*, 5(4), pp 629–642.

Clover, D.E. and Markle, G. (2003). Feminist arts practices of popular education: Imagination, counter-narratives and activism on Vancouver

Island and Gabriola Island. *New Zealand Journal of Adult Education*, 31(2), pp 36–52.

Clover, D.E., Dzulkifli, S., Gelderman, H. and Sanford, K. (eds) (2020). *Feminist adult educators guide to aesthetic, creative and disruptive practice in museums and communities*. https://onlineacademiccommunity.uvic.ca/comarts/feminist-adult-educators-guide/

Eisner, E. (2008). Persistent tensions in arts-based research. In M. Cahnmann-Taylor and R. Siegesmund (eds), *Arts-based research in education* (pp 16–27). Routledge.

Greenwood, J. (2019). *Arts-based research*. https://oxfordre.com/education/display/10.1093/acrefore/9780190264093.001.0001/acrefore-9780190264093-e-29

Hein, H. (1990). The role of feminist aesthetics in feminist theory. *The Journal of Aesthetics and*

Art Criticism, 48(4), pp 281–291.

Knowles, J. and Cole, A. (eds) (2008). *Handbook of the arts in qualitative research*. Sage Publications.

Lisahunter (2017). If You See What I Mean? Visual Narratives – Stories Told Through, With And By Visual Images. In R. Dwyer, I. Davis, and emerald, e. (eds) Narrative research in practice (pp 89–116). Springer Science+Business Media Singapore.

Leavy, P. (ed.) (2017). *Handbook of arts-based research*. Guilford Press.

McNiff, S. (2008). Arts-based research. In J. Knowles and A. Cole (eds) *Handbook of the arts in qualitative research* (pp 29–40). Sage Publications.

Sanford, K. and Clover, D.E. (2022). A wasteland of climate anxiety: Installations and meaningful (teacher) education. In A. Farrell, C. Skyhar and M. Lam. (eds) *Teaching in the Anthropocene: Education in the face of environmental crisis* (pp 269–281). Canadian Scholars Press.

Schallié, Charlotte (ed.) (2002). *But I Live: Three Stories of Child Survivors of the Holocaust.* New Jewish Press.

Schönweger, A. and Clover, D.E. (2020). The critical advocacies and pedagogies of women's museums. In K. Sanford, D.E. Clover, N. Taber and S. Williamson (eds) *Feminist critique and the museum: Educating for a critical consciousness* (pp 250–266). Brill.

Ward, J. and Shortt, H. (eds) (2020). *Using arts-based research methods: Creative approaches for researching business, organization and humanities*. Palgrave MacMillian.

Whitson, R. (2017). Painting pictures of ourselves: Researcher subjectivity in the practice of feminist reflexivity. *The professional geographer*, 69(2), pp 299–306. https://doi.org/10.1080/00330124.2016.1208510

Chapter 6

Banks, J.A. (1998). The lives and values of researchers: Implications for educating citizens in a multicultural society. *Educational* Researcher, 27(7), pp 4–17.

Brayton, J., Ollivier, M., and Robbins, W. (n.d.). Introduction to feminist research. Retrieved from https://parl.ext.unb.ca/research.htm

Cook, J. and Fonow, M.M. (1986). Knowledge and women's interests: Issues of epistemology and methodology in feminist sociological research. *Sociological Inquiry*, 56(4), pp 2–29.

Cooke, B. and Kothari, U. (2001). *Participation: The new tyranny?* Zed Books.

Darroch, F. and Giles, A. (2014). Decolonizing Health Research: Community-based participatory research and postcolonial feminist theory. *The Canadian Journal of Action Research*, 15(3), pp 22–36. https://doi.org/10.33524/cjar.v15i3.155

Frisby, W., Maguire, P., and Reid, C. (2009). The 'f' word has everything to do with it: How feminist theories inform action research. *Action Research,* 7(1), pp 13–29.

Global Education Monitoring Report. (2020). *A new generation: 25 years of efforts for gender equality in education*. UNESCO.

Hall, B.L., Mushi, P.A., and Sanga, P.L. (eds). (2022). *Reigniting Hope: 50 Years of Adult Education in Tanzania*. Dar es Salaam University Press.

Harding, S. (1995). Just add women and stir? In *Missing links* (pp 295–307). IDRC.

Johnson, P.A., Widnall, S.E., and Benya, F.F. (2018). *Sexual harassment of women: Climate, culture, and consequences in academic sciences, engineering, and medicine*. The National Academies Press.

Joseph, J. (2015). Sexual harassment in tertiary institutions: A comparative perspective. *Temida*, 18(2), pp 125–144. https://doi.org/10.2298/tem1502125h

Khan, S. (2024). More sensitisation on POSH, consent and sexual harassment on campuses. *Education Times* (June 1). https://www.educationtimes.com/article/campus-beat-college-life/99735685/more-sensitisation-on-posh-consent-and-sexual-harrasment-on-campuses

Lenette, C. (2022). *Participatory action research: Ethics and decolonization*. Oxford University Press.

Lokot, M., Hartman, E., and Hashmi, I. (2023). Participatory approaches and methods in gender equality and gender-based violence research with refugees and internally displaced populations: A scoping review. *Conflict and health*, 17(1), p. 58. https://doi.org/10.1186/s13031-023-00554-5

Ollivier, M. and Tremblay, M. (2000). *Questionnements féministes et méthodologie de la recherche.* L'Harmattan.

Chapter 7

Bibi, A. (2 April 2020). *Are we invisible? Domestic worker Anjuman Bibi asks, in light of lockdown.* https://www.marthafarrellfoundation.org/blog/are-we-invisible-domestic-worker-anjuman-bibi-asks-in-light-of-lockdown/

Boyd, R.D. (1989). Facilitating personal transformation in small groups. *Small Group Behavior,* 20, pp 459–474.

Crenshaw, K. (1991). Mapping the margins: Intersectionality, identity politics, and violence against women of color. *Stanford Law Review,* 43(6), pp 1241–99.

Daloz, L. (1999). *Mentor: Guiding the journey of adult learners.* Jossey-Bass.

Dirkx, J.M. (1998a). 'Knowing the Self Through Fantasy: Toward a Mythopoetic View of Transformative Learning'. Proceedings from the Adult Education Research Conference. San Antonio, TX.

Dirkx, J.M. (1998b). Transformative learning theory in the practice of adult education: An overview. *PAACE Journal of Lifelong Learning,* 7, pp 1–14.

Domestic Workers' Action Network. (2020). *My life as an informal migrant worker during the COVID-19 pandemic: A participatory research by Domestic Workers' Action Network.* PRIA and Martha Farrell Foundation.

Etmanski, C., Dawson, T., and Hall, B. (2014). Introduction. In C. Etmanski, B. Hall, and T. Dawson (eds), *Learning and teaching community-based research: Linking pedagogy to practice* (pp 3–22). University of Toronto Press.

Etmanski, C., Krause, W., and Bandyopadhyay, K. (2024). Participatory pedagogy online: Reflections from a Global Leadership virtual field school. In T. Cappiali and J. Jean-Pierre (eds), *Promoting inclusion and justice in university teaching* (pp 76–89). Edward Elgar Publishing.

Farrell, M. (2014). *Engendering the workplace: Gender discrimination and prevention of sexual harassment in organisations.* PRIA: Uppal Publishing House.

Freire, P. (2003). *Pedagogy of the oppressed* (Rev ed.). Continuum. (Original work published 1970).

Hall, B.L. (1975). Participatory research: An approach for change. *Convergence,* 8(2), pp 24–32.

Hooks, B. (1994). *Teaching to transgress: Education as the practice of freedom.* Routledge.

Israel, B.A., Schulz, A.J., Parker, E.A., Becker, A.B., Allen, A. and Guzman, J.R. (2003). Critical issues in developing and following community-based participatory research principles. In M. Minkler and N. Wallerstein (eds), *Community-based participatory research for health* (pp 56–73). Jossey-Bass.

Jha, V., Vaishnava, B and Bandyopadhyay, K.K. (2011). *Citizen leadership: Deepening democratic accountability in India, Brazil, and South Africa*. Academic Foundation.

Krause, W. (2022). Implications of Islamic women's mobilisations in Egypt. *Globalizations,* pp 1–15. https://doi.org/10.1080/14747731.2022.2035060

Kucukaydin, I. and Cranton, P. (2012). Critically questioning the discourse of transformative learning theory. *Adult Education Quarterly,* 63(1) pp 43–56. doi: 10.1177/0741713612439090

Mezirow, J. (1991). *Transformative dimensions of adult learning.* Jossey-Bass.

Mezirow, J. (1994). Forum: Understanding transformation theory. *Adult Education Quarterly,* 44(4), pp 222–232.

Nagpal, A. and Bandyopadhyay, K.B. (2020). Knowledge and participation: Empowering Indian urban poor for accessing public services. *International Education Journal, Comparative Perspectives,* 19(1), Special Edition.

Royal Roads University. (2021, Nov. 2). Global Leadership Digital Field Study with India. https://www.royalroads.ca/global-leadership-digital-field-study-india

Stevens-Long, J., Schapiro, S.A. and McClintock, C. (2012). Passionate scholars: Transformative learning in doctoral education. *Adult Education Quarterly,* 62(2), pp 180–198. doi:10.1177/0741713611402046

Tandon, R. (1988). Social transformation and participatory research. *Convergence,* 21(2-3), pp 5–18.

Tandon, R. (2002). *Participatory research: Revisiting the roots.* Mosaic Books.

Tandon, R. and Mohanty, R. (2002). *Civil society and governance.* PRIA.

Yorks, L. and Kasl, E. (2006). I know more than I can say: A taxonomy for utilizing expressive ways of knowing to foster transformative learning. *Journal of Transformative Education,* 4(1), pp 22–43.

Chapter 8

Banks, S., Armstrong, A., et al., (2013). Everyday ethics in community-based participatory research. *Contemporary Social Science,* 8(3), pp 263–277. https://doi.org/10.1080/21582041.2013.769618

BC Ministry of Education and First Nations Education Steering. (2006). *First Peoples Principles of Learning.*

Castleden, H., Garvin, T., and ND Hobson, H. (2008). Aboriginal good practice and research: A community-based participatory research approach in Canada. *Canadian Journal of Public Health,* 99(2), pp 73–77.

Castleden, H., Morgan, V.S., and Lamb, C. (2012), 'I spent the first year drinking tea': Exploring Canadian university researchers' perspectives on community-based participatory research involving Indigenous Peoples. *The Canadian Geographer,* 56, pp 160–179.

Chilisa, B. (2012). *Indigenous research methodologies*. Sage Publications.

Chrona, Jo. (2022). *Wayi wah! Indigenous pedagogies. An act for reconciliation and anti-racist education*. Portage & Main Press.

Community-Based Research Canada (CBRC) Website: https://www.communityresearchcanada.ca/

First Nations Information Governance Centre (FNIGC), which focuses on OCAP (Ownership, Control, Access, and Possession). https://fnigc.ca/

Israel, B.A., Schulz, A.J., Parker, E.A., Becker, A.B. and Community-Campus Partnerships for Health (2001). Community-based participatory research: policy recommendations for promoting a partnership approach in health research. *Education for health* (Abingdon, England), 14(2), pp 182–197. https://doi.org/10.1080/13576280110051055

Kovach, M. (2009). *Indigenous methodologies: Characteristics, conversations, and context*. University of Toronto Press Inc.

Lepore, W., Hall, B.H. and Tandon, R. (2021). The Knowledge for Change Consortium: A decolonising approach to international collaboration in capacity building in community-based participatory research. *Canadian Journal of Development Studies*, 42(3), pp 347–370. https://doi.org/10.1080/02255189.2020.1838887.

McGregor, D., O'Flaherty, K and Wonnacott, D. (2018). Indigenous research: A review of the literature and directions for future research. *The Canadian Journal of Native Studies*, 38(1), pp 63–89.

Potts, K. and Brown, L. (2005) *Becoming an Anti-Oppressive Researcher.* In: Brown, L. and Strega, S. (eds), *Research as resistance: Critical, Indigenous, and anti-oppressive approaches*, Canadian Scholars Press, pp 255–286.

Smith, L.T. (2012). *Decolonizing methodologies: Research and indigenous peoples* (2nd ed.). Zed Books.

Strega, S., and Brown, L. (2015). Research as resistance: Revisiting critical, indigenous, and anti-oppressive approaches. In Brown, L. and Strega, S. (eds), *Research as resistance: Revisiting critical, indigenous, and anti-oppressive approaches*, Canadian Scholars Press, pp 3–22.

Tri-Council Policy Statement (TCPS 2): The TCPS 2 provides ethical guidelines for research involving humans in Canada, including specific sections on community-based research. It is essential reading for understanding ethical considerations in CBR. https://ethics.gc.ca/eng/policy-politique_tcps2-eptc2_2018.html

Wilson, S. (2008). *Research is ceremony: Indigenous research methods.* Fernwood Publishing.

Chapter 9

Burke, J.G., Hess, S., et al. (2013). Translating community-based participatory research principles into practice. *Progress in Community Health Partnerships*, 7(2), pp 115–122. https://doi.org/10.1353/cpr.2013.0025

Gaudry, A. (2011). Insurgent Research. *Wicazo SA Review* 26, no. 1, pp 113–36. Accessed 10 March 2024. https://www.academia.edu/619243/Insurgent_Research

Holliman, R. (2017). Supporting excellence in engaged research. *Journal of Science Communication*, 16(5). Accessed 15 April 2024. https://jcom.sissa.it/article/pubid/JCOM_1605_2017_C04/

Horowitz, C.R., Robinson, M., and Seifer, S.D. (2009). Community-Based participatory research from the margin to the mainstream. Circulation, 119(19), pp 2633–2642. https://doi.org/10.1161/circulationaha.107.729863

Lepore, W., Hall, B.H. and Tandon, R. (2021). The Knowledge for Change Consortium: A decolonising approach to international collaboration in capacity building in community-based participatory research. *Canadian Journal of Development Studies*, 42(3), pp 347–370. https://doi.org/10.1080/02255189.2020.1838887.

Rubin, C.L., Martinez, L.S., et al. (2012). Community-engaged pedagogy: a strengths-based approach to involving diverse stakeholders in research partnerships. *Progress in Community Health Partnerships*, 6(4), pp 481–490. https://doi.org/10.1353/cpr.2012.0057

Tembo, D., Hickey, G., et al. (2021). Effective engagement and involvement with community stakeholders in the co-production of global health research. *BMJ*, no. 178. https://doi.org/10.1136/bmj.n178

Chapter 10

Ahuja, S. and Yadav, D. (2019). Effect of digital pedagogy interventions in rural areas. *MIER Journal of Educational Studies Trends & Practices*, 9(2), pp 227–240.

Ayesha Nadeem, Naha Rajgaria, Payaswini, and Upasana Singh. (2017). Relevance of the verse '*Sa Vidya Ya Vimuktaye*' in the contemporary education system and its impact on the Indian society. *Explore – Journal of Research*, vol. IX, pp 274–287.

Babbar, S.K. and Johannsdottir, L. (2024). India's ancient philosophy on holistic education and its relevance for Target 4.7 of the United Nations Sustainable Development Goals. *Discover Sustainability*. 5(51). https://link.springer.com/article/10.1007/s43621-024-00225-2

Bhatnagar, Anjoo. (2023). Optimizing early childhood growth, development and education in holistic nurturing care environment: A six year follow up study. Euro-Global Conference on Pediatrics and Neonatology (5th edition). 28–29 August, London, U.K.

DEI. (2019). DEI Vision Book. https://www.dei.ac.in/dei/files/notices/2019/IOE.pdf

DEI. (2020a). 15 Year Strategic Plan for Institute of Eminence. https://www.dei.ac.in/dei/edei/files/DEI%20Progress-MHRD-May-22-2020.pdf

DEI. (2020b). Jugaad: The DEI Way. https://www.dei.ac.in/dei/files/notices/2020/JUGAADNEW.pdf

Dua, P., Dhir, A., Naranyan, A. and Allamraju, A. (2023). *A Holistic Approach to Achieving SDGs: A Case Study of Dayalbagh, India*. https://uwspace.uwaterloo.ca/ handle/10012/19181

Gautam, S. and Kumar, K. (2023). Environmental awareness, psychological wellbeing and spiritual values: A correlational study. 46th (Inter) National Systems Conference (NSC) on Evolution of Homo Sapiens to Homo Spiritualis for Better Worldliness. 27–29 June.

Government of India. (2011). *Report of the Subcommittee on Community Engagement*, Planning Commission, Government of India.

Government of India. (2020). *National Education Policy 2020*. Ministry of Human Resource Development. Government of India. https://www.education.gov.in/sites/upload_files/mhrd/files/NEP_Final_English_0.pdf

Higher Education Quality Committee (HEQC) South Africa. (2004). *Criteria for Institutional Audits*. Council on Higher Education.

Mahmoudi, S., Jafari, E., Nasrabadi, H. and Liaghatdar, M. (2012). Holistic education: An approach for 21st Century. *International Education Studies*, vol. 5, pp 178–86. https://files.eric.ed.gov/fulltext/EJ1066819.pdf

Panwar, H., Singh, K. and Saraswat, S. (2023). The success story of DEI feeding millet-based diet to the last, the least, the lowest, and the lost. Presented at the International Agribusiness Conclave on Production, Processing, and Value Addition of Millets, 21–22 March 2023, Rajasthan Agricultural Research Institute, Jaipur.

Satsangi, P.S. and Dhir, A. (2024). *Role of Communities in Achieving Sustainable Development*, Academic Foundation India.

Shankar, D. (2021). University-Society Connect. *Quality Mandate for Higher Education Institutions in India*. University Grants Commission (pp 79–88).

Sharma, M., Kalra, P.K., Soami Daya, K., and Verma, J.K. (2021). Systems Approach to Skilling and Vocational Education in India. *Quality Mandate for Higher Education Institutions in India*. University Grants Commission (pp 236–258).

Tandon, R. (2014). Occasional Paper, *Fostering Social Responsibility in Higher Education in India*. Available at: *1531475111_Fostering_Social_Responsibility.pdf*

Thompson, B. and Kinne, S. (1990). Social change theory: Applications to community health. In Bracht, N. (ed.). *Health Promotion at The Community Level* (First edition, pp 45–65). Sage.

University Grants Commission (2020). Fostering Social Responsibility and Community Engagement in HEIs in India. *National Curriculum Framework and Guidelines*. University Grants Commission.

University Grants Commission (2022). *Guidelines for Fostering Social Responsibility and Community Engagement in Higher Educational Institutions in India 2.0*. University Grants Commission.

Chapter 11

Blundo, R. (2000). *Participatory Research and Service-Learning: A Natural Match for the Community and Campus*. https://www.researchgate.net/publication/242177919

Bush, P.L., Hamzeh, J. and Macaulay, A.C. (2017). Community-based participatory research. In *Oxford Bibliographies*. Oxford University Press. Retrieved from https://www.oxfordbibliographies.com/view/document/obo-9780199756797/obo-9780199756797-0126.xml

Chika-James, T.A., Salem, T. and Oyet, M.C. (2022). *Our Gains, Pains and Hopes: Community Partners' Perspectives of Service-Learning in an Undergraduate Business Education*. SAGE Open, 12(1). https://doi.org/10.1177/21582440211069390

Cowden, Kimberly J., McDonald, L. and Littlefield, R. (2013). Using community based participatory action research as service-learning for tribal college students. *Journal of Indigenous Research*, 2(1). https://doi.

org/10.26077/fqvk-t411

Davidson, N. and Major, C.H. (2014). Boundary crossings: Cooperative learning, collaborative learning, and problem-based learning. *Journal on Excellence in College Teaching*, 25(3-4), pp 7–55.

DeHaven, M.J., Gimpel, N.E., Dallo, F.J. and Billmeier, T.M. (2011). Reaching the underserved through community-based participatory research and service learning: Description and evaluation of a unique medical student training program. *Journal of Public Health Management and Practice*, 17(4), pp 363–368. https://doi.org/10.1097/PHH.0b013e3182214707

Furco, A. (1996). Service-learning: A balanced approach to experiential education. Service Learning, General, 128. Retrieved from https://digitalcommons.unomaha.edu/slceslgen/128

Gimpel, N., Kindratt, T., Dawson, A. and Pagels, P. (2018). Community action research track: Community-based participatory research and service-learning experiences for medical students. *Perspectives on Medical Education*, 7(2), pp 139–143. https://doi.org/10.1007/s40037-017-0397-2

Haidet, P., Kubitz, K. and McCormack, W.T. (2014). Analysis of the team-based learning literature: TBL comes of age. *Journal of Excellence in College Teaching*, 25(3-4), pp 303–333.

Hatcher, J.A. and Bringle, R.G. (1997). Reflection: Bridging the gap between service and learning. *College Teaching*, 45(4), pp 153–158. https://doi.org/10.1080/87567559709596221

Juliana, J.F., Gauthier, M., Ghezeljeh, A., Leandro, L.L., Keats, K., Sholanke, D., Zachari, D. and Gutberlet, J. (2022). The power of community-based participatory research: Ethical and effective ways of researching. *Community Development*, 53(1), pp 3–20. https://doi.org/10.1080/15575330.2021.1936102

Israel, B.A., Schulz, A.J., Parker, E.A. and Becker, A.B. (2001). Community-campus partnerships for health: Community-based participatory research: policy recommendations for promoting a partnership approach in health research. *Educ Health*, 14, pp 182–197.

Kendall, J.C. (1990). Combining service and learning: A resource book for community and public service, Volume 1. National Society for Internships and Experiential Education. https://books.google.com/books/about/Combining_Service_and_Learning.html?id=m4adAAAAMAAJ

Krishnan, A., Tandon, R., and Nongkynrih, B. (2020). Relevance of community-based participatory research in community medicine training. *Indian Journal of Community Medicine*, 45(3), pp 256–260. https://doi.org/10.4103/ijcm.ijcm_343_19

Marcus, M.T., Taylor, W.C., Hormann, M.D., Walker, T. and Carroll, D. (2011). Linking service-learning with community-based participatory research: An interprofessional course for health professional students. *Nursing Outlook*, 59(1), pp 47–54. https://doi.org/10.1016/j.outlook.2010.10.001

McKeachie, W.J. (1999). *Teaching Tips: Strategies, Research, and Theory for College and University Teachers.* Houghton Mifflin.

Moore, S. and Donaldson, L.P. (2022). Incorporating community based participatory action research in social work graduate education. *Journal of Teaching in Social Work*, 42(4), pp 409–422. https://doi.org/10.1080/08841233.2022.2117761

Reinschmidt, K.M., Maez, P., Iuliano, J.E. and Nigon, B.M. (2019). Using active learning strategies linked to CBPR principles in a semester-long class project to teach qualitative research methods in public health. *Pedagogy in Health Promotion*, 5(1), pp 36–44. https://doi.org/10.1177/2373379918761976

Resch, K. and Schrittesser, I. (2023). Using the service-learning approach to bridge the gap between theory and practice in teacher education. International Journal of Inclusive Education, 27 (10), pp 1118–1132. https://doi.org/10.1080/13603116.2021.1882053

Sigmon, Robert L. Spring (1979). Service-learning: Three Principles. Synergist National Center for Service-Learning, *ACTION*, 8(1), pp 9–11.

Smith, K.A., Sheppard, S.D., Johnson, D.W. and Johnson, R.T. (2005). Pedagogies of engagement: Classroom-based practices. *Journal of Engineering Education*, 94, pp 87–100.

Stanton, T.K., Giles, D.E. and Cruz, N.I. (1999). *Service-learning: A Movement's Pioneers Reflect on Its Origins, Practice, and Future.* Jossey-Bass.

Stewart, T. and Wubbena, Z.C. (2015). A systematic review of service-learning in medical education: 1998–2012. *Teach Learn Med*, 27, pp 115–122.

Suresh, A., Wighton, N.M., Sorensen, T.E., Palladino, T.C. and Pinto-Powell, R.C. (2022). A hybrid educational approach to service learning: Impact on student attitudes and readiness in working with medically underserved communities. *Medical Education Online*, 27(1). https://doi.org/10.1080/10872981.2022.2122106

Tandon, R. (2002). Introduction: Revisiting the roots. In Participatory Research: Revisiting the Roots (pp 7–8). Mosaic Books.

Tantia, V., Valarmathi, S., and Kareem, J. (2024). The Integration of service-learning andragogy for achieving learning outcomes and cultivating 21st century skills in the commerce domain. In S. Valarmathi, J. Kareem, V. Tantia, K. Babu, and P. Lucas (eds), *Effective and Meaningful Student Engagement Through Service Learning* (pp 188–210). IGI Global. https://doi.org/10.4018/979-8-3693-2256-7.ch011

Valarmathi, S., Kareem, J., and Tantia, V. (2024). Exploring student perspectives on service learning: Their expectations, challenges, and perceived benefits. In S. Valarmathi, J. Kareem, V. Tantia, K. Babu and P. Lucas (eds), *Effective and Meaningful Student Engagement Through Service Learning* (pp 61–80). IGI Global. https://doi.org/10.4018/979-8-3693-2256-7.ch004

Chapter 12

Johnson, D., Johnson, R., and Holubec, E.J. (1993). *Cooperation in the Classroom.* (7th ed.). Interaction Book Company.

Lou, Y. and MacGregor, K. (2004). Enhancing Project-Based Learning Through Online Between-Group Collaboration. *Educational Research and Evaluation,* 10(4), pp 419–440.

Muñoz, F. y Jiménez, J. (2015). *Paz imperfecta y empoderamiento pacifista. En P. Cabello, y J. Moreno (Ed.) Diversas miradas. Un mismo sentir: Comunicación, Ciudadanía y Paz como retos del siglo XXI.* Plaza y Valdez. pp 49–66.

Nacional Unidas (2018). *La Agenda 2030 y los Objetivos de Desarrollo Sostenible: una oportunidad para América Latina y el Caribe.* CEPAL (LC/G. 2681-P/Rev.3), Santiago.

Schmidt, S. and Ralph, D. (2016) The Flipped Classroom: A Twist on Teaching. *Contemporary Issues in Education Research*, vol. 9, No 1, First Quarter.

Tandon, R., Hall, B., Lepore, W., and Singh, W. (2016) *Training the Next Generation of Community Based Researchers: A Guide for Trainers.* PRIA and University of Victoria.

PIIOM Misión Ciencia para la Paz (2003). Ministerio de Ciencia y Tecnología. Gobierno de Colombia. Piiom Misión Ciencia Para La Paz.

Vygotsky, L. (1981). Pensamiento y Lenguaje. Buenos Aires: La Pléyade.

Chapter 13

Araujo, O. (2013). Proyecto Educativo Institucional. *Entorno Geográfico, 2.* https://doi.org/10.25100/eg.v0i2.7586

Brennan, J. (2008). Higher education and social change. *Higher Education*, 56(3), pp 381–393. https://doi.org/10.1007/s10734-008-9126-4

Dirkx, J.M. (2012). Self-formation and transformative learning: A response to 'calling transformative learning into question: some mutinous thoughts,' by Michael Newman. *Adult Education Quarterly*, 62(4), pp 399–405. https://doi.org/10.1177/0741713612456420

Flores, I., González, L.F, Astaiza, A., and Lopera, D. (2023). Towards transdisciplinarity in the co-construction of knowledge: The Peace and

Region Program at the University of Ibagué K4C Hub, Colombia. In W. Lepore, B. Hall, and R. Tandon (eds), *Bridging Knowledge Cultures: Rebalancing Power in the Co-Construction of Knowledge*, Brill, pp 232–255. https://brill.com/display/title/69418

Ibrahim, S.S. (2006). From individual to collective capabilities: The capability approach as a conceptual framework for self-help. *Journal of Human Development*, 7(3), pp 397–416. https://doi.org/10.1080/14649880600815982

Navarro Barros, N.I. and Uribe Sarmiento, J.J. (2019). *La retaguardia en disputa Monográfico del conflicto en la provincia Sur del Tolima*.

Orozco, L.E. and Reyes Alvarado, A. (2021). *La Universidad Necesaria. Una propuesta de resignificación de la Universidad de Ibagué*.

Parra, F. and Álvarez, M. (2020). Unibagué: Una historia de desarrollo humano. In *40 años construyendo región* (pp 53–74).

Rosenthal, M.S., Lucas, G.I., et al. (2009). Teaching community-based participatory research principles to physicians enrolled in a health services research fellowship. *Academic Medicine*, 84(4), pp 478–484. https://doi.org/10.1097/ACM.0b013e31819a89e8

Sen, A. (1999). *Development as Freedom*. Oxford University Press.

Sisselman-Borgia, A.G. and Torino, G.C. (2017). Innovations in experiential learning for adult learners. *Journal of Applied Learning in Higher Education*, 07(Spring), pp 3–12. https://doi.org/10.57186/jalhe_2017_v7a1p3-12

Star, S.L. and Strauss, A. (1999). Layers of silence, arenas of voice: The ecology of visible and invisible work. *Computer Supported Cooperative Work*, 8(1-2), pp 9–30. https://doi.org/10.1023/A:1008651105359

Stoddart, M.C.J. (2007). Ideology, hegemony, discourse : A critical review of theories of knowledge and power. *Social Thought & Research*, 28(250), pp 191–225.

Tunnermann Bernheim, C. (2007). Los desafíos de la universidad en el siglo XXI. In *La universidad necesaria para el siglo XXI* (pp 19–37).

Chapter 14

Government of India (1968, 1986, 2020), *National Policy on Education*. Ministry of Education, Government of India.

Ministry of Education, (n.d.) *Unnat Bharat Abhiyan*. https://unnatbharatabhiyan.gov.in

University Grants Commission. (2022). *Guidelines for Fostering Social Responsibility and Community Engagement in Higher Education Institutions in India*. https://www.ugc.ac.in/pdfnews/9944839_Guidelines-for-Fostering-Social-Responsibility-and-Community-Engagement-in-Higher-Education-Institutions-in-India.pdf

UGC Reports on Training of Master Trainers in Community-Based Participatory Research

- Nagpur University, Maharashtra from 20th to 22nd April 2022
- Madurai University, Tamil Nadu from 27th to 29th April 2022
- Central University of Odisha, Koraput from 7th to 9th June 2022
- Bhopal University, Madhya Pradesh from 16th to 18th June 2022
- Agra University, Uttar Pradesh from 15th to 17th July 2022
- Kurukshetra University, Haryana from 19th to 21st July 2022
- Tezpur University, Assam from 26th to 28th July 2022

UGC Annual Reports

- https://www.ugc.gov.in/pdfnews/5789724_UGC_AR_2020-21_FNL.pdf
- https://www.ugc.gov.in/pdfnews/7167021_English-Annual-Report-2021-22.pdf
- https://www.ugc.gov.in/oldpdf/annualreport/AR.2022-23.English_WEB.pdf
- https://onlinecourses.swayam2.ac.in/ugc24_ge05/preview

Chapter 15

Hall, B., Tandon, R., et al. (2016). *Knowledge and Engagement: Building Capacity for the Next Generation of Community Based Researchers*. PRIA and University of Victoria.

Lepore, W., Tandon, R., and Hall, B. (eds.) (2024). *Bridging Knowledge Cultures: Rebalancing Power in the Co-Construction of Knowledge*. Brill https://doi.org/10.1163/9789004687769

NOTES ON CONTRIBUTORS

Mónica del Pilar Álvarez is academic coordinator of the Peace and Region Semester at University of Ibagué, Colombia, and cultural mediator of the National Project Peace Takes the Word. She undertakes formal education initiatives in higher education and popular education, and participatory research in communities and rural contexts on issues related to rural women, memory and peace building. She is a member of the Colombia IAPaz Hub.

Kaustuv Kanti Bandyopadhyay is Director at Participatory Research in Asia (PRIA), New Delhi, where he provides strategic leadership, oversees impact-driven programs, and fosters partnerships both nationally and internationally. With over 30 years of experience, his research focuses on the intersectionalities of participation, civil society ecosystems, social accountability, sustainable urbanisation, and climate resilience. Kaustuv has made significant contributions to strengthening the non-profit sector. He holds a PhD in Anthropology.

Sarah Banks is professor of Applied Social Sciences and co-founder of the Centre for Social Justice and Community Action, Durham University, UK. She coordinates the ethics working group of the International Collaboration for Participatory Health Research and has a long-standing interest in practical ethics in social work, community development and participatory research.

Nandita Pradhan Bhatt is Director at Martha Farrell Foundation, where she is responsible for program delivery and management of the Foundation. She also heads the gender programs in Participatory Research in Asia (PRIA). She has nearly 30 years of experience in the space of gender mainstreaming and inclusion. A trained CBPR mentor, alumni of the first Mentor Training Program in 2017 under the Knowledge for Change (K4C) Program, Nandita also mentors the K4C Hub in Pt. Ravi Shankar Shukla University, India.

Tanya Clarmont, Teme-Augama Anishnabai, and French Canadian from the Ottawa Valley, is Director of Community Action and Learning with the Victoria Native Friendship Centre, which includes work with leadership and advocacy projects, learning curriculums for community, research, and community services like the Bruce Parisian Library and a legal clinic. She has worked with Friendship Centres for 23 years and has held positions at the national, provincial and local levels. She is a founding mentor of the UNESCO K4C Salish Sea Hub.

Darlene E. Clover, PhD, is a professor at the University of Victoria, Canada. Her areas of focus include feminist and nonformal adult education, arts-based adult education and research, community development, cultural leadership. Since the late 2000s, her research has centred on museum education and learning and their contributions to social and gender (in)justice. Her current focus is exhibitions as research and knowledge mobilisation and specifically, how feminist strategies in museums such as animation, herstorying, reframing, recentring, rescripting, naming, gender bending and revisualising shatter entrenched masculine narratives and make very different histories/perspectives visible, hearable, feelable, knowable and discussable.

Catherine Etmanski is a passionate educator who creates inclusive and engaging learning opportunities for adult learners from all backgrounds. Her areas of scholarship include collaborative leadership, transformative learning, and the use of arts-based methods in promoting social change. In 2014, she co-published the book *Learning and Teaching Community-Based Research*.

Irma Alicia Flores-Hinojos, PhD, is an associate professor in the Faculty of Education at the University of Los Andes, Colombia. Her professional focus is research and teaching, specifically in teacher training encompassing qualitative and participatory research, ethnoeducation, popular and rural education, inclusion, diversity, and curricular transformation. She actively engages in mentoring within the community-based research program under the UNESCO Chair in Community-Based Research and Social Responsibility in Higher Education, and is coordinator of the Colombia IAPaz Hub within the K4C Consortium.

John Gaventa is a political sociologist, educator and civil society practitioner with over 40 years of experience in research, teaching and organisational leadership in the North and South. He is currently a Research Fellow at the Institute of Development Studies (IDS), UK. He previously served as Director of Research at IDS (2015–2019), and as Director of the Coady International Institute and Vice President of International Development at StFX University in Canada (2011–2014). He has written extensively on subjects of power, participation and participatory research.

Jyoti Gogia, PhD, is professor of Economics at the Dayalbagh Educational Institute (Deemed to be University) in Agra, India. She serves as the coordinator of the Dayalbagh K4C Hub and as the nodal officer for the Association of Indian Universities-Dayalbagh Educational Institute-Academic and Administrative Development Centre (AIU-DEI-AADC). Her research is primarily focused on gender issues, food systems, food security, and sustainable development.

Luisa Fernanda González Pineda holds a biological and chemical degree from the University of Caldas and an MEd and PhD in Education from the University of the Andes. Her work as a professor and researcher focuses on qualitative research in inclusive education, training and supporting educational actors, and evaluating teaching, curriculum, educational practices, public policies, and social responsibility in higher education. She is also a mentor in the community-based research program at the Colombia IAPaz Hub under the K4C Consortium.

Anshuman Karol, PhD, currently working as Lead – Governance and Climate Action with Participatory Research in Asia (PRIA), New Delhi, has multi-functional experience of over 24 years in decentralised planning, participatory research and evaluation, capacity building, and training. He is a certified mentor on community-based research within the K4C Consortium.

Wanda Krause is associate professor, and Program Head of Global Leadership, at Royal Roads University, Canada. She has more than 20 years of experience as a scholar-practitioner investigating how courageous individuals collaborate to lead and mobilise change. Her PhD is in politics of the Middle East and focused on women's contributions to civil society and political change in challenging environments.

Walter Lepore is assistant professor in the School of Public Administration at the University of Victoria (Canada), and co-founder of the Salish Sea K4C Hub that provides training in community-based research and Indigenous research methodologies. He is also the Director of Research for the UNESCO Chair in Community-Based Research and Social Responsibility in Higher Education, and former coordinator of the K4C Consortium.

René Oosthuizen, PhD, is an academic at Rhodes University, South Africa, and the academic lead of the K4C hub at the university. Her research emphasises engaged scholarship and community-based participatory research for decolonising higher education. She develops curricula, facilitates training, contributes to panels and publications fostering transdisciplinary collaborations to address societal challenges through collaborative research practices.

Diksha Rajput, PhD, is deputy secretary at University Grants Commission (UGC), India. She has 22 years of service at the UGC where she has been instrumental in advancing ICT initiatives, e-content development, SWAYAM MOOCs, teacher training, community-based participatory research and e-governance projects. An alumna of Delhi University, Indian Institute of Mass Communication (IIMC), and Dr. Bhimrao Ambedkar University, Agra, she actively contributes to implementation of India's National Education Policy (NEP) 2020 and capacity building for UGC employees. Prior to her tenure at the UGC, she worked in the Indian Information Service (IIS), Information and Broadcasting (I&B) Ministry, Government of India, and at the Indian National Trust for Art and Cultural Heritage (INTACH).

Wafa Singh holds a doctoral degree in community engagement in higher education from the Durban University of Technology. Her research interests include community-based participatory research and academic social responsibility. She has co-edited the book *Community Engagement in Higher Education: From Theory to Practice* (Routledge, 2023).

Tariqa F. Tandon is a researcher and development practitioner whose interests converge around the fields of political science, gender, migration and anticolonialism. Tariqa holds a master's degree in political science from Carleton University, Ottawa, Canada, and a bachelor's degree in political science from McGill University, Montreal, Canada.

Crystal Tremblay, settler of European and French-Canadian descent, is an associate professor in the Department of Geography, and director of CIFAL Victoria at the University of Victoria. She is a social geographer and a community-based scholar with over 15 years of international experience in sustainable development, environmental stewardship and livelihood enhancement. Strongly rooted in community-driven, decolonial and participatory methodologies, she is passionate about cultivating spaces for the co-creation of knowledge leading to environmental, economic and social equity. She is a founding mentor of the UNESCO K4C Salish Sea Hub.

Sharon Valarmathi, PhD, is associate professor in the Department of Commerce, and director of the Centre for Service Learning at CHRIST (Deemed to be University). She specialises in taxation law and management, and has over 20 years of teaching experience. Passionate about community-based participatory research, she actively engages with communities, integrating immersive and practical learning into her courses. Dr Valarmathi also guides PhD scholars and leads service learning initiatives.

INDEX